ADVA

Game-Based Learning in Action

"Following a group of innovative tech-savvy teachers, Matthew Farber unearths a close-knit tribe of passionate educator-scholars actively using games in their classrooms. This community applies scholarly research on game-based learning to their own teaching and presents their results at academic conferences and teacher workshops. Farber's book introduces you to the teachers, the tools, and their techniques, and ties it together with current cutting-edge research. At the end of each chapter you'll find yourself excited to dive into an overflowing toolbox of techniques to try, games to play, and papers to read. Farber covers a vast landscape, pulling resources together and presenting them to you in a thorough and easy to follow format. Press start!"

—Mark DeLoura, Engineer, Game Developer, Former Senior Advisor for Digital Media in the White House Office of Science and Technology Policy

"Matthew Farber's book sheds a fascinating light on a dispersed group of educators who bring radical educational practices into conventional settings. More importantly, this book portrays how this small but effective global community supports one another, both personally and professionally, and provides the foundation required to integrate games-based learning into on-going coursework. For those new to games-based learning, Farber shows us how classroom learning can be transformed when educators work together to understand their students then design curriculum that speaks to their passions."

—Barry Joseph, Associate Director for Digital Learning at the American Museum of Natural History

"*Game-Based Learning in Action* by Matthew Farber is an excellent and timely book. It offers fresh and imaginative solutions that are all too rare in charting the future of American education. By documenting an innovative tribe of remarkable teachers who have proven, compelling ways to use games to revolutionize twenty-first century teaching, learning and assessment, Farber has done the field a real service. Chock full of practical insights on ways to catalyze the 'playful learning movement' the book delivers the passion, knowledge and 'game plan' of the real heroes who can, if given a shot, transform America's classrooms."

—Michael Levine, Founder and Executive Director of the Joan Ganz Cooney Center at Sesame Workshop

"If you want to become an expert on games for learning, I know no better way than *Game-Based Learning in Action*. It makes research accessible, and is full of thoughtful case studies on exemplary games as well as great advice about how to integrate all of it into a classroom. It is rare to find a book that is great for researchers, game designers, and teachers, but here it is!"

—Jesse Schell, CEO Schell Games, and Distinguished Professor of Entertainment Technology at Carnegie Mellon University

Game-Based Learning in Action

Colin Lankshear and Michele Knobel
General Editors

Vol. 80

The New Literacies and Digital Epistemologies series
is part of the Peter Lang Education list.
Every volume is peer reviewed and meets
the highest quality standards for content and production.

PETER LANG
New York • Bern • Frankfurt • Berlin
Brussels • Vienna • Oxford • Warsaw

Matthew Farber

Game-Based Learning in Action

How an Expert Affinity Group Teaches With Games

Foreword by James Paul Gee

PETER LANG
New York • Bern • Frankfurt • Berlin
Brussels • Vienna • Oxford • Warsaw

Library of Congress Cataloging-in-Publication Data
Names: Farber, Matthew, author.
Title: Game-based learning in action: how an expert affinity group teaches with games /
Matthew Farber.
Description: New York: Peter Lang.
Series: New literacies and digital epistemologies; vol. 80 | ISSN 1523-9543
Includes bibliographical references and index.
Identifiers: LCCN 2017017243 | ISBN 978-1-4331-4474-5 (pbk.: alk. paper)
ISBN 978-1-4331-4471-4 (ebook pdf) | ISBN 978-1-4331-4472-1 (epub)
ISBN 978-1-4331-4473-8 (mobi)
Subjects: LCSH: Educational games.
Educational technology.
Teachers—Professional relationships.
Classification: LCC LB1029.G3 F36 | DDC 371.33/7—dc23
LC record available at https://lccn.loc.gov/2017017243
DOI 10.3726/b11291

Bibliographic information published by **Die Deutsche Nationalbibliothek**.
Die Deutsche Nationalbibliothek lists this publication in the "Deutsche
Nationalbibliografie"; detailed bibliographic data are available
on the Internet at http://dnb.d-nb.de/.

The paper in this book meets the guidelines for permanence and durability
of the Committee on Production Guidelines for Book Longevity
of the Council of Library Resources.

© 2018 Peter Lang Publishing, Inc., New York
29 Broadway, 18th floor, New York, NY 10006
www.peterlang.com

All rights reserved.
Reprint or reproduction, even partially, in all forms such as microfilm,
xerography, microfiche, microcard, and offset strictly prohibited.

Printed in the United States of America

CONTENTS

List of Figures	ix
Foreword by James Paul Gee	xi
Acknowledgments	xiii
Introduction	1
Structure of This Book	4
References	5
Part I: An Affinity Group of Game-Based Learning Educators	**7**
Chapter 1: The Tribe	9
Red Bandanas and Educational Anarchists	9
The Tribe as Community of Practice	12
The Games in Education Symposium as Affinity Space	14
Selecting the Keynote Speakers	17
The Speakers' Dinner	18
Birds of a Feather Play Together	20
Birds of a Feather Tweet Together	21
Chapter Summary	24
References	24

Chapter 2:	Learning From the Experts	27
	The Inner Circle	27
	The Tribe as Affinity Group	29
	Taking Risks and Changing Paradigms	31
	Game-Based Learning Evangelism	33
	Pioneering Practitioners	35
	Trusting the Experts	36
	The Trouble With Experts	37
	Chapter Summary	39
	References	40
Chapter 3:	Games in School	41
	The "Horizontal Learning Space" in *Quest Atlantis*	42
	Minecraft Mentors	44
	Balanced Learning Games	46
	Epistemic Games	47
	Gamification	48
	Game-Like Learning	50
	Games as Designed Spaces	52
	The Intersection of Games and Learning	53
	The Business of Games4Ed	54
	Chapter Summary	56
	References	56

Part II: A Close Look at The Tribe in Action — 61

Chapter 4:	"The Godmother of Educational Gaming"	63
	Room 339: Home to Epic Learners	65
	Teaching Her Heroes	67
	Thursday	67
	Friday	72
	References	77
Chapter 5:	"For the Next 3 Hours, You Have a License to Snoop Around the House"	79
	Gone Home	80
	The School	82
	Observing *Gone Home* in the Classroom	83
	References	94
Chapter 6:	"Life Just Got Epic!"	95
	Room 322: Iterative Design and Student Choice	96

Day 1	97
Day 2	104
References	110

Part III: "Go Where the Game Takes You!" — 111

Chapter 7:	Playful Learning	113
	Play Theory	114
	Play Theory in Practice	115
	Balancing Play and Game	118
	Montessorian, by Design	121
	Playful Learning Environments	122
	Chapter Summary	124
	References	124
Chapter 8:	Gameful Learning	127
	Gameful Learning Practices	128
	Making School Replayable	130
	Learner Agency	133
	Meaningful Role Play	135
	Scaffolding Student Choice	137
	Designing Branched Quests	140
	Chapter Summary	141
	References	142
Chapter 9:	Games as High Quality Curricular Materials	145
	Video Games as Text	146
	Video Games and Literary Devices	149
	Humanities Games as "Standalone Pieces"	151
	The Versatility of Humanities Games	153
	Turning Literature Into Role-Playing Games	154
	Reskinning Games	156
	Chapter Summary	159
	References	159
Chapter 10:	"How Can I Twist This Game to My Purposes?"	161
	How *World of Warcraft* Became Sheehy's Curriculum	162
	Contextual Transposition	165
	The Malleability of *Minecraft*	166
	Cell Games	168
	Applying the EPIC Framework	171

Using *The Walking Dead* to Teach Ethics	172
Chapter Summary	173
References	174
Chapter 11: The Case for Experiential Learning	175
Shared Experiences	176
Games as Digital Field Trips	177
Lesson Planning for Experiences	179
Games and Mentorship Learning	181
Virtual Internships	183
Virtual Internship Authorware	186
How The Tribe Engaged Students in Affinity Groups	187
Chapter Summary	189
References	190
Chapter 12: Open-Ended Assessments for Open-Ended Games	191
Games, the Curriculum, and Assessments	192
The Tribe's (Non)Use of Dashboard Analytics	194
"The Ultimate Assessment"	196
The Case for Schönian Reflective Practices	198
Narrativizing Game Events	200
Unobtrusive Assessments	201
Games and Dispositional Behaviors	203
Chapter Summary	205
References	205
Chapter 13: The Role of the Game-Based Teacher	209
The Teacher as Game-Master	210
Flash Lessons and Teaching on the Fly	212
The Game Explosion	214
The Husøy/Staaby Pendulum	215
Teachers as Learning Designers	218
Chapter Summary	219
References	219
Conclusion	221
Lessons Learned	222
Follow—and Join—The Tribe!	224
Index	227

FIGURES

Figure 1.1. One of the red bandanas, this one signed, "Thank you!" up by the knot.   12
Figure 1.2. Panel at the 2012 Games in Education Symposium: *Expanding the Conversation: How Does Playing Online Games Foster Safety?*   15
Figure P 2.1. Steve Isaacs, Paul Darvasi, myself, and Peggy Sheehy   62
Figure 4.1. Circle area in Sheehy's classroom   66
Figure 5.1. Screenshot from Darvasi's Haiku page   87
Figure 5.2. Screenshot of blank game evidence chart   88
Figure 5.3. Foyer of the Greenbriar house   89
Figure 6.1. Isaacs' classroom   97
Figure 6.2. Students designing with Project Spark and Disney Infinity   102
Figure 6.3. Student-designed Makey Makey controller   103
Figure 8.1. Elements of gameful learning   129
Figure 13.1. The Husøy/Staaby Pendulum   217

FOREWORD

Lots of teachers tell me they want to get into game-based teaching and learning. Then they me ask how they can start. I always tell them, don't do it alone; find a group of other teachers who are making things happen on their own and join them.

Lots of teachers ask me how we could ever reform our schools for real; how we can finally get past our fetish for facts and tests and sorting. I tell them, it will never be done by professors, policy makers, politicians, or Schools of Education. It will only happen when teachers take back their own profession and act together in the name of real innovation and not in the name of fame and fortune for people who do not spend their day teaching kids.

Today, there is a teaching and learning revolution going on outside of school. Everyday people, young and old, often together, join interest-driven websites to teach and learn from each other and to resource each other for making, doing, participating, and innovating. These people are joined together by a shared affinity for something, not first and foremost by age, race, class, gender, or politics. Their shared affinities are limitless: making media; citizen science; public journalism; women's health; raising chickens; modding video games; anime; fan-fiction; robotics; activism of all sorts, and on and on and on.

If people have a passion—say, for modding (modifying, re-programming) video games—they often have a home-base website—organized by their favored social norms for interaction—but this site links to many other sites and to resources all across the internet and the real world. They meet in and link to real world spaces, as well, and thereby meld the "real" and the virtual.

I call home bases, and all the spaces and clusters of spaces they are linked to, "affinity spaces"—they are spaces within spaces, like neighborhoods within towns within cities within states and countries. In affinity spaces, people distribute teaching and learning across multiple people and tools. Sometimes you teach; sometimes you learn. Sometimes you lead; sometimes you follow. You get expert at some things—sometimes well past the expertise of credentialed experts—but you often return to being a novice in a new area. People never stop teaching, learning, and growing.

All people in an affinity space share an interest. Some go beyond interest and share a passion and it is this passion that is the attractor to the space. It is this passion that ultimately organizes real change in the world. People today can be parts of many different affinity spaces to feed various interests—and they often make vital contributions in this way—but we hope, too, they each find a passion, as well.

Teaching and learning is now often organized more powerfully outside of school than it is in it. But there is no reason that interest, passion, and affinity cannot move to school and expand the school's relationship to the real and virtual worlds of diverse people, interests, and passions. But teachers will have to be the attractors. Don't wait for the professors, politicians, or publishers.

Now when teachers ask me how and where they can start, I can, thankfully, say: Well, there's finally a manual. This book is it.

James Paul Gee, Mary Lou Fulton Presidential Professor
of Literacy Studies, Regents' Professor, and author of *What Video Games
Have to Teach Us About Learning and Literacy* (2003; 2007).

ACKNOWLEDGMENTS

This book would not have been possible without the support of many people. I would like to thank my dissertation chair, Christopher Shamburg, and the entire committee: Leonid Rabinovitz, Muriel Rand, and Rebecca Rufo-Tepper. I am also grateful to my series editors, Michele Knobel and Colin Lankshear, for their continued faith in my vision.

This journey would not have been possible without the support of The Tribe, my community of practice. I would like to express my gratitude to my new colleagues in the School of Teacher Education at my new home: The Technology, Innovation and Pedagogy Department at the University of Northern Colorado.

On a more personal note, I would like to thank my wife, Laura, for her patience throughout the duration of this research; my curious son, Spencer; and our playful dog, Lizzie. A special thank-you is extended to my parents, Gary and Judith Farber. And thanks to my wife's parents, Virginia Fisher and Frank Fisher.

> An early version of some paragraphs and sections, including Chapters 4, 5, and 6, appears on ProQuest Dissertation and Theses. All rights reserved.

INTRODUCTION

Middle school teacher Steve Isaacs was the International Society for Technology in Education (ISTE) Outstanding Teacher of the Year in 2016. That year he was also New Jersey's PBS Digital Innovator, and he became a Microsoft Innovation Expert. Isaacs has been twice invited to the White House, met with Satya Nadella, CEO of Microsoft, and he helped to organize Minefaire, a *Minecraft*-themed convention. Peggy Sheehy is another transformational teacher-leader. In the past several years she has led keynote addresses in Sydney, Australia and Mumbai, India, and *USA TODAY's* Greg Toppo devoted an entire chapter of his (2015) bestselling book *The Game Believes in You: How Digital Play Can Make Our Kids Smarter* to her teaching. In her 6th grade humanities class, students learn by playing by the massive multiplayer online (MMO) video game *World of Warcraft*. Toronto-based English teacher Paul Darvasi is the more cerebral educator of the three, having authored several articles about his use of pervasive and serious games. In late 2016 he wrote *Empathy, Perspective and Complicity: How Digital Games Can Support Peace Education and Conflict Resolution* for UNESCO's Mahatma Gandhi Institute for Education for Peace and Sustainable Development (MGIEP). The CBC Radio's *The Current*, in Canada, highlighted Darvasi's findings in a feature titled, *Can Video Games Promote Empathy?*, in March 2017.

Isaacs, Sheehy, and Darvasi are three teacher-leaders making international inroads to evangelize how and why games drive learning. In late 2015, I embedded myself into each of their classrooms. I discovered that each did quite a bit more than teach with games: they were also expert practitioners in an inner circle of a game-based learning community of practice, where members "have multiple levels of participation" (Lave & Wenger, 1991, p. 98). Part of a group nicknamed "The Tribe," they mentor and apprentice new members by openly sharing their best practice in game-based learning education.

So how did I select these teachers to study? I began by conducting theoretical sampling to guide me to their network. Theoretical sampling pertains "to conceptual and theoretical development of analysis; it is *not* about representing a population or increasing the statistical generalizability of your results" (Charmaz, 2014, pp. 198–199).

Initially, my research pertained to Isaacs, Sheehy, and Darvasi—participants in my doctoral dissertation. These three teachers were selected because they led keynote addresses at the Games in Education Symposium, a conference in upstate New York. The theoretical sampling was, therefore, completed vis-à-vis the conference committee's vetting process. This book builds upon that research, expanding outwards into their community of practice.

In this book, The Tribe describes the teachers who read—and then apply in practice—scholarly research on game-based learning. They share best practice at academic conferences, as well as at teacher training workshops, and they lead online communities of practice. Each are also friends who support one another in an ever-changing educational system. This book is their story.

Created by Darvasi in July 2017, The Tribe has a Facebook Group. Being part of it helped broaden my scope of study. The following people's insights helped make this book possible. Each was generous, freely sharing anecdotes and reflecting on experiences about game-based learning. Some are classroom teachers, while others are academics, researchers, and designers. All are thought-leaders in game-based learning communities of practice. Alphabetically, they are:

- Adam Bellow—Cofounder of BreakoutEDU
- Sande Chen—Writer and game designer; co-author of *Serious Games: Games That Educate, Train, and Inform* (2005)
- Mark Chen, part-time game developer, part-time lecturer, games scholar, and author of *Leet Noobs: The Life and Death of an Expert Player Group in World of Warcraft* (2011)

- Dan Curcio—Special education science coordinator in New Jersey
- Paul Darvasi—English and media studies teacher in Toronto, Canada
- Seann Dikkers—Associate professor of education at Bethel University, Minnesota; author of *Teachercraft: How Teachers Learn to Use Minecraft in their Classrooms* (2015)
- John Fallon—English teacher in Connecticut
- Barry J. Fishman—Professor at the University of Michigan
- C. Ross Flatt—Manager of programs at the Institute of Play
- Zack Gilbert—Social studies teacher in Illinois; host of the EdGamer podcast
- Lucas Gillispie—Director of academic and digital learning for Surry County Schools in North Carolina; co-author of the *World of Warcraft in Schools* curriculum
- Kip Glazer—Learning technologist, and school administrator in California
- Mark Grundel—5th grade teacher in New Jersey
- Chris Haskell—Clinical assistant professor at Boise State University in Idaho
- Carrie Ray-Hill—Director of content at iCivics
- Aleksander Husøy—English teacher in Bergen, Norway
- Glen Irvin—High school Spanish teacher in Minnesota
- Steve Isaacs—Video game design and development teacher in New Jersey
- Jeremiah (Remi) Kalir—Assistant professor at the University of Colorado, Denver
- Robert Kalman—Middle school computer technology teacher from New Jersey; educator-in-residence at Pixel Press, creator of Bloxels
- Marianne Malmstrom—Educator from New Jersey who has since relocated to teach in New Zealand
- Matt Nolin—Game developer at 1st Playable Productions in Troy, New York; board member of the Games in Education Symposium
- James Pike—Teacher at the Sycamore School in Malibu, California
- Melissa Pilakowski—English teacher, and moderator of the Games4Ed Twitter chat
- Peter Quigley—Games coordinator for the Epistemic Games Group
- Meenoo Rami—Manager of *Minecraft* Education at Microsoft
- Marc Ruppel—Senior Program Officer at the National Endowment for the Humanities

- Tobi Saulnier—Founder and CEO of 1st Playable Productions; cofounder of the Games in Education Symposium
- Karen Schrier—Associate professor, and director of Games and Emerging Media at Marist College
- David Williamson Shaffer—Professor at the University of Wisconsin, Madison, and game scientist at the Wisconsin Center for Education Research
- Peggy Sheehy—Middle school humanities teacher in Suffern, New York
- Tobias Staaby—Religion and ethics teacher in Bergen, Norway
- Benjamin Stokes—Assistant professor at American University; cofounder of Games for Change
- Bron Stuckey—Researcher of game-based communities of practice in Australia
- Mark Suter—High school computer teacher in Ohio
- Caro Williams-Pierce—Assistant professor at the University at Albany; editor of the book *Teacher Pioneers: Visions from the Edge of the Map* (2016)
- A. J. Webster—Teacher and cofounder of the Sycamore School in Malibu, California
- Mitch Weisburgh—Founder of Academic Business Advisors and Games4Ed

Structure of This Book

This book is a deep dive into the praxis of teachers in The Tribe—those whose everyday pedagogy engage students with games. It is divided into 3 parts. Part I is about The Tribe—the moniker educator Peggy Sheehy gave to this particular community. (I capitalize "The" throughout. There are other tribes of likeminded educators; however, because Sheehy emphasizes "The" in "The Tribe," so will I!) Part II is a close look into Darvasi, Isaacs, and Sheehy's classrooms. Finally, Part III analyzes the data from those three classrooms, and then synthesizes it with conversations from more members in this affinity group.

Aside from sharing resources, this book contains authentic teaching strategies from expert educators. There is a lot of game analysis, too! Some games observed were digital, while others were tabletop. Games were sometimes pervasive—taking place beyond screens and game boards. And, in some cases, students had opportunities to create games.

Ultimately, this book is about the intersection of excellent teaching practice with high-quality game-based learning. I hope you learn from these experts as much as I did!

References

Charmaz, K. (2014). *Constructing grounded theory* (2nd ed.). London: Sage.
Lave, J., & Wenger, E. (1991). *Situated learning: Legitimate peripheral participation*. Cambridge: Cambridge University Press.
Toppo, G. (2015). *The game believes in you: How digital play can make our kids smarter*. New York, NY: Palgrave Macmillan Trade.

PART I
AN AFFINITY GROUP OF GAME-BASED LEARNING EDUCATORS

This book starts with the story of how game-based learning grew to be more than a nontraditional teaching approach; it is a grassroots movement to transform education to be more meaningful and engaging for all stakeholders.

These experts posted successes immediately on social media outlets, like Twitter and Facebook. This created a positive feedback loop of encouragement from other likeminded educators in their network. These teachers spent weekends, holidays, and summers attending, speaking, and keynoting conferences. They also freely shared their best practice with one another. As a result, perceived risk-taking from using novel teaching strategies like game-based learning became just that: a perception. To this affinity group, the practice of teaching was intrinsically rewarding—both joyful and meaningful, like the experience of playing a really good game.

· 1 ·
THE TRIBE

The Tribe is an affinity group of true practitioners, an affiliation of teachers that evolved to become a thriving community of practice.

When you speak to leaders in game-based learning communities, you may hear about how education can be transformed by the play games afford. When observed in the classroom, these transformational teacher-leaders lead from behind, as foot soldiers, putting their expertise into practice. I discovered classrooms that resembled Petri dishes to test new products and ideas. This chapter begins with an origin story. Next, I analyze how this group of like-minded people mentor one another, both online and in person.

Red Bandanas and Educational Anarchists

Search Peggy Sheehy's résumé on LinkedIn and you will discover the following entry: "Team Leader of the Red Bandana Project." So, what exactly is the Red Bandana Project? Fortunately, there is a description:

> The Red Bandanas community supports this site, and the awarding of the red bandana is in recognition of educational change agents. These are people brave enough to break out of the constraints of our systems and whose work has inspired others to

greater risk taking and new adventures. In the end, it's all about creating the best of learning environments that we can offer our kids! (Sheehy, 2013)

I contacted Marianne Malmstrom in December 2016 to learn more about the Red Bandana Project, which she cofounded with Sheehy. Both had met virtually in Second Life, a once popular multi-player environment where users created avatars—or digital representations of themselves—and then chatted in real time. Second Life was (and still is, for that matter) an open-world without the goals, challenges, or rules typically associated with video games. That's basically it. Oh, and there was e-commerce too! There were lots and lots of in-game purchases, including outfits for avatars and virtual real estate.

In 2007, ISTE "built" a virtual island in Second Life. There, members met to have live conversations. They even used digital lounge chairs and couches! (Although Second Life has waned in popularity, the ISTE Island is still used for professional development. I led a virtual talk there in 2015. Or at least my avatar—SecondMatt Lupindo—did!)

Anyway, as the story goes, Malmstrom "met" Sheehy (AKA "Maggie Marat") for the first time on that ISTE Island. "My computer was so old I couldn't even hear her—but I could read her text chats," she recalled. "All I knew was that I had to find this woman. I didn't know that she lived up the road from me." At the time, Malmstrom lived in northern New Jersey, while Sheehy taught in Rockland County, New York. "So, I got on the phone to her school and said, 'I need to see you.'"

From there, Malmstrom's view of education changed. Malmstrom and Sheehy soon migrated to play *World of Warcraft*—"a real video game"—together. Then more educators began to play in their guild (or team) of players.

Frustration with education's fetishism of standardized testing and teacher accountability led Malmstrom to relocate to New Zealand in 2016. Nonetheless, from half a world away, she maintains her affiliation with The Tribe. "The connections made in Second Life were pretty darn strong," she continued. "It was the first time I found my tribe. Up until then I was working in an absolute bubble." Malmstrom was amongst a new breed of educators trying to break the status quo, attempting "to figure out what would work in an environment where we had no map."

Second Life was where Malmstrom realized that there were others who understood the power of how games teach. She had found her affinity group. "One of the most liberating and exciting times in my career was when I found other people," Malmstrom said. "We would stand around in the [virtual] circle talking to each other. Every night, people would hop on and tell stories about what was going on in their classrooms, sharing their ideas and challenge."

Soon enough, Malmstrom and Sheehy spent time together socially. At an ISTE Conference they discussed how to push the conversations from the island to the real world. "Somewhere in that conversation we came up with the idea of red bandanas to symbolize educational anarchists," she said.

Like the Jolly Roger pirate flag adorned with a skull-and-crossbones insignia, the red bandanas symbolized nontraditional approaches Sheehy and Malmstrom favored—particularly using game worlds and virtual environments in the classroom. When they met other likeminded educators, they awarded them red bandanas. Scott Merrick was one such teacher. In a blog post, he recounted the ritual of receiving his red bandana at the 2013 ISTE Conference:

> Sunday morning, up at 5:00 a.m. to an alarm and into the fitness room for a long stationary bike ride. Quick shower and out to the Hyatt Ballroom A to meet up with the EPIC Leadership team. I met Chris Haskell for the first time, got my first ISTE hug from dear Anne Collier, Bron Stuckey, and met several new pals. We were issued event T-shirts and red bandanas, which we were instructed to wear and to customize with a sharpie message. (Merrick, 2013)

That previous summer, in 2012, Matt Nolin and Tobi Saulnier—organizers of the annual Games in Education Symposium in upstate Troy, New York—were awarded red bandanas. "Peggy and Marianne, and a couple of other folks, had these red bandanas that they would wear," Nolin recalled, when we spoke in November 2016. "The bandanas physically represented that they were in this tribe together. They gave one to Tobi and myself. It was an invitation: You guys do so much for us; you're a part of our tribe."

The red bandanas were literally just that: red cloth kerchiefs (see Figure 1.1). There were no sewn-in logos, nor were there formal rituals or secret handshakes. These are teachers, after all—not a secret society like the Illuminati! "We went to the craft store and got these bandanas and markers, and marked them up," Malmstrom said. Hers remains in her posession—I spotted it pinned to her backpack when we videoconferenced on Skype. She continued:

I've always had it on my backpack. It's this idea: when we spotted people we thought were pushing the conversation forward, we would award them a red bandana. We tried to systemize it more, but it's really hard to create a community non-organically. We did it for that one ISTE, and, after that, other conferences we went to. But we didn't sustain it because we were all in separate places. But the idea was to say, "Yeah, you're changing the conversation, and you're an educational anarchist, too!"

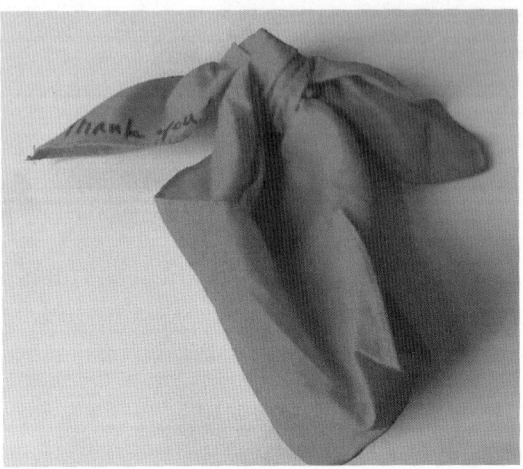

Figure 1.1. One of the red bandanas, this one signed, "Thank you!" up by the knot. Image courtesy of Matt Nolin.

Red bandanas represented a stand against teacher-led direct instruction that lacked affordances for play, students' interests, or, for that matter, fun. It signified a move towards gameful learning practices, which positions play and fun upfront as drivers of learning. As the years rolled on, others joined this affiliated alliance of forward thinking educators. Together this is an affinity group of passion-driven educators who evangelize how games can be used to teach, engage, and inspire learning.

The Tribe as Community of Practice

Bron Stuckey is a close friend of Malmstrom and Sheehy, and she is a researcher of communities of practice. Like most thriving communities of practice, there are leaders in the inner circle, as well as new members who are mentored to become experts. "Over time, these people found each other online," Stuckey said, when we spoke in late 2016. Because Stuckey lives in

Australia, we also conversed on Skype. "The Tribe has always been globally inclusive."

Stuckey also first met Sheehy online in Second Life. "It was a playful virtual space. I was researching [the educational virtual world] *Quest Atlantis* at the time, and I was doing teacher professional development in Second Life. That's where I met Peggy, Marianne, and a bunch of people who were engaged in gameful practices. Second Life was significant to The Tribe."

I next asked Stuckey about her thoughts on the significance of awarding red bandanas to likeminded educators. "We think of ourselves as a tribe because we recognize rituals in our experiences," she replied. "We recognize different roles and progressions in what we do, and we celebrate together. We support each other in learning new things and progressing the tools we use."

Sheehy echoed Stuckey's sentiment. "The Tribe shares a philosophy about virtual worlds, games, new technologies, new environments, new approaches to learning," Sheehy said, in late 2015. "We share a philosophy. We often attend the same conferences, and we tweet each other. Each is a conference compatriot."

Sheehy is a firm believer in a teachers' need to have a community of practice. And by believer, I intend that in the literal sense! I happened upon a video on YouTube in which Sheehy shared her mantra about the importance of finding one's tribe. From 2010, it is less than 30-seconds in length. And, as of November 2017, it has been viewed more than 1,700 times. Titled, "ISTE Interview with Peggy Sheehy: Finding your Tribe," she says:

> I have a mantra, which is, "Get thee to ISTE [the annual conference]." Are you new to Second Life? Get thee to ISTE. Are you new to education? Get thee to ISTE. You've moved to a new department, you're no longer in the classroom, but in a library setting? Get thee to ISTE. You will find your affinity group. You will find your tribe. (Sheehy, 2010)

The moniker, "The Tribe," can be traced back to the (2009) bestselling book, *The Element*, which TED Talk speaker Ken Robinson coauthored with Lou Aronica. In the chapter, "Finding Your Tribe," the authors advised passionate people to seek out likeminded individuals. In a subsequent book, *Finding Your Element*, Aronica & Robinson further posited, "Finding your tribe is a powerful validation of your own interests and passions. It affirms and reinforces your commitment to what you're doing and can relieve the sense of isolation that people sometimes feel without such a commitment" (2014, p. 193).

An ethos of free and open sharing of best practices within and outside of the community of practice is common for those in The Tribe. Stuckey attributed this spirit to virtual world communities, which engender a spirit of generosity. "When you see kids play Minecraft, the first thing you see is that they want to teach someone else what they learned, they want to share it and celebrate what they experienced," she said. "The Tribe has that spirit."

The Tribe is intentionally welcoming by design. I observed how game-based learning functions best when a network of passionate educators works together. I once suggested to teacher Lucas Gillispie that The Tribe is like a cooperative board game, which are games with a common player goal. In this case the cooperative goal is to bring playful learning experiences to all classrooms. Gillispie replied with a laugh, then he referenced the cooperative board game Forbidden Island. To win, players work together to retrieve hidden treasures before an island sinks into the sea. "Education is sinking," he mused. "And we are here to help shore it up!"

The Games in Education Symposium as Affinity Space

Each summer members of The Tribe converge at the Games in Education Symposium to lead presentations and give workshops on game-based learning best practices (see Figure 1.2). More than a conference, it also serves as an affinity space for The Tribe. Slightly different than a community of practice, an affinity space pertains more on the place where members meet; communities of practice theory focuses on group affiliation (Gee, 2005).

Since 2006, the Games in Education Symposium has been held in upstate New York. It is one of Troy-based game design studio 1st Playable Productions' community service initiatives. A couple of years ago, it was spun-off to become its own separate nonprofit entity. WMHT, the local public television affiliate in Albany, New York, and the Capital Region Board of Cooperative Educational Services (BOCES) cosponsor the conference. It is one of very few that has the express purpose of training teachers. Its stated mission is to:

- Enable and empower forward thinking educators with knowledge, practical in-service experiences, and connections to other pioneering educators;

Figure 1.2. Panel at the 2012 Games in Education Symposium: *Expanding the Conversation: How Does Playing Online Games Foster Safety?* Panelists featured many in The Tribe. Pictured from left to right: Marianne Malmstrom, Chris Haskell, Bron Stuckey, Sheehy, and Lucas Gillispie, and Anne Collier, at the podium. Malmstrom, Stuckey, and Sheehy are wearing red bandanas. Image courtesy of Matt Nolin.

- Bring nationally recognized practitioners in education to share techniques and outcomes associated with use of computer/video games to enhance classroom education and student achievement; and
- Provide a forum for educators to gain hands-on familiarity with the latest technology, share experiences and ideas with their peers, and acquire an understanding of how games complement and inspire students' interest in learning. (Games in Education, 2015, "Mission")

Tribe member Dan Curcio attends the Games in Education Symposium with the express purpose of having immediate takeaways for his students. "I create a lot [of game-based lessons] by myself," he said, early in 2017. "But nothing grew more for me then when I started attending conferences and joined in on Twitter. I am part of a tribe, and follow what others are doing. That's where I take ideas and bring it back to the classroom."

In 2016, Curcio attended a workshop I led on adapting the card game *One Night Ultimate Werewolf* to the classroom. In the game, players sit in a circle and try to deduce who in the group is the werewolf. In the classroom, I had used the game's social deduction mechanic to teach students about the Salem Witch Trials. That school year, Curcio purchased the game, and then used it as an icebreaker with his special education students. He continued:

> *Werewolf* became a great way to assess verbal levels of my students. We have so many limitations, such as cognitive processing issues. Some kids have dyslexia, but they have great verbal comprehension. Just playing that game gave me a feeling for what kids understood, like who understood how to bluff. I learned right there who comprehended what was happening. Of course, some kids were less limited in being capable of bluffing; they understood the game and took the lead. As a special ed teacher, this game became my informal assessment tool.

Chris Haskell credits his growth in The Tribe to Games in Education board member Matt Nolin. Haskell is a clinical assistant professor of educational technology at Boise State University, and he led the keynote talk at the 2017 conference. "Matt [Nolin] had the vision to say, 'Let's get some cool people together—not just theoreticians in the space, but people who are doing stuff, so they can talk about practice,'" Haskell said, in November 2016.

The organizers of Games in Education recruit teacher-practitioners as its core group of presenters. The conference functions as an idea forum for like-minded educators. "The hardest thing is bringing people into this fold," Nolin explained. "We have to take this risk. You go through this vetting process."

As a summer intern, Nolin began his career designing games at 1st Playable Productions back in 2009. After observing how committed the company was to community service, he decided to work there full-time. "There is a devotion to helping out, volunteerism, and social responsibility," Nolin said. He continued:

> 1st Playable Productions helps grow and develop the area of games in education through people who are practicing it and doing it in classrooms. The conference then provides an opportunity for teachers on the frontlines to network with others, and to share their practice with the grassroots teachers—to get these pioneers really excited in front of other teachers.

The organizers of the Games in Education Symposium seek to identify presenters who can provide attendees with immediate takeaways—useful sets of ideas to put into practice right away. "We heavily weigh whether [a potential presenter] has classroom experience," Nolin said. "But it's a variety of things. We have core tenets, like, is it practical? Can you impact teachers that are practicing right now in a positive way? Do you have experience educating yourself in some way?"

Nolin and the organizers also ask speakers for referrals. In 2016, Haskell recommended one of his former students, Minnesota-based teacher Glen Irvin, to lead a session on how he uses *Minecraft* in a Spanish learning classroom. "I guess I have been one of the linchpins of The Tribe, so to speak!" Haskell declared.

Sometimes Nolin and his team discover presenters through blogs and newspapers. "The E. K. Theater machinima group was in the *New York Times*," Nolin recalled. Like puppeteers, E. K. Theater's performers student add live voiceovers to video game footage, retelling classics from William Shakespeare and Edgar Allan Poe. "We wanted to share this with teachers because it can open so many minds about what you can do [with games], aside from applying historical texts and recreating them with games." A few months after E. K. Theater performed at the 2015 Games in Education Symposium, The Tribe's Paul Darvasi published an article for MindShift about the troupe.

Selecting the Keynote Speakers

Many members of The Tribe—like Haskell, Darvasi, Isaacs, and Sheehy—have served as keynote speakers at the conference. Curious about the vetting process, I asked 1st Playable cofounder Tobi Saulnier to explain it. "We choose keynotes on the basis of people having an authentic classroom perspective/story to share (so this rules out academic and game dev [development] folks), and who have been recommended as being dynamic speakers who can get people talking early in the conference," she wrote, via email, in January 2016. "Nowadays we have audience survey feedback from prior years that influences the choice, too."

As of 2017, Darvasi had been a keynote speaker on two separate occasions. "Paul presented a workshop one year, and we had a lot of positive feedback from the session, as well as from the volunteer staff," Nolin said. "Paul is a really dynamic speaker." Nolin next explained how Darvasi went from session presenter to keynote speaker:

> Usually we try to get folks we are familiar with, and have seen present—maybe not even at Games in Education. We want to be able to verify that they are going to bring what is important to our conference and to the attendees. We want them to have things that are big picture, and to set the tone for the two days. And they all should be practicing teachers, which is weighted very heavily. They can speak directly to the challenges and opportunities you've come across to other teachers. It's hard to replicate that when you're on the outside. Peggy has been involved from a number of years, and was excited on what she had to share. And Steve [Isaacs] has been a previous presenter with his hands-on workshops and presentations.

Isaacs led the 2015 Symposium with a keynote talk themed on student choice and voice. In my (2017) revised edition of *Gamify Your Classroom: A Field Guide to Game-Based Learning*, Isaacs shared his experience meeting those in

The Tribe. It all took place in the hotel where the Games in Educations Symposium speakers were staying. Because of its relevance, I am including his quote here, as well. Isaacs said:

> I came down for breakfast at the hotel. I saw an open seat at a table. I asked to sit down and was immediately welcomed. Eating at that table was Sheehy, Malmstorm, Lucas Gillispie, and Chris Haskell. Over the years we became dear friends. There is nothing I love more than interacting with people who are passionate about game-based learning. When I travel to conferences, the best part is connecting with my tribe. These are the people I want to surround myself with. We are an extensive support system of affirmations, guidance, and feedback. If I have a question about something, I throw it out there to them. Also, these people tend to be outside of my school because I do something very different. I'm immersed in games in the classroom. Most of what I learned is the 'outside' community of practice, and this has led to deep friendships. We play together, and laugh together. I wouldn't be nearly as inspired or excited without this community to interact with. (as stated in Farber, 2017, p. xix)

The Speakers' Dinner

Typically, there are two social events at the Games in Education Symposium. The first is the Speakers' Dinner, an opportunity for presenters to share a meal with the conference organizers. The second event is a social mixer, on the second night of the conference. At the mixer, the speakers are again invited, as are all of the conference attendees.

The speakers are often at the same the hotel, and many can be found in the lobby playing board games together. The whole thing has the vibe of an annual class reunion. "What we're really able to do—because we are a smaller conference—is to have these pioneers, who are on the cutting edge, come together," Nolin said. "And because they are all physically located together, we then give them opportunities to meet and talk to each other. We've had some great relationships blossom."

"My favorite night is the Speakers' Dinner," Nolin then confessed. "One reason is that we cover the dinner for all of the speakers that come. That alone sets us apart—and it sets up a general theme for the conference. We take care of everyone who comes to the conference." The Symposium is free for all attendees and speakers—even lunches are typically provided. "We try to make it warm and welcoming for everyone to engage with each other, to network and to be part of this community."

The Games in Education Symposium has maintained its unique focus on practitioner educators, and it has been quietly building up a network of cutting edge, innovative teachers. "The goal is to reward teachers [with hotel and meals], and to give them some time away from everything else," Nolin continued. "It is a dedicated time to be with other people who are doing interesting things. And hopefully they foster a network of amazingly talented people." Chris Haskell concurred, stating:

> They do something very clever there. They bring in a lot of really smart folks to run these sessions. Then they put the speakers together. They host a number of events that are primarily for the speakers, but they do give the teachers [conference attendees] a chance to swing by.
>
> The Speakers' Dinner places us together at a table. That's something we don't often get to do together. At big conferences, we wander into each other, we chat briefly, we maybe make plans to do things later. We're never sequestered together. And when someone is feeding you—you're obligated to converse! That's when we start sharing practice, and we start sharing experiences. And you start to connect to one another's networks.

It was at the Speakers' Dinner where Darvasi first connected with John Fallon. Both teachers created alternate reality games at all-boys private schools. Alternate reality games are like "pervasive games," which take place in the real world. (In the summer of 2017, Fallon was elevated from conference presenter to keynote speaker.)

"A story Paul and I like to tell—which you probably heard a lot—was that we showed up to Games in Education thinking we were these mad scientist oddballs who did these alternate reality games," Fallon said. "We realized that we had been going in the same exact direction, and that's where our friendship and partnership started."

Darvasi and Fallon now codeliver *The Blind Protocol*, an alternate reality game about digital privacy, at each of their respective schools. They plan the game on Skype, as well as asynchronously, on their own schedules, using Google Docs. "We text each other with live updates to solve problems we run into." Both copresent at conferences together, too. They give practical advice, so that others can similarly teach with games. "We frame the message in the way of concrete takeaways," Fallon continued. "If a teacher can't walk out of a presentation with a path of how to do it in their classroom, it is a lost opportunity. This game-based learning community is good about that. It's always been about, 'How can we get more teachers to use games?'"

Birds of a Feather Play Together

When a teacher decides to use games, it may be because he or she plays games. Takeuchi and Vaala's (2014) report featured levels of proficiency of teachers who taught with games. Game-using teachers were compared to non-game-using teachers. Results indicated 82% of surveyed teachers were self-described game players, and 78% of that group taught with games (n = 694; Takeuchi & Vaala, 2014). Game-using teachers reported that some games were more effective than others as learning tools. Takeuchi and Vaala also suggested that teachers who had experience playing video games may be more prone to teach with them. Additional teacher training, as well as creating a common language between educators and developers, was recommended (Takeuchi & Vaala, 2014).

Takeuchi and Vaala stratified the groups of teachers, sorting game-using teacher-participants as either "dabblers" or "naturals." Non-game-using teachers were not totally resistant to teaching with games; however, the percentage that utilized games to teach was smaller, at 55% (Takeuchi & Vaala, 2014). This was evident in my field observations, too: participant teachers were gamers, or "game-using teachers" in their personal lives (Takeuchi & Vaala, 2014, p. 17). While not part of the Takeuchi and Vaala (2014) study, members of The Tribe would be "naturals" in the game-using category.

Members of The Tribe play games in their free time and had a deep understanding of play within games, as well as how play drives learning. The literature supports this notion: It is "imperative that teachers know the game" they are using (Squire, 2011, pp. 138–139). "By playing a game in practice, teachers can think about what it is about the game that is engaging, and what types of strategies they want to use?" Darvasi said. He told me this the day after we met at Snakes and Lattes, a board game café in Toronto.

Playing together and talking about games is part of The Tribe's identity as a community. At the 2016 Games in Education Symposium, John Fallon brought several board games with him. And in the lobby of the hotel, The Tribe played the trivia game *You Don't Know Jack*. Before the Speakers' Dinner, a group played *Pokémon GO* around downtown Troy, New York. Being gamers and teachers affords these members the opportunity to gain a deep understanding of the mechanics, processes, and semiotic language of games.

Birds of a Feather Tweet Together

Dan Curcio shared an anecdote about how Twitter brought him from lurker to expert practitioner. Initially hesitant to join Twitter, Curcio now regularly shares ideas on the social media site. "We had a tech consultant come in," he recalled. "She said we really had to get on Twitter." He already liked technology, but he was an outlier at his school. Curcio continued:

> I said to the consultant, "I don't care about [singer and frequent Twitter user] Justin Bieber." She then said that there were also communities of teachers, communicating with each other, and sharing. I got on and started with @cybraryman1 [teacher Jerry Blumengarten's Twitter handle], who I've become good friends with over the years. This got me into different chats and hashtags. I came upon @mr_isaacs [Isaacs' handle] early on, and he was talking about games. I then realized that there were other people doing this type of thing: nontraditional ways of teaching.

About one year after following one another on Twitter, Curcio discovered that his wife taught at the same school as Isaacs. Curcio has since become good friends with Isaacs. "Steve was the bridge to meet more people," he continued. "He followed me Twitter, as did Peggy [Sheehy], and Lucas [Gillispie]. What's really important is having these group conversations about what is happening in classrooms."

Stewarding is the process and practice of administrating an online community of practice (Wenger, White, & Smith, 2012). Isaacs frequently acts as the steward of The Tribe. He is a conduit, connecting people to one another. For example, Isaacs stewarded Ohio-based computer technology teacher Mark Suter. They met through the online doctoral program at a Boise State University, led by Haskell, and they stayed connected on Twitter. "We were in the same online project groups together, and we discovered that we both teach game design using GameMaker: Studio," Suter recalled.

Like Isaacs, Suter uses game design as a lens to teach computer science education. "I took a Code.org approach, which is to make it fun, and then they [students] will want to learn computer science," he said. Students make video games using the iterative design process, which mirrors Isaacs' approach (see Chapter 6). "Steve and I have our students send each other their games to evaluate one another's. We use Google Forms, which is fun because they are different age ranges now." As a result, an online apprenticeship model exists between Suter's and Isaacs' students.

Those who decide to adopt nontraditional teaching methods need the guidance of a community of practice. Online communities are learning spaces in which members learn "from and with each other" (Wenger et al., 2012, p. 7). Belonging to online communities of practice is integral to teaching effectively with games. Because game-based learning teachers are often not located in the same school building—or even time zone—they depend on social media as the affinity space to share achievements.

Both Twitter and Facebook are platforms, or "sandboxes" for sharing best practices. A platform is a technology package that incorporates various tools for community members to utilize (Kraut & Resnick, 2011; Wenger et al., 2012). Twitter's real-time conversations help create a system of apprenticeship by enabling members to cement online relationships (Wenger et al., 2012). Another is the Facebook Group, eponymously called The Tribe, created by Darvasi in July 2017. It counts scholar James Paul Gee and *USA TODAY* education writer Greg Toppo as active members. At the time of this writing there were over 125 members in it, posting ideas daily. Topics range from competing definitions of game-based learning to recommendations of games to play.

The Games4Ed chat, launched on September 10, 2015 by Mallory Kesson and Melissa Pilakowski, is Twitter-based community. Every Thursday at 8:00 p.m. Eastern Time, users meet to answer questions posed by guest moderators. "There was not a game-based learning chat at the time," co-organizer Pilakowski recalled, when we spoke in February 2017. Pilakowski is an English teacher from Nebraska, and she volunteers her time to organize the Games4Ed chats.

The name of the chat—Games4Ed—is related to the start-up nonprofit, Games4Ed.org, which includes Isaacs. In 2015, Kesson reached out to him to secure the use of the name. Like many new to online communities of practice, Pilakowski "felt like a total lurker, helping Mallory to get it going." At first, Kesson wanted the chat to be a personal resource, so she could learn more about game-based learning and gamification from experts online—like Isaacs. But Kesson's teaching schedule caught up with her, and she stopped running the chats, leaving Pilakowski at the helm.

Twitter is an appealing avenue to get professional development because it is easily accessible. "It is easy to pop in and out of communities throughout the day," Pilakowski explained. "In our chat we can pop in, share some information, pick up a kernel or two, and there is no an obligation to stay in if something comes up. That's something we understand as educators in our community." Many participants return each week; however, some "ebb and flow—they learn some things, and then they go off for a while."

One could argue that, for some users, all of Twitter is a community. "As Twitter educators, we are part of a larger community," Pilakowski said. "We support each other, join each other's chats, and build up each other's communities." To that end, there is a constant demand for guest chat moderators. Sometimes Pilakowski receives recommendations from myself or from Isaacs. "I'm always on the lookout for moderators," she concluded.

Mark Grundel had been a lurker in the Games4Ed community, reading other's tweets and following along. Soon enough, he began contributing to the hashtagged conversations. Whenever he was free, he'd join in. "If it was 8 o'clock on a Thursday evening, I'd hop on the Games4Ed chat," he recalled, early in 2017.

Soon enough, Grundel noticed that his tweets were frequently being retweeted (shared) by someone named MineGage. "So, I started messaging with Garrett [MineGage is the educational gaming company led by Garrett Zimmer]. I told him that I had this New Year's resolution: I wanted to start a Twitter chat about game-based learning." Zimmer reminded him that there was already the Games4Ed chat. Then Zimmer suggested they both launch a *Minecraft* in education chat: #MinecraftEdu.

The MinecraftEdu chat has continued nonstop for over two years. Mentored under the tutelage of Zimmer, as well as Isaacs, Grundel moved from lurker to participant to community leader (Wenger et al., 2012). He continued:

> That's when I started hooking up with the other serious game-based educators. And you know Steve! He's just been phenomenal, helping me, taking me under his wing. He's really been a mentor in the truest sense. He helped me get connected with the [Microsoft] PlayCraftLearn team because he was one of the original *Minecraft* mentors—and now I am one too. In terms of community, it stems from Twitter and those educational chats.

In an attempt to reach more teachers, in February 2017 Grundel wrote an article in New Jersey's teachers' union magazine, the *NJEA Review*. In it, he invited teachers statewide to join the chat. Titled, *The Minecraft Phenomenon in Education*, he wrote:

> If you are nervous about getting started, whether with the regular edition or the Education Edition, there is a vast community of educators who are more than willing

to support you. Microsoft has produced a brilliant website, education.minecraft.net, that houses engaging conversations, vast worlds, detailed lesson plans, and a variety of training videos. Furthermore, if you are on Twitter, you can follow the hashtag #MinecraftEdu and pose your questions to the community. (Grundel, 2017)

Chapter Summary

The Tribe is a community of practice of likeminded educators. As such, it is an affinity group for best practices in game-based learning. These teachers are passion-driven.

The Games in Education Symposium is an affinity space in which The Tribe meet face-to-face, share ideas, and mentor newcomers. The Tribe's affinity space extends online to social media (e.g., Twitter chats), as well. The next chapter frames what teachers new to game-based learning can learn from following the experts.

References

Aronica, L., & Robinson, K. (2009). *The element: How finding your passion changes everything.* New York, NY: Penguin Group.

Aronica, L., & Robinson, K. (2014). *Finding your element: How to discover your talents and passions and transform your life.* New York, NY: Penguin Group.

Farber, M. (2017). *Gamify your classroom: A field guide to game-based learning.* New York, NY: Peter Lang.

Games in Education Symposium. (2015). Retrieved from http://gamesineducation.org

Gee, J. (2005). Semiotic social spaces and affinity spaces. In D. Barton & K. Tusting (Eds.), *Beyond communities of practice.* (pp. 214–232). Cambridge, MA: Cambridge University Press.

Grundel, M. (2017, February). *The Minecraft phenomenon in education.* Retrieved from https://www.njea.org/teaching-and-learning/classroom-tools/toolbox

Kraut, R., & Resnick, P. (2011). *Evidence-based social design: Mining the social sciences to build online communities.* Cambridge, MA: MIT Press.

Merrick, S. (2013, June). *The best ISTE day ever: Day 2 reflections, part 1.* Retrieved from http://scottmerrick.blogspot.com/2013/06/the-best-iste-ever-day-2-reflections.html

Sheehy, P. (2010, August 24). *ISTE interview with Peggy Sheehy: Finding your tribe.* Retrieved from https://www.youtube.com/watch?v=PRgTf5WJ-xU

Sheehy, P. (2013, April). *Team leader, red bandana project.* Retrieved from https://www.linkedin.com/in/psheehy

Squire, K. (2011). *Video games and learning: Teaching and participatory culture in the digital age*. New York, NY: Teachers College Press.

Takeuchi, L. M., & Vaala, S. (2014). *Level up learning: A national survey on teaching with digital games*. New York, NY: The Joan Ganz Cooney Center at Sesame Workshop.

Wenger, E., White, N., & Smith, J. D. (2012). *Digital habitats: Stewarding technology for communities*. Portland, OR: CPsquare.

· 2 ·

LEARNING FROM THE EXPERTS

As discussed in Chapter 1, The Tribe enables members to learn together, to discover new games and ideas, and to share personal experiences through the lens of game-based learning. When they collaborate and share common interests, members branch out, creating new communities (e.g., the MinecraftEdu community; Wenger, White, & Smith, 2012).

This chapter begins with anecdotes from members of The Tribe who recount how they moved from outside the community into the inner circle. I speak with community of practice expert Bron Stuckey about what we can learn—and what we cannot learn—from experts. Then I continue with a conversation with Caro Williams-Pierce and Seann Dikkers, both alumni of the Games Learning Society program, which had run at the University of Wisconsin, Madison.

The Inner Circle

Etienne Wenger in known for his seminal work in situated cognition theory, and the importance of communities of practice. One of the benefits of belonging to a community of practice is that there is often a meaningful exchange of ideas. "Etienne might describe The Tribe as the inner circle of a community of practice, which is very important to the health of the community," Bron Stuckey began, in late 2016. "In a community of practice, the first thing you establish is an inner circle of practitioners."

Members of The Tribe serve as mentors to teachers new to game-based learning. The community offers learning opportunities to those who are familiarizing themselves with the community before they become fully engaged (Wenger et al., 2012). "When you find someone who is not part of The Tribe, but is independently kind of moving along on the same track, you pull them in and say, 'Hey, we're doing this too,'" Lucas Gillispie said, in 2016. "We are a very giving, transparent, and generous group of people because we're very passionate about it. I don't know anyone who is doing games for learning who is not passionate about learning."

To participate in a community of practice, learners engage in experiences and become practitioners themselves (Lave & Wenger, 1991). Teachers in The Tribe practice game-based learning; they are not solely theoreticians. Through situated spaces, they "connect with the history of the practice and participate more directly in its cultural life" (Lave & Wenger, 1991, p. 101). In a 2015 interview, Paul Darvasi told me that he recommends that teachers new to game-based learning spend time playing games. By playing games, teachers learn by becoming part of a social practice—"knowledge takes on value for the learner in the fashioning of identities of full participation" (Lave & Wenger, 1991, p. 43). "While they [teachers] play games, [they should] think about the experience critically," Darvasi explained. "To think about what it is about games that are engaging. What's the learning goal? And, then based on that, to start acquiring knowledge of what games are available, and then to tailor those to their needs."

Darvasi's insights are drawn from his own experience. He discovered the video game *Gone Home*—which I observed in practice—on Twitter. "There was a scholar named Ian Bogost who was commenting on it and I got curious," Darvasi said. "I bought it and played it and thought it would be a great text." After playing, he decided *Gone Home* sustained "a great narrative that would solicit the type of thinking that would be in line with an English literature class."

Darvasi places a high degree of value on sharing best practices with a community of practice. In social practice, knowledge is shared within a community (Lave & Wenger, 1991). To Darvasi, sharing with the community is an obligation. He said:

> The most important thing is to create viable models by teachers who use games in their practice and share their results, through blogs, through formal papers. And

allowing other teachers to share their successes and failures. I believe that also empowers teachers also to experiment in their classes. Teachers who are unfamiliar with games and are reticent to use games in their practice as a result of that are much more likely to incorporate a game element if they have an experience that shared with them in detail. Then they can not only see the value of incorporating a game in their practice, but they also see the procedural steps that have to take place in order to succeed in that endeavor.

Other teachers I spoke to in this community of practice echoed this notion. Steve Isaacs credited his personal and professional learning network as his "idea-generating machine." Peggy Sheehy stated, "I learn about games from The Tribe—which is what I call my friends, who are also gaming teachers."

The Tribe as Affinity Group

Designing games is something A. J. Webster has always enjoyed. I know firsthand: I attended his and Christy Durham's 2016 Games in Education Symposium workshop on remixing the commercial card game *Fluxx* to fit curriculum (more on this in Chapter 9!). We spoke in December 2016.

"When I started teaching, I played lots of games with the kids," Webster recalled. "I designed a game to teach Latin verb conjugations. I had kids design games to talk about mythology. Games were always there."

In 2009, Webster came across a magazine article about a new school in Manhattan called Quest to Learn. Webster had been drawn in by the fact that it used game-based learning embedded in its pedagogical approach. "I also read Jim Gee's book [*What Video Games Have to Teach Us About Learning and Literacy* (2007)]. I read everything I could about game-based learning. I slowly found the community more and more through that." Reflecting on his experience of finding others who had a similar vision for education, Webster said:

> Upon reading an article, I realized that what I was doing was 'a thing,' and that there were other people were doing this. And, there's a term for it! It's not this crazy thing I do alone. There is a tribe out there; there are people out there. I jumped on a plane over my spring break and I camped out on Quest to Learn's doorstep. This was their first year, before they had protocols. They let me come in and sit and ask a bunch of questions.

That summer Webster cold-called the staff at GameDesk, a now defunct game-based learning start-up. (Tribe member Jim Pike once designed game-based lessons for GameDesk. In 2017, he joined the school where Webster teaches.) Founded by Lucien Vattel, GameDesk launched the short-lived PlayMaker

School in Los Angeles. Webster had volunteered at GameDesk that summer, and then he taught at PlayMaker, alongside teacher Ted Wakeman.

In 2015 Webster and Wakeman cofounded the Sycamore School, in Malibu. When Webster attended the Games in Education Symposium, he befriended Isaacs, Sheehy, Darvasi and other members of The Tribe. Webster recalled his experience joining The Tribe. He said:

> All of us are excited that other people are excited. All of us in The Tribe care about student experiences. All of us see that this is fun. Because we're teachers, we like learning, and we like sharing learning, especially when you have kids say, "Learning doesn't have to be painful? It can be something I enjoy?" I think all of us are invested in that. I don't need to get paid per diem for that. I want to bond with other people who get excited by that too. I guess that's The Tribe's mentality. We're all in this thing together—to make learning better for everyone.

While the Games in Education Symposium is a hive to bring together like-minded educators in a face-to-face setting, social media brought Norwegian teacher Aleksander Husøy to this community. In particular, the connection was Darvasi's blog, Ludic Learning; Husøy had read about Darvasi's adaptation of the video game *Gone Home*. This was shortly after Husøy made his own early ventures into using games in his classroom. "I was using *Civilization IV* in social studies and English at that point," he recalled, in December 2016. "I read about the *Gone Home* unit he did, and I was attracted to the idea of working with a short story-like game in that way."

Husøy reached out to Darvasi on Twitter. They formed a kinship, and both decided to try deliver the unit together, even though they were a continent apart. "It worked where our students would collaborate as they were analyzing the game. And now we're running the same unit for the third time!"

As with others I interviewed, Husøy discovers games to adapt to his classroom from affinity spaces. "The way I find games is through The Tribe—my personal learning network of other educators who are also interested in the use of games in education," he said. "Unfortunately, we don't have too many [game-based learning educators] in my school or city. So, most of the people I interact with are through social media."

Tobias Staaby teaches with Husøy in Bergen, Norway. In 2014, he made international news after he adapted the zombie video game *The Walking Dead* into his high school religion and ethics class. "That got translated into English news sites, and then it just exploded into the gaming news outlets," Staaby said, when we spoke in November 2016. Like Husøy, Staaby credits online communities—in particular, Twitter—as the space for discovering and growing his game-based teaching practice. He explained:

> I engage with the community—mostly through Twitter, actually. That's where I connected to you guys—to Paul [Darvasi]. That made me want to go the GLS [Games Learning Society] Conference. Aleks and I went there and met some of The Tribe. But Twitter is definitely my main platform. Without Twitter, I probably wouldn't be where I am today.

John Fallon also discovers games on social media and on blogs. "When a big RPG [role-playing game] comes out from certain developers, I will check that out," Fallon said, also in late 2016. "I look for games that are off-the-radar, particularly recommendations from people I know who play games. I'm also a big fan of outlets like [the gamer news website] *Polygon*. I see what the conversations are about."

Members of The Tribe laud each other's accomplishments. Darvasi published blog posts for MindShift about Sheehy and Issacs, and about Husøy and Staaby. Sheehy, in turn, has written about Darvasi. Sheehy wrote:

> It takes a seasoned teacher, who "gets" games, like Lucas Gillispie or like Paul Darvasi (Toronto, Canada), to play the game long enough to unearth the pedagogy. Paul's work with the indie game, *Gone Home*, is a consummate example of the powerful potential these games, not initially intended for education, can contribute to the classroom when a skilled educator is at the helm. (2015, para. 24)

Taking Risks and Changing Paradigms

Current research suggests that positive emotions from achieving lesson goals result in "low perceived risk" (Gigliotti & Howard, 2015, p. 8). The potential reward of being an effective game-based learning educator is the social recognition in the various communities of practice that each participant engages in. Positive feedback from social media outlets, like Twitter, is often immediate. Regarding the implementation of educational technology tools, risk can occur when teachers have a "predisposition," or an "openness to change" (Baylor & Ritchie, 2002, p. 399). Risk taking teachers are willing to try "new instructional innovations, a belief that they can take risks in teaching" (Baylor & Ritchie, 2002, p. 399).

Members of The Tribe have a willingness to try new things, to take risks. As Isaacs told me in late 2015, it is the educational system that does not take enough risks to lead new paradigms of teaching. While he saw value in "testing the waters" of nontraditional methods, such as using commercial games to teach, he noted setbacks when choosing "low hanging fruit." When trying a game "in an afterschool club or with only gifted and talented students," the "workflow"—where the game fits in to the trajectory of a learning unit—can be difficult to identify. As a video game design teacher, Isaacs reported few barriers to using games in his classroom. Nonetheless, he takes the opposite approach to selecting games that have a low barrier to adoption in a traditional school setting. Isaacs continued:

> I think that there's great value in being bold, as long as there's learning in it. To quote Marianne Malmstrom for a second, her notion is to "follow the learning." In other words, games are designed as great learning environments. Watch the kids play and explore and see how that learning takes place. Then design around that.

Lucas Gillispie was an early adopter in bringing commercial games into the classroom. He went as far as cowriting a *World of Warcraft* curriculum, which I observed implemented by Peggy Sheehy (see Chapter 4). "Having a partner like Peggy and Steve is great because you feel like you're not the only one doing this, when you are moving into unchartered waters."

Gillispie's point is that when using novel practices—like adapting a commercial online video game into a middle school classrooms—who can you ask when something goes wrong? You can't necessarily seek advice from neighboring teachers or local administrators. A teacher that bleeding edge *requires* a network of likeminded teachers. "What happens, and what do you do, if kids steal money from another player in the game?" Gillispie continued. "How do you deal with that? Those kinds of conversations, and the camaraderie—the ability to tell war stories about experiences—have been absolutely invaluable."

Implementing innovative teaching strategies, such as game-based learning, comes with the potential for administrator-related barriers. A principal or school board member may not share Gillispie's or Sheehy's enthusiasm to bring *World of Warcraft* to school children. But the teachers I interviewed actually reported few obstacles; they expressed autonomy and agency to select materials that would give students access to their school's curriculum. In fact, Sheehy's principal is in her *World of Warcraft* guild! "He understands the power of games; he understands the hidden curriculum," Sheehy said. She next told me about a PowerPoint presentation she keeps ready to show to any skeptical newly elected Board of Education member, which includes academic research on games and learning. She continued:

It amazes me that people who are so invested in education, and the health and welfare of our children, don't understand the power that a well-designed game—under the tutelage of a caring and knowledgeable teacher—can have on children. It can be immense. It can change everything. It changes the whole picture for them [students]. It gets them [students] excited about learning again.

C. Ross Flatt, from the Institute of Play, spoke to me in early 2016 about teachers who take risks. "We want teachers to take risks, to be able to try to new things," he began. "That is very important." To Flatt, teachers need freedom to test new things needs. They also require time for feedback and reflection—"but not unlimited freedom." He continued:

> In a public school setting it's difficult to give everyone carte blanche to try what they want. There's a difference between the work that you and I are doing, or the teachers at HistoryQuest [a history-themed game-based professional development program] are doing, versus anybody who wants to try out their crackpot theory in schools. Administrators and bureaucracies need to think about how they are assessing and teachers need to be rewarded for taking risks. Teachers need to be given chances to fail. It's very easy as an administrator to go into a classroom and play Monday morning quarterback with a lesson experience you might never have tried. What is that feedback going to do for you?

Herein lies the balance between administrator oversight and teacher autonomy. If a teacher is overly concerned about earning a perfect score on an observer's report, then that culture might send a message that it may not be okay to take risks. After all, good games are designed to be unpredictable. For that matter, any lesson embedded playful affordances—including project-based learning—can be wrought with moments when teachers may need to veer off plan. "Administrators need to support teachers taking risks, but teachers do need to get feedback—that's how you grow in a profession," Flatt said.

When Flatt was a teacher at Quest to Learn, a game-based school the Institute of Play founded, he codesigned the geography game *Galactic Mappers* with a full team of collaborators. "Designers need feedback. I would argue that designers are hypercritical of one another, but in a good way. It's part of the culture. Create a culture of openness and honesty—with feedback to let teachers know that it is okay to take certain risks."

Game-Based Learning Evangelism

Transformational leaders attempt to "influence whole organizations or even cultures" (Northouse, 2013, p. 186). They seek to "change and transform people" (Northouse, 2013, p. 185). Leaders in this style are often charismatic, using their personalities to empower people, and to convert other people's ways of thinking (Northouse, 2013). The Tribe's teachers fit the definition of transformational leadership.

Marianne Malmstrom spoke to me about how she evangelizes game-based learning to other teachers. "What breaks those boundaries is when you help people see things differently—especially when it seems so contrary to what people hold in their heads," she began. "Gaming is a really good example of that. But it's not the only thing in education we are up against."

Like others in The Tribe, she spoke of game-based learning as if it were a political cause. So, what exactly are "we up against"? Malmstrom clarified:

> There's such a negative perception of games and play. We come to it not just because we're gamers, but because we understand that play is the biological way that we learn. Well-designed games are really complex and can teach us, as educators, a lot about learning. It's hard to come to that conversation with somebody who is really against games. A good example of this is somebody who was doing research into student autonomy and agency and came across my work. But they then said they didn't go through my work because it was about games. I replied, "It's not about games, but the importance of agency." For me it's about letting people see what it looks like and let them come to it on their own.

At Malmstrom's former school, Elizabeth Morrow, her class was in the computer lab; geographically, it was central to the school. "You had to cut through it to get to the kitchen," she said. Other teachers and administrators would go through the lab and "hear the sound of learning." The conversations stopped people. "They got curious, and that became an opportunity to talk about it. It's always better when teachers discover it [game-based learning] for themselves, when they see you do that in your classroom. Then they're open and ready for that conversation."

Darvasi said there remained "stigmas associated with video games." When we spoke in 2015, he noted a "cultural shift." Soon enough, more teachers would decide to use video games in their classrooms. Isaacs expressed a similar sentiment regarding taking risks to change the educational paradigms:

> [One] thing that I think is going to help [the cause] is that the [U.S. Department of Education's] Office of Ed Tech is entirely behind the value of using games in the classroom. I think that's going to bring more of the mainstream; it used to be all of us renegades that were into getting games into the classroom. If it becomes mainstream, that'll help the cause for sure.

Isaacs was referencing Barack Obama's administration, which actively supported game-based learning. Under his term, Eric N. Martin, the young "video game czar" and Mark DeLoura, former Senior Advisor for Digital Media to the Director of Technology and Innovation, organized the White House Education Game Jam. Only time will tell whether President Donald Trump's team will do the same. Regardless, there are networks in place nationally that support the implementation of games and learning in classrooms. Of note is the Connected Learning Summit, launched in 2018 to combine resources from the Digital Media Learning Conference with the Games Learning Society (GLS) Conference and the Sandbox Summit. Meeting each summer, it convenes stakeholders together, from academics to designers to teachers.

Pioneering Practitioners

William Kist's (2005) seminal book *New Literacies in Action: Teaching and Learning in Multiple Media* shared findings about teachers who innovated by embedding new media literacy into their everyday practice. In it, he identified by name his teacher-participants, describing "how they took these pioneering steps" (Kist, 2005, p. 17).

Like Kist, Caro Williams-Pierce shed light on teacher pioneers, in particular those who use games in everyday practice. Several teachers in The Tribe contributed chapters to her (2016) book, *Teacher Pioneers: Visions from the Edge of the Map*. And many of the contributors were also in my research. So, in the spirit of The Tribe's ethos of openness, we compared findings.

Her book began when she was editing conference proceedings for the (then annual) GLS Conference (it was last held in 2016). Conference. She was on the conference committee, and she took note of the stories she heard from teachers in the field. "Steve [Isaacs] was definitely one of those people—and Paul Darvasi too." We spoke in November 2016, days before her book was published. "They all came to GLS. I kept seeing these presentations, or reading these things when I was co-chairing the conference."

In particular, Williams-Pierce was struck by "the brilliant things being born not only of the literature, game principles, and thinking about the ways that games and people interact, but also coming naturally and organically from the classroom constraints that these teachers are in."

When I pressed Williams-Pierce to define what teacher pioneers actually are, she resisted. "I don't define teacher pioneers—I let teachers define themselves as teacher pioneers," she replied. "I came up with the name from a quote I used liberally from math educators who talk about teachers who push against the border of the map of what's known done, and what's useful in classrooms." Here is the quote Williams-Pierce is referencing:

> Teachers often must play the part of the pioneer if changes are to be made. Pioneers forge ahead in spite of difficulty, learning all they can before striking out for new territory. They study maps, anecdotal records, and talk to those on the edge of the frontier. They take old knowledge with them, but expect to develop new strategies, solve novel problems, create new language to describe what they see, and share what they learn with those who have not yet made the journey. Pioneers learn as they go. (Armstrong & Bezuk, 1995, p. 89)

Upon publishing her book, she co-authored an article in which she reflected and connected commonalities of her book's teacher-contributors. Teacher pioneers:

- Use carefully designed and flexible contexts that provide parameters, while also leaving ample space for learner creativity, thoughtfulness and autonomy.
- Design opportunities for practice in contexts that become more advanced, complex and challenging as the learner progresses.
- Provide opportunities for learners to demonstrate their increased capacity by applying it to meet constantly more complex problems.
- Support a joyful and exhilarating exploration into the complexities of topics, through deep analysis of and connections to other aspects of the topic and the world.
- Design contexts that support learners in authentic (and often messy) investigation, discussion and practice.
- Afford their learners space to try, fail and try again, learning from each experience. (Swartz & Williams-Pierce, 2016, pp. 272–278)

Trusting the Experts

Seann Dikkers' (2015) *Teachercraft: How Teachers Learn to Use Minecraft in their Classrooms* connected areas of commonality across different groups of educators who use *Minecraft*. "One of those elements was this sense of community," Dikkers said. We spoke in December 2016.

An associate professor of education at Bethel University, Dikkers moderated a 2015 panel at the GLS Conference that included myself, Isaacs, and BrainPOP's Jessica Millstone. Dikkers also has led two keynote presentations at the Games in Education Symposium, and he contributed a chapter to Williams-Pierce's book. "Not all of the teachers I researched were gamers. To me that was fascinating. How can you not be a self-defined gamer, yet you do innovative things with *Minecraft* in your classroom?"

In each of the cases in Dikkers' research where a teacher was not a gamer, he or she reported a friend who was a gamer. One example was a teacher in Gillispie's school who "trusted him implicitly" to take care of the technology in her classroom. "This was a teacher who barely looked at games," Dikkers explained. That teacher had a good friend whom she trusted—Lucas Gillispie—to say that a game-based approach would work. "That teacher trusted someone in her tribe, so to speak. I can't say that this is the case with all teachers, but there are a certain number of teachers that don't need things proven to them prior to integration." He continued:

> In a profession and environment where we say there we don't have enough time, or we're trying to teach to the test and standards, it's fascinating that there are people who rely on those that they know and trust as great teachers. And teachers are still looking for new and better ways to cover content that engages and motivates students. That hasn't gone away at all. In my research, I saw that it was absolutely the case that not only do expert teachers want to share what they do with others, but some of those friends will adopt those practices without a sense of how it's going to work.

Perhaps more teachers would use games in practice if it were formally embedded into their mentorship training. "We trust that our student teaching supervisors and cooperating teachers have expertise that we don't, and therefore we mimic," Dikkers continued. "That's not necessarily a bad thing if you are mimicking best practice. I'd be curious to see what happens if one mimics poor practice, but we don't identify those teachers."

The Trouble with Experts

One time at a conference in New Zealand, Bron Stuckey overheard teachers as they exited a session about game design remarking about how the talk was motivating, but because the conference was on a Friday afternoon, come Monday, they might not recall how to integrate the new approaches.

Stuckey is skeptical of positioning expert practitioners to represent an entire community. "I think we made a mistake in promoting experts," she said. "I know experts are important and give a lot of vision. You go to a conference and you see someone give a fabulous talk and you get really excited."

Rather than experts sharing best practice, Stuckey wants to see more stories of "near novices"—the people who are just a step ahead of those that are just starting new practice. "I've seen Peggy [Sheehy] present here in Australia, in the USA, and around the world," she said. "I say to her at the end, 'Do you realize how many acronyms and insider jargon you used in that presentation?'"

An expert game-based learning teacher might use terms like "digital badges" or "XP" [experience points]. While digital badges are common in video games, in fitness tracker apps, and on social media, "83% of adults do not have much awareness" of what they actually are (Horrigan, 2016, p. 8). "The gamers in the room understand, but the problem is teachers who have not stepped into that practice. They won't understand." Thus, experts may unintentionally "separate their expert knowledge from the room." Stuckey continued:

> Peggy is in a school where her principal is a *World of Warcraft* player. As soon as she says tells people that, teachers will take a lot of what she said and put it in the "too hard basket." They'll say, "Oh, I don't have that principal. I don't have that kind of school sanction for what I want to do." Look at a school like where Marianne [Malmstrom] was—Elizabeth Morrow—a school where a lot of privileged things were happening. She had, for most of the time, an independent lab. Those are the things that a novice teacher will use to put a barrier between them and the practice. They would say, "Well, that's really great for Peggy—she's in a school already where her principal is a gamer." Or, "Marianne's in a really privileged school, and we could never do that." They won't take those first steps, and for a lot of good reasons. Especially elementary school with such an overcrowded curriculum, something has to go for something new to come in. They haven't yet realized that this [game-based learning] is not something new, it's a pedagogical change. It's not a new subject.

Those in The Tribe might inspire teachers to use games in practice, but more accounts of near novices are certainly needed. How did the people who broke the ground in their school get to where they are? Master practitioners do not often tell novices how difficult it was to achieve expertise.

"Community of practice research shows that when experts speak from the center of the community, they can't get remember what it was like to be novice," Stuckey explained. "This goes back to Socrates. The best person to teach you was not the master, but one of the journeymen—one of the people on the journey to becoming a master. They could remember what it was like, and the questions needed to get you started."

Stuckey champions the notion of having two teachers implement new approaches together, locally in the same school building. After all, not all teachers actively participate in Twitter chats or spend weekends at conferences.

This is the case with HistoryQuest, the Institute of Play's history teacher professional development program facilitated with the Woodrow Wilson Teaching Foundation. Its goal was to recruit two teachers per school. "We tried to make sure someone comes with somebody because you are trying a risky thing," C. Ross Flatt explained. "With another person, you have an ally in your school. If there is another teacher in your department that was taking the same risks that you were taking, administration, supervisors, parents, and students are not going to see that it is just one lone person." (I was recruited into the first HistoryQuest cohort, and I was the only one from my school to attend. But I was the exception—almost all teachers came with a department colleague.)

Some members of The Tribe have taken steps to make game-based learning more accessible. At the 2016 Games in Education Symposium, A. J. Webster and Christy Durham engaged teachers in a workshop in which participants remade the card game *Fluxx*. Upon hearing this anecdote, Stuckey told me about a keynote speaker she recently saw who played the party game *Taboo* with the audience. She also uses commercial card games in trainings. For example, she plays along *Metagame*, "which is a little adult, but works well with teachers." Designed by Colleen Macklin, John Sharp, and Eric Zimmerman it challenges players to argue, debate, and defend opinions. It is sort of like *Apples to Apples*, but about knowledge of popular culture.

"Teachers, in a lot of respect, lost touch with their own sense of fun," Stuckey said. "I get them to play *Metagame* as it is, at a table. Then we brainstorm ways to adapt it for a subject area." With history, one could argue was Cleopatra more powerful than Napoleon. "They start thinking gamefully. Teachers have always used games, but somehow, they've missed that digital leap. Reminding them of games and how to adapt a game for learning is the hump to get over."

Chapter Summary

This chapter examined the inner circle of game-based learning as a community of practice. Others may perceive these teachers as risk-takers; however, this affinity group supports one another socially. They know their methods are nontraditional, yet they witness firsthand how engaging games can be for learning. As a result, The Tribe takes a transformational leadership role, evangelizing how more teachers should also teach with games.

References

Armstrong, B. E., & Bezuk, N. (1995). Multiplication and division of fractions: The search for meaning. In J. T. Sowder & B. P. Schappelle (Eds.), *Providing a foundation for teaching mathematics in the middle grades* (pp. 85–119). Albany, NY: State University of New York.

Baylor, A. L., & Ritchie, D. (2002). What factors facilitate teacher skill, teacher morale, and perceived student learning in technology-using classrooms? *Computers & Education, 39*(4), 395–414. doi:10.1016/S0360-1315(02)00075-1

Dikkers, S. (2015). *Teachercraft: How teachers learn to use Minecraft in their classrooms.* Pittsburgh, PA: ETC Press.

Gee, J. P. (2007). *What video games have to teach us about learning and literacy* (rev. ed.). New York, NY: Palgrave Macmillan.

Gigliotti, A., & Howard, S. (2015). Having a go: Looking at teachers' experience of risk-taking in technology integration. *Education and Information Technologies.* doi:10.1007/s10639-015-9386-4

Horrigan, J. (2016, September). *Digital readiness gaps.* Pew Research Center. Retrieved from: http://www.pewinternet.org/2016/09/20/2016/Digital-Readiness-Gaps/

Kist, W. (2005). *New literacies in action: Teaching and learning in multiple media.* New York, NY: Teachers College Press.

Lave, J., & Wenger, E. (1991). *Situated learning: Legitimate peripheral participation.* Cambridge: Cambridge University Press.

Northouse, P. G. (2013). *Leadership: Theory and practice* (6th ed.). Thousand Oaks, CA: Sage.

Sheehy, P. (2015, November 23). *Getting schooled at Filament Games.* Retrieved from Filament Games website: https://www.filamentgames.com/blog/getting-schooled-filament-games

Swartz, T. F., & Williams-Pierce, C. (2016). Learning by design: Teacher pioneers. *On the Horizon, 24*(3), 268–279. doi:10.1108/oth-05-2016-0024

Wenger, E., White, N., & Smith, J. D. (2012). *Digital habitats: Stewarding technology for communities.* Portland, OR: CPsquare.

Williams-Pierce, C. (Ed.). (2016). *Teacher pioneers: Visions from the edge of the map.* Pittsburgh, PA: ETC Press.

· 3 ·

GAMES IN SCHOOL

As in some classrooms today, one century ago, students sat in rows listening to direct instruction from a lecturing teacher. John Dewey (1916) espoused the virtues of learning from playing and experimenting with abstract concepts (e.g., mathematical symbols) in a school setting. Dewey (1916) proposed that schools should be "equipped with laboratories, shops, gardens, where dramatizations, plays, and games are freely used, opportunities exist for reproducing situations of life, and for acquiring and applying information and ideas in the carrying forward of progressive education" (p. 190). He was one of the more notable progressive educators; he was an early proponent of experiential learning.

Fast-forward 100 years, and the conversation of reinventing schools persists. Factory models of education, in which children are grouped in grades based on birth year and learn in distinct content disciplines, have been called into question (Gray, 2014). The paradigm of active learning, rather than passive "sit-and-get" education, seems possible due to digital technology (Adams Becker, Estrada, Freeman, & Johnson, 2014, p. 8). Computers can create personalized learning environments that adapt to student ability (Adams Becker et al., 2014).

The promise of game-based learning is that it can "harness the spirit of play to enable players to build new cognitive structures and ideas of substance"

(Klopfer, Osterweil, & Salen, 2009, p. 5). Game-based learning "structures learning activities around real-world or fictional challenges that compel learners to take on a variety of roles as they actively identify and seek out the tools and multi-disciplinary information they need to generate solutions" ("Institute of Play," 2015).

This chapter opens with the story of how teachers participated in a community of practice around the game *Quest Atlantis*, a research project led by Sasha Barab one decade ago. Next, I speak to Microsoft's Meenoo Rami about *Minecraft*'s thriving teacher community. Several members of The Tribe happen to serve in Microsoft's official Global *Minecraft* Mentor Program. Also included in this chapter is a discussion about epistemic games. For that, I speak with David Williamson Shaffer, the foremost expert on the topic.

The "Horizontal Learning Space" in *Quest Atlantis*

The game *Quest Atlantis* was among the first to use "socially responsive design" (Barab, Dodge, & Thomas, 2005, p. 89). It enabled participants to play within the contextual setting of a virtual world (Barab et al., 2005). Conceived as an afterschool product, *Quest Atlantis* was developed in a participatory design program with the Bloomington Boys and Girls Club, in Indiana. *Quest Atlantis'* goals included teaching social responsibility through the game's social interactions (Barab et al., 2005), and putting students into sociocultural learning experiences (Barab, Squire, & Steinkuehler, 2012; Shaffer, 2006).

Activity theory was also embedded in *Quest Atlantis*. Activity theory describes how learning happens when one interacts with something in his or her environment (Daniels, 2001; Lave & Wenger, 1991; Vygotsky, 1978). Family Quest was a mission that applied activity theory by pairing parents with children in playful scenarios (Barab, Downton, & Siyahhan, 2010). Barab et al. (2010) findings suggested that playing the game promoted intergenerational play and apprenticeship learning.

Bron Stuckey and I spoke in December 2016 about *Quest Atlantis'* community of practice, and its apprenticeship learning models. "Those kids, right from the very beginning, were telling Sasha [Barab] and the design team exactly what they wanted, and what they wanted to see and have in a virtual world design space," Stuckey recalled. "It started out to be a learning space—but not an online textbook, like many other products in that period. We had strong elements to have it global from the get-go, and schools all over the world could use it. The fact that it was free got a lot of schools interested."

Teachers were restricted from bringing *Quest Atlantis* into a school without prior training. "Sasha said I trained around 5,000 teachers around the world," she said. "We didn't want teachers to get it on their own. We knew from the Second Life environment—and other games—like *River City* [the multi-user virtual environment developed at Harvard]—that there were too many 'Lone Rangers.'" By "Lone Ranger," Stuckey was referring to early adopters of new technologies who often do so on their own. Early adopters can do little to grow a community within a school.

"Our training required two teachers to attend," Stuckey continued. "We made efforts from the beginning to ensure the program was community-based for teachers." When a teacher returned to his or her school, there was a support network to use the product. In addition to local networks, *Quest Atlantis* launched a Facebook community, and an email listserv to further support teachers.

The *Quest Atlantis* team created rules and norms for student behavior. "It wasn't a list of dos and don'ts," Stuckey said. "That was deliberate. It was a list of what it looks like to be a good person, thoughtful, kind, and caring." They knew this was a social experiment, and it needed some structure. "We monitored all of the chats. Teachers were sent chat transcripts in case there was anything of concern." Chat transcripts became necessary because *Quest Atlantis* was open 24/7—students could be online anytime of the day, even when teachers weren't. But a teacher could read the transcripts later. "Teachers across the globe loved that."

Over the course of 12 years, the *Quest Atlantis* team discovered three children who posted thoughts of self-harm. "We were able to contact the schools and let them know to get counselors in. Principals in each of these three cases were happy because those chats could have happened somewhere where nobody would notice—outside of a trusted space."

The virtual environment of *Quest Atlantis* was a "horizontal learning space," placing teachers and students on equal footing. Teachers and students did not have separate, or distinct avatars (graphical representations of players). "We did not want teachers to be the police in the world," Stuckey said. The design decision was to create a space of sociocultural learning opportunities. She continued:

> That was an important point—the teachers had to come in as colearners in this space. Their avatars looked like the kids' avatars. Students only knew if you were a teacher by dialogue with you in the world. In the first year I was involved, if you told someone you were a teacher, they would run far away to the farthest part of the world

they could get to. After we had enough kids and teachers in, you then became a point of contact. Kids would ask where your kids are, or what do you teach, what age do you teach, what was your students' favorite boy band? When will your kids be on so we can meet them? You became a point of interest for kids as a teacher.

It was important for the designers and researchers to ensure that teachers didn't bring their "power role" from the classroom into the virtual space. "Teachers were the trusted adults," Stuckey said. There were design elements in place for building positive norms. Students were encouraged to be positive with others and to learn coping strategies. "And this is over 12 years ago. We're still doing the same things in *Minecraft* today. Kids need these experiences."

Minecraft Mentors

We see reverberations of Stuckey's research today in *Minecraft: Education Edition*'s teacher community. That is no coincidence; Stuckey consulted with the team at Microsoft Education when it launched its Global *Minecraft* Mentor Program back in 2016.

Similar to *Quest Atlantis*, when a teacher uses *Minecraft* with students, his or her onscreen avatar resembles the students'. But unlike *Quest Atlantis*, the students are likely the experts in the virtual space—not the teachers. "The leveling between teachers and students is interesting," Meenoo Rami said. Rami works with the *Minecraft* Education community at Microsoft. We spoke in early 2017. "It goes beyond leveling; it's not even on par with teachers." Having students as experts changes the dynamic in the system of a classroom. Rami continued:

> The students actually come in as already experts of this experience. The teacher has to figure out how to not let that expertise get to them—or overwhelm them. How do I use that expertise to make connections to the curriculum or the content or the concepts or ideas I want my students to discover? Students are mostly past the teachers' expertise in *Minecraft*, and the roles are reversed.

Not a self-described gamer, nor a hardcore *Minecraft* player, Rami is a former teacher at Philadelphia's Science Leadership Academy. She also served as a teaching fellow with the Bill and Melinda Gates Foundation. "I embody the spirit of the community," she said. "It shares commonly held beliefs like kids should be creating, not just consuming. Kids can be amazing problem solvers if given the chance to do so. Their work should be shared and published and celebrated for more than just a grade in a gradebook."

Those foundational beliefs about teaching and learning support why Rami, as well as those in The Tribe, feel comfortable to connect with people—whether it is across the hall or across the world. *Minecraft* is not an easy thing to pick up, like planning a traditional lesson. "You do need support. When you are adapting this for your students it's really important to have a community to lean on."

Rami supports teachers who use the resources created by the *Minecraft* teacher community, like shared worlds or lesson plans. "Whether it is a single teacher or an entire district buying the game, Neil [Manegold, her colleague at Microsoft] and I help them get started on their *Minecraft* journey," she said. "Teaching with *Minecraft* is always more powerful with someone else on the journey with you." Some teachers who use *Minecraft* are confident to learn with and from their students. Rami also pointed out an unintended benefit: teachers gain a sense of empathy for their students. "You see how it is when you feel lost or overwhelmed or confused."

On the *Minecraft: Education Edition* website, a teacher can connect with a mentor, review shared lessons, and even download a premade map of a game world. The mentorship program is a competitive program that pairs teacher experts with new community members. Rami looks for educators who want to be part of something bigger. "That hunger and curiosity to seek to make connections, and to want to learn from other teachers," she said. "Every single person we selected this year is kind and decent. I wanted people who are bighearted and big minded. It isn't about us—it's about the students that we get to serve."

To learn more about the mentorship program, I spoke to Mark Grundel. A member of The Tribe, Grundel teaches 5th grade in New Jersey. "The way I see being a *Minecraft* mentor is that I can get teachers comfortable using the game," he said, in early 2017. "The mindset is that you [a newly onboarded teacher] don't need to know everything, and that it is okay to just be the facilitator. You're not going to be an expert—unless you quit your day job!"

As a mentor, Grundel's goal is to get teachers to be comfortable using the game in their classrooms. "*Minecraft* is very community-driven. Without the community *Minecraft* wouldn't be what it is—not just the educator community, but also the YouTube community, and the modding and building community."

Balanced Learning Games

A game's core mechanics can be defined as the repeated actions performed during play (Fullerton, 2008; Salen & Zimmerman, 2003). The degree of effectiveness of an educational game can be analyzed by matching core mechanics to learning goals (Beall, Clarke-Midura, Groff, Owen, & Rosenheck, 2015). In other words, a good geometry game should not quiz players about postulates and theorems; instead, a balanced game should engage the player in the actions of doing geometry.

Balanced games align "learning goals, game mechanics and judgments about learner play and performance" (Beall et al., 2015, p. 7). To proceed to challenging game levels, players master leveled challenges within the constraints of the game's system. Mastering a core mechanic in a balanced game may indicate mastery of a learning goal. Data from player progress can then be analyzed to "assess students' understanding of the content" (Beall et al., 2015, p. 9).

SimCityEDU: Pollution Challenge! is a balanced game. Published by GlassLab Games, it is an educational modification of the commercial version. Players are put in the role of city manager solving authentic problems. A series of four increasingly complex missions, *SimCityEDU: Pollution Challenge!* is aligned to both Common Core State Standards and the Next Generation Science Standards. To succeed, players need to master a city's interconnected system. Eliminating coal-burning facilities results in a cleaner city, but also results in a higher unemployment rate.

Mars Generation One: Argubot Academy is another balanced game from GlassLab. It teaches argumentation schemes using a trading card mechanic, and it was designed to reward students for linking evidence to claims (*Field Study Results: Mars*, 2015). Writing claims-based arguments is in the Common Core State Standards for English language arts ("Common Core," 2017). After playing *Mars Generation One: Argubot Academy*, 65% of students improved from pretest to posttest after playing for 2 hours (*Field Study Results: Mars*, 2015). Promising data has also been reported in early research pertaining to GlassLab's middle school math game, *Ratio Rancher*. After playing for 3 days, student participants showed "significant learning gains in their understanding of ratios and proportions"—a Common Core mathematics skill ("Common Core," 2017; *Field Study Results: Ratio*, 2015, p. 1).

My observations and interviews with members of The Tribe indicated that they rarely sought out educational games with core mechanics that were matched to singular content goals. Instead, many selected commercial, off-the-shelf games (e.g., *Minecraft*, *World of Warcraft*), award winners (*Gone Home*) or tabletop games adapted to meet several desired objectives.

In a November 2015 interview, Darvasi commented to me about how a teacher could appropriate a game's core mechanics (actions of play, like guessing or jumping) to match learning goals. He said:

> Can you map [core] mechanics to learning mechanics? Mechanics that have been identified and isolated that have definite learning attached to them ... I think that's where the research is going to go in the next decade in games and learning—to understand how the individual components of the game bestow a pedagogical value on the experience *in addition* [emphasis added] to the content. I'm a firm believer in Marshall McLuhan's phrase that "the medium is the message," and the mechanics constitute the structural elements of the game. They convey knowledge, certain elements, certain affordances and restrictions. Understanding that is only going to better position us as educators who want to use games in a meaningful and productive way in our classrooms.

Epistemic Games

Epistemics study the processes in which people speak and act in the workforce, and *epistemic games* apply that to make learning authentic (Arastoopour, Bagley, Chesler, D'Angleo, & Shaffer, 2013). A genre of balanced video games that apply sociocultural learning principles, to play an epistemic game, one must master the epistemic grammar, or semiotic language (Gee, 2007a; Shaffer, 2006). This is a tenet of sociocultural theory: learning occurs once there is an understanding of semiotics—the language of the situation, or workplace (Daniels, 2001; Gee, 2007a; Vygotsky, 1978).

The value of epistemic games is that learning is presented in schema models, which can then be tested again in different scenarios (Shaffer, 2012). These types of games put players in authentic settings in which situated learning must take place in order to progress (Shaffer, 2006). Players succeed only if they master the semiotic grammar needed to be a part of a particular community of practice or workforce culture (e.g., in *SimCity* the player acts as a city manager; Gee, Halverson, Shaffer, & Squire, 2005; Shaffer, 2006).

Epistemic games are "based on the ways in which professionals acquire their epistemic frames may thus provide an alternative model for organizing our educational system" (Shaffer, 2006, p. 223). An *epistemic frame* is the lens in which one views an experience (Shaffer, 2006). Epistemic frames describe the skills, knowledge, identity, and values—wrapped in a particular epistemology—which learners use to solve complex problems (Shaffer, 2006). Many in The Tribe assessed learning outcomes by asking students to test out their epistemic frames—which were situated in a game's space—to other contexts outside of the game world.

To learn more about epistemic games, I spoke with the Epistemic Games Group's David Williamson Shaffer in January 2017. "More than having the parts of an epistemic frame, what actually matters is the ways those things are connected to one another," Shaffer began. He continued:

> The idea of the epistemic frame is that you have skills, knowledge, identity, and values. I can talk about understanding that I have to please the stakeholders in the city when I'm doing urban design [in a city-planning game, like *SimCity*]. That means is that I also understand that [pleasing the stakeholders] is related to the land use choices we have, the environmental constrains that we're under, and the social and economic goals the city has.

Shaffer noted the importance of contemplation while in a task—the reflection-in-action—and after the experience, the reflection-on-action (Schön, 1983). "We care about students understanding how ideas are related to one another." I observed members in The Tribe using reflection-on-action strategies as a method for students to apply epistemic grammar to settings outside of the game's space (Schön, 1983). Their students played games, then they reflected on decisions and consequences.

Gamification

Socratic Smackdown is a gamified debate game from the Institute of Play. I regularly had students play to debate current events. To play, a small group of students sit in a circle, and then engage in a Socratic-style argument about a topic. "At the end of the day, *Socratic Smackdown* is a book club discussion," the Institute of Play's C. Ross Flatt explained to me in late 2016. "There are points and rules associated with it, and there are rewards that make it a game on the surface—but really, it's a book talk."

Gamification takes elements associated with games and places them in non-game contexts (Kapp, 2012). It "incorporates the use of rewards to drive action" (Anderson & Rainie, 2012, p. 1). Critics point out that mechanics can extrinsically motivate (Kapp, 2012; Sheldon, 2012). Nonetheless, gamification shows promise in its effectiveness for increasing student outcomes and motivation (Salinas, Sanchez, & Sturges, 2015).

The aspects of games that may draw teachers into adopting gamification techniques may include the reward and incentive systems built into gaming experiences. Digital badges are one example. A component of many video games, digital badges signify skill mastery ("Open Badges for Lifelong Learning," 2012). Digital badges are also an increasing element in education, which can help personalize learning achievements (Adams Becker, Estrada, Freeman, & Johnson, 2015).

Some teachers might be more easily drawn to the reward structures typical with gamification than by using video games as their focal point of instruction. I spoke to Melissa Pilakowski about why that might be. An English teacher and moderator of the Games4Ed Twitter chat, we spoke in February 2017. "I think game-based learning is harder for some teachers to wrap their brains around," she replied. "Gamification is easier for teachers. They can take what they are doing right now and add a layer. With game-based learning, you change the way you teach—not just the incentives of how you teach. It's a bigger risk."

Classcraft is an example of a gamified layer that some members of The Tribe reported using in their classrooms. Classcraft groups students into teams, a bit like the guild structures in the video game *World of Warcraft*. The rewards range from eating snacks in class to asking the teacher for test answers. The Classcraft website suggests that teachers use the system to engage learning and manage student behavior ("Classcraft," 2015). Of its teacher users, "98% reported playing increased student engagement; 99% reported a positive impact on the classroom behavior; 88% reported an increase in academic performance; and 89% reported an increase in overall efficiency in the classroom" ("Classcraft," 2015, "After Sampling 100's of Teachers").

Special education science teacher Dan Curcio uses gamification to structures create student teams. Rather than Classcraft, he opted to put his "skeletal framework" on the learning management platform Edmodo. "I post research questions there, and I have folders on there with interactive content," he said, early in 2017. "They can score points by doing things." Some of those "things" range from projects in *Minecraft* to online science games available on the PhET website [a series of science and math interactives from the University of Colorado, Boulder].

"The goal [of gamification] is to create a climate of collaboration for students," Curcio explained. "Let's say we're studying cell structures. We will put together a giant cell, modeled as a working city in *Minecraft*." Then he gamifies it by adding a team dynamic. Teams have to answer questions, and then they make a *Minecraft* world based on those questions. Curcio also has students complete graphic organizers to assess learning outcomes. "At the beginning of the year we build a rapport. That's where team building comes in. They learn to become part of a team that is not athletic."

When teams are created, Curcio connects assigned research topics to his science curriculum. "This year it was climatology, and students had to find terminology on natural disasters, climate terms, and endangered animals." After they find enough "buzzwords," they create a team name and mascot based on those findings. "That's how I roll into the year, by developing a team, using the content I am using that year. The classroom environment is developed so it will have collaboration."

Game-Like Learning

Games can situate learning and bring equity to the classroom (Gee, 2007a). This may include using "game-like learning" techniques, in which parts of the game's system become parts of the system of a classroom (Gee, 2007b, p. 207). Students in this setting would then have chances to approach the same complex problem differently, in authentic contexts (Gee, 2007b). Members of The Tribe may be drawn in by these constructivist views. But this approach has different meanings depending on the game used.

Game-like learning describe the philosophy used at Quest to Learn, the public school in New York City cofounded by Katie Salen, coauthor of *Rules of Play: Game Design Fundamentals* ("Institute of Play," 2015; Salen & Zimmerman, 2003). The curriculum also embeds design thinking and systems thinking (Rufo-Tepper, Salen, Shapiro, Torres, & Wolozin, 2011). Learning trajectories are housed in a mission and quest structure. Missions are several weeks, while quests have goals that are achievable in 1 or 2 days (Rufo-Tepper et al., 2011). Quest students also take part in "boss levels," the culminating task to apply all that was taught (Rufo-Tepper et al., 2011, p. 73).

The Quest to Learn philosophy is built on game-like learning principles, which are ingrained in curriculum development ("Institute of Play," 2015). Game-like doesn't have to be a game; instead, students are using playful concepts to engage in larger experiences. The Game-like Learning Principles—which were observed in The Tribe's classrooms—are:

1. Everyone is a participant.
2. Challenge is constant.
3. Learning happens by doing.
4. Feedback is immediate and ongoing.
5. Failure is reframed as iteration.
6. Everything is interconnected.
7. It kind of feels like play. (Q Design Pack Games and Learning, 2013, p. 49)

Games can be used to model how interconnected systems in the world function (Rufo-Tepper et al., 2011). When students are using games for learning, they "pay explicit attention to the status of games as dynamic learning systems, as rule-based models supporting specific ways of knowing and doing" (Rufo-Tepper et al., 2011, p. 85). The ability to understand interconnected systems is a 21st century skill that games can be used to teach effectively ("Framework for 21st Century Learning," 2015; Gresalfi, Peppler, Santo, & Salen-Tekinbaş, 2014). A systems thinker is able to "analyze how parts of a whole interact with each other to produce overall outcomes in complex systems" ("Framework for 21st Century Learning," 2015, p. 4).

Playing, modifying existing rules, and designing new games are methods to teach systems thinking experientially (Gee, 2007a; Gresalfi et al., 2014; Salen & Zimmerman, 2003; Torres, 2009). In a 20-month study of Quest students, there was significant growth shown in responses to pretest to posttest questions pertaining to systems thinking skills (Shute, Torres, & Ventura, 2013). Learning outcomes were "primarily a function of being part of Quest to Learn" (Shute et al., 2013, p. 64).

Game-like Learning Principles resonated with the C. Ross Flatt. He trains teachers on game-like learning through the Institute of Play's TeacherQuest professional development program. The Game-like Learning Principles allow him to consider whether an experience he brings to teachers is actually game-like. "It gave language to something I valued, and it contextualized it," he said. "It doesn't have to hit on all of those principles, but it does let me think more deeply if I am using game-like learning or is it fancy dressing."

Game-like experiences are not teacher-directed quiz shows, like classroom *Jeopardy!*; rather, they feel playful and are immersive. All students should be learning by doing. And it should seem fun. No wonder the infographic of the Game-like Learning Principles is the Institute's most tweeted image!

Games as Designed Spaces

Game-based learning proponents—like those in The Tribe—note the potential games have to bolster a child's creativity, innovative thinking skills, and problem solving abilities—all of which are 21st century skills ("Framework for 21st Century Learning," 2015; King, 2011). Games are designed spaces (Squire, 2006). Playing video games requires a deep understanding of the game's semiotic domain—as prescribed by the designer—in order to progress (Gee, 2007a).

When playing a digital game, there are affordances, signifiers, and constraints in which players interact. Affordances invite people to interact with a real or virtual object (Norman, 2013). In a video game, an affordance may be the image of a door, which may suggest that the player should pass through to the next room. A signifier is more direct in stating what actions a person should take (Norman, 2013). Signifiers in a video game can be written text or blinking arrows. When the screen is tinted red in the war game *Call of Duty*, loss of health points is being signified. Constraints are the rules that structure the design of a game's system (Norman, 2013; Salen & Zimmerman, 2003). Learning the constraints is part of the engagement of playing video games.

There are clear connections to game level design and the zone of proximal development, in which problems are ordered in increasing complexity (Vygotsky, 1978). Good games increase task complexity to keep players engaged (Gee, 2007a). Stealth assessments are embedded into the code of a video game and assess without stopping the actions of play (Shute, 2011). In the physics game *Newton's Playground*, stealth assessments were analyzed—specifically player persistence to find solutions (Shute, 2011). Regarding physics concepts (e.g., velocity, gravity), there was a significant relationship between persistence to achieve in the game to posttest assessed learning outcomes (Kim, Shute, & Ventura, 2013).

Cognitive, motivational, emotional, and social benefits have been observed when youth play video games (Engels, Granic, & Lobel, 2014). Of teens aged 13–17, 83% play video games together in-person, and 75% play together online (Anderson, Duggan, Lenhart, Perrin, & Smith, 2015). Social and emotional learning (SEL) skills are another promise offered by advocates of game-based learning. The mobile game *If You Can* (2015) was intentionally designed to teach SEL skills. Code was embedded to assess play using evidence-centered design methodology ("If You Can," 2015). The game connects player choices to SEL goals, which include tools for regulation, grit and persistence, and emotional management ("If You Can," 2015).

The Intersection of Games and Learning

There is mounting research on video games as new digital media literacy, and on teacher attitudes regarding the use of games to teach (Fishman, Plass, Riconscente, Snider, & Tsai, 2014). The A-GAMES study is particularly useful in reporting how teachers use the assessment reports in balanced games designed specifically for learning. It was also used to analyze responses of the teachers who were "enthusiastic" about game-based learning (Fishman et al., 2014, p. 27). Of the teachers surveyed, 18% were clustered in this group (Fishman et al., 2014). Teachers in this segment (Cluster 1) "use games more often than teachers in other clusters for understanding student learning and making instructional decisions" (Fishman et al., 2014, p. 27).

Games used in The Tribe's classrooms serve to drive experiential learning. Students were presented with optimally challenging, meaningful choices in situated contexts (Gee, 2007a; Salen & Zimmerman, 2003). The games had an agreed-upon codified rule-set and a goal; they were "games with rules" (Piaget, 1962, p. 146). Games with rules are social and rule-dependent (Piaget, 1962). Strategy, competition, and games of chance are examples. Games with rules are the most common in middle childhood and are "almost the only ones that persist at the adult stage" (Piaget, 1962, p. 146).

As a tool, games can be used as a drill-and-skill rote memorization, or games can be authentic spaces of inquiry that inspire deeper learning experiences (Gee, 2007a). Games are "a system in which players engage in an artificial conflict, defined by rules, that results in a quantifiable outcome" (Salen & Zimmerman, 2003, p. 80). "Good" video games "are crafted in ways that encourage and facilitate active and critical learning and thinking" (Gee, 2007a, p. 38). Good games can engage students in the process of meta-cognition; players often hypothesize how a designer would think in order to solve a presented problem (Gee, 2007a). Video games are "designed experiences" in which players take agency of a role and learn by doing (Gee, 2007a, p. 41; Squire, 2006).

Games can also be used to provide a personalized opportunity to learn curriculum (Gee, 2007b). The process of thinking like a game designer creates a sense of equity for students in the 21st century (Kafai & Peppler, 2012). Learner equity is also a function of the student's support system at home (Gee, 2007b). Poor children lack the same opportunity to have experience-based, situated learning outside of the school day (Gee, 2007b). Regarding the video game *Portal 2* and situated learning, Gee (as cited in Herron, 2012) asserted:

> If one kid has 10,000 hours of experience with the stuff the book's about—like 10,000 hours of playing [the video game] *Portal*—that kid has a much better opportunity to learn than the kid that has 14 minutes. Opportunity to learn is not the book—it's whether you can bring experience to the book. (para. 16)

In *Portal 2*, players take agency of a character that must solve a series of progressively complex physics puzzles by testing and hypothesizing solutions, applying the scientific method in the system of a game (Gee, 2007a; Ke, Shute, & Ventura, 2015). *Portal 2* has been shown to improve cognition because problems are presented in a situated context and environment (Ke et al., 2015). Learning outcomes related to physics improved more from *Portal 2* than with brain-training games, which did not evoke player agency or role-play (Ke et al., 2015).

The Business of Games4Ed

Mitch Weisburgh is a partner at Academic Business Advisors, an educational technology consultant company, as well as the cofounder of the nonprofit Games4Ed. Weisburgh might be the member of The Tribe with the most business acumen. He is also a regular attendee at the Serious Play Conference, the ISTE Conference, and the Games in Education Symposium. We spoke in March 2017 about the challenges of making and distributing good learning games.

Although active in educational technology for decades, Weisburgh's involvement with learning games dates back just a few years—2014 to be precise. That year, Ed Metz, program director of the Small Business Innovation Research (SBIR) grant program for the Department of Education, invited Weisburgh, amongst many others, to Washington, D.C. to discuss the potential for games in education.

As Weisburgh explains it, monies from the SBIR program originate at the Small Business Administration (SBA). From there, funds are allocated through federal departments, including the aforementioned Department of Education (through the Institute of Education Sciences, or IES), the National

Science Foundation, (NSF), and the National Institute of Health (NIH). "The idea is to grant monies that will spur new and innovative research," he said. "These ideas should be big. Ideas that are too risky for venture capital or private equity to finance, but could have a big return."

SBIR grants have two phases: Phase I pertains to feasibility, and the award is in the $100,000 range; Phase II is about $800,000. "The money is a grant, not a loan," Weisburgh continued. "Money can be used for development—but some also has to be used for research."

Weisburgh estimated the total market for U.S. schools to purchase games at about $150 million. Herein lies the problem. Creating a polished high quality video game can cost millions of dollars. Getting a return on that investment is hardly guaranteed. "Very few educational games can span more than one or two grade levels," he said. "And generally games are very narrow in range, like a game about photosynthesis or a certain way of handling an algebraic concept."

The idea of SBIR-granted educational games is to support development early on, lowering some of the financial barriers to innovation. But there still are obstacles. While at the Ed Games Expo in 2014—an exhibition fair of SBIR-supported games—Weisburgh recalled thinking, "When I looked at each game, I thought, there is no way that they could make it in the education market. There's no way it can scale. None will get enough traction to reach kids."

After the Expo, Weisburgh headed to a meeting at the White House. The purpose was to discuss how to make games more successful in schools. When word got out that the Bill and Melinda Gates Foundation intended to invest in game-based learning, the tone of the meeting shifted. "It went from how do we get games more successful in schools to how do we get money from Gates Foundation." Weisburgh left disappointed.

On the train ride home, Weisburgh spoke to Larry Cocco, who was New Jersey's director of educational technology. Weisburgh asked Cocco, "What if we got together educators, administrators, researchers, developers and figure things out like we should've yesterday, at the White House?"

And they did. A few months later, just before the Future of Education Conference (FETC), in Orlando, Florida, Weisburgh and Cocco organized the Games4Ed group. Weisburgh's connection to The Tribe was the Games4Ed group. Nowadays there are three people on the Games4Ed board of directors: Weisburgh, Lucas Gillispie, and FableVision's Shelby Marshall. Weisburgh's role is to look for opportunities to help people who are good at game-based learning (i.e., those in The Tribe) to share best practices. Melissa Pilakowski moderates the weekly #Games4Ed Twitter chat, which is one of the idea forums for likeminded teachers to share game-based learning methods.

Chapter Summary

As a tool for teaching, games could potentially create learner equity, giving all children access the prescribed academic curriculum—the underlying tenet of several teacher effectiveness models. Playing games creates an opportunity to learn. But how do expert teachers of game-based learning use games in their classrooms? And how do these expert teachers of game-based learning view the effectiveness of this teaching technique?

Part II of this book takes a deep dive into three classrooms. My field research into Paul Darvasi, Steve Isaacs, and Peggy Sheehy's classrooms reveal that they played in the same horizontal learning space as their students. For example, Sheehy joined her students in their *World of Warcraft* guilds, and she played the card game *Guillotine* with some of her students. Part III connects my field research to additional interviews with others in The Tribe. It also shares best practice ideas from this affinity group of experts.

References

Adams Becker, S., Estrada, V., Freeman, A., & Johnson, L. (2014). *NMC horizon report: 2014 K–12 edition*. Austin, TX: The New Media Consortium.

Adams Becker, S., Estrada, V., Freeman, A., & Johnson, L. (2015). *NMC horizon report: 2015 K–12 edition*. Austin, TX: The New Media Consortium.

Anderson, J., & Rainie, L. (2012, May 18). *The future of gamification*. Retrieved from Pew Internet & American Life Project website: http://www.pewinternet.org/Reports/2012/Future-of-Gamification.aspx

Anderson, M., Duggan, M., Lenhart, A., Perrin, A., & Smith, A. (2015, August). *Teens, technology and friendships*. Pew Research Center. Retrieved from http://www.pewinternet.org/2015/08/06/teens-technology-and-friendships/

Arastoopour, G., Bagley, E. A., Chesler, N., D'Angleo, C., & Shaffer, D. W. (2013). Design of a professional practice simulator for educating and motivating first-year engineering students. *Advances in Engineering Education*, 3(3), 1–29.

Barab, S., Dodge, T., & Thomas, M. (2005). Making learning fun: Quest Atlantis, a game without guns. *Educational Technology Research & Development*, 53(1), 86–107. doi:10.1007/BF02504859

Barab, S. A., Downton, M. P., & Siyahhan, S. (2010). Using activity theory to understand intergenerational play: The case of family quest. *International Journal of Computer-Supported Collaborative Learning, 5*(4), 415–432.

Barab, S., Squire, K., & Steinkuehler, C. (Eds.). (2012). *Games, learning, and society: Learning and meaning in the digital age.* Cambridge, MA: Cambridge University Press.

Beall, M., Clarke-Midura, J., Groff, J., Owen, V. E., & Rosenheck, L. (2015). *Better learning in games: A balanced design lens for a new generation of learning games.* Retrieved from MIT Scheller Teacher Education Program website: http://education.mit.edu/post-news/new-guide-from-lgn-and-education-arcade-informs-next-generation-of-game-design/

Classcraft Homepage. (2015). Retrieved from http://www.classcraft.com/

Common Core Homepage. (2017). Retrieved from http://www.corestandards.org

Daniels, H. (2001). *Vygotsky and pedagogy.* London: Routledge Falmer.

Dewey, J. (1916). *Democracy and education.* New York, NY: Macmillan.

Engels, R., Granic, I., & Lobel, A. (2014). The benefits of playing video games. *American Psychologist, 69*(1), 66–78. doi:10.1037/a0034857

Field Study Results: Mars Generation One. (2015, February 20). Retrieved from GlassLab Games website: http://about.glasslabgames.org/wp-content/uploads/2014/08/ResearchMGOFull.pdf

Fishman, B., Plass, J., Riconscente, M., Snider, R., & Tsai, T. (2014). *Empowering educators: Supporting student progress in the classroom with digital games part I: A national survey.* Ann Arbor, MI: University of Michigan.

Framework for 21st Century Learning. (2015). *About us.* Retrieved from Partnership for 21st Century Learning website: http://www.p21.org/about-us/p21-framework

Fullerton, T. (2008). *Game design workshop: A playcentric approach to creating innovative games* (2nd ed.). Amsterdam, The Netherlands: Elsevier Morgan Kaufmann.

Gee, J. P. (2007a). *What video games have to teach us about learning and literacy* (rev. ed.). New York, NY: Palgrave Macmillan.

Gee, J. P. (2007b). Game-like learning: An example of situated learning and implications for opportunity to learn. In J. P. Gee, E. H. Haertel, P. A. Moss, & L. J. Young (Eds.), *Assessment, equity, and opportunity to learn* (pp. 200–221). New York, NY: Cambridge University Press.

Gee, J. P., Halverson, R. R., Shaffer, D. W., & Squire, K. D. (2005). Video games and the future of learning. *Phi Delta Kappan, 87*(2), 105–111.

Gray, P. (2014). *Free to learn: Why unleashing the instinct to play will make our children happier, more self-reliant, and better students for life.* New York, NY: Basic Books.

Gresalfi, M., Peppler, K. A., Santo, R., & Salen-Tekinbaş, K. (2014). *Gaming the system: Designing with Gamestar mechanic.* Cambridge, MA: MIT Press.

Herron, K. (2012). *Jim Gee on the use of video games for learning about learning.* Retrieved from Spotlight on Digital media and Learning website: http://spotlight.macfound.org/blog/entry/jim-gee-on-the-use-of-video-games-for-learning-about-learning/

If You Can. (2015). Retrieved from http://www.ifyoucan.org/how-does-if-teach-sel/

Institute of Play. (2015). Retrieved from http://www.instituteofplay.org

Kafai, Y. A., & Peppler, K. A. (2012). Developing gaming fluencies with Scratch: Realizing game design as a design process. In S. Barab, C. Steinkuehler, & K. Squire (Eds.), *Games learning society: Learning in the digital age* (pp. 355–380). Cambridge, MA: Cambridge University Press.

Kapp, K. M. (2012). *The gamification of learning and instruction: Game-based methods and strategies for training and education*. San Francisco, CA: Pfeiffer.

Ke, F., Shute, V. J., & Ventura, M. (2015). The power of play: The effects of Portal 2 and Lumosity on cognitive and noncognitive skills. *Computers & Education, 80,* 58–67.

Kim, Y. J., Shute, V. J., & Ventura, M. (2013). Assessment and learning of qualitative physics in Newton's playground. *The Journal of Educational Research, 106,* 423–430.

King, E. M. (2011). *Guys and games: Practicing 21st century workplace skills in the great indoors* (Doctoral dissertation). Retrieved from ProQuest Dissertations & Theses Full Text; ProQuest Dissertations & Theses Global. (Order No. 3488741) http://search.proquest.com/docview/917951417?accountid=12793

Klopfer, E., Osterweil, S., & Salen, K. (2009). *Moving learning games forward*. Retrieved from MIT Education Arcade website: http://education.mit.edu/wp-content/uploads/2015/01/MovingLearningGamesForward_EdArcade.pdf

Lave, J., & Wenger, E. (1991). *Situated learning: Legitimate peripheral participation*. Cambridge: Cambridge University Press.

Norman, D. A. (2013). *The design of everyday things* (rev. and expanded ed.). New York, NY: Basic Books.

Open Badges for Lifelong Learning. (2012, January 23). Working paper. Retrieved from MozillaWiki website: https://wiki.mozilla.org/images/5/59/OpenBadges-Working-Paper_012312.pdf

Piaget, J. (1962). *Play, dreams and imitation in childhood*. New York, NY: Norton Library.

Q Design Pack Games and Learning. (2013). Retrieved from http://www.instituteofplay.org/wp-content/uploads/2013/09/IOP_QDesignPack_GamesandLearning_1.0.pdf

Rufo-Tepper, R., Salen, K., Shapiro, A., Torres, R., & Wolozin, L. (2011). *Quest to learn: Developing the school for digital kids*. Cambridge, MA: MIT Press.

Salen, K., & Zimmerman, E. (2003). *Rules of play: Game design fundamentals*. Cambridge, MA: MIT Press.

Salinas, A., Sanchez, J., & Sturges, D. L. (2015). Gamification as a teaching strategy: Is it effective? *HETS Online Journal* (pp. 22–47). Retrieved from http://draweb.njcu.edu:2048/login?url=http://search.ebscohost.com/login.aspx?direct=true&db=eue&AN=103664855&site=ehost-live

Schön, D. A. (1983). *The reflective practitioner*. London: Temple Smith.

Shaffer, D. W. (2006). Epistemic frames for epistemic games. *Computers and Education, 46*(3), 223–234.

Shaffer, D. W. (2012). Models of situated action: Computer games and the problem of transfer. In C. Steinkuehler, K. Squire, & S. Barab (Eds.), *Games learning society: Learning in the digital age* (pp. 403–431). Cambridge, MA: Cambridge University Press.

Sheldon, L. (2012). *The multiplayer classroom: Designing coursework as a game*. Boston, MA: Course Technology/Cengage Learning.

Shute, V. J. (2011). Stealth assessment in computer-based games to support learning. *Computer Games and Instruction, 55*(2), 503–524.

Shute, V. J., Torres, R., & Ventura, M. (2013). Formative evaluation of students at Quest to Learn. *International Journal of Learning and Media, 4*(1), 55–69.

Squire, K. (2006). From content to context: Video games as designed experiences. *Educational Researcher, 35*(8), 19–29. Retrieved from http://website.education.wisc.edu/~kdsquire/tenure-files/18-ed%20researcher.pdf

Torres, R. J. (2009). *Learning on a 21st century platform: Gamestar mechanic as a means to game design and systems-thinking skills within a nodal ecology* (Doctoral dissertation). Retrieved from ProQuest Dissertations & Theses Full Text; ProQuest Dissertations & Theses Global. (Order No. 3361988) http://search.proquest.com/docview/304957106?accountid=12793

Vygotsky, L. S. (1978). *Mind in society: The development of higher psychological processes.* Cambridge, MA: Harvard University Press.

ns the variations game-based learning takes. "Game design is a huge piece of it.
PART II
A CLOSE LOOK AT THE TRIBE IN ACTION

In late 2015, I embedded myself into Peggy Sheehy, Paul Darvasi, and Steve Isaacs' classrooms. I had the unique opportunity to observe them in action as they taught with games. Each used games differently: as a text to be critically analyzed, as a shared experience, and as a model with which to draw inspiration for student designs. After my visit I interviewed them, and surveyed their students. Lastly, I coded my data and looked for lessons learned from these leaders and experts in this game-based learning community. The analysis appears in Part III, which expands to include more interviews with others in The Tribe.

After my field research, I reunited with my original dissertation participants at the 2016 Games in Education Symposium (see Figure P 2.1). I had discovered that game-based learning was baked differently into each of their classrooms. "Steve, Peggy, and Paul all use games, and have different approaches," Marianne Malmstrom, told me in late 2016. She reflected on the variations game-based learning takes. "Game design is a huge piece of it. Or games like *World of Warcraft*—for narrative and a whole range of literacies. You can connect it to literature to help with writing. Or do what Paul Darvasi does [with *Gone Home*] and take them on a whole intellectual journey to get them to think differently—not only at literature, but at the context of their lives."

Figure P 2.1. Steve Isaacs, Paul Darvasi, myself, and Peggy Sheehy (from left to right). Picture taken at the Games in Education Symposium in 2015, the summer after I visited their classrooms.

· 4 ·
"THE GODMOTHER OF EDUCATIONAL GAMING"

Peggy Sheehy is the cofounder of the WoWinSchool Project, which integrates the MMO game *World of Warcraft* into a classroom experience. Her 6th grade humanities lessons are a "massive series of 'quests,' each built around key skills and ideas" (Toppo, 2015, p. 133). Sheehy is "in demand at teacher's conferences, having laid out her vision before adoring crowds in Mumbai, San Francisco, and Sydney, among many others" (Toppo, 2015, p. 129). In August 2015, she served as a Teacher Fellow at Filament Games, an educational game company in Madison, Wisconsin.

Beginning the last week in September, students in Sheehy's classroom play *World of Warcraft*. It is then played for the duration of the school year. Only a few students have played it at all prior to my observation of her in 2015. She explained that several students wind up purchasing a subscription to the game after they are promoted from her room to 7th grade.

Sheehy takes in-game experiences and asks students to compare and contrast decisions to her course text (*The Hobbit*), as well as to their personal quests in adolescent life. This can take the form of whole class discussions or written assessments (e.g., reflection papers and prompts). Sheehy does not test her students, nor does she grade their reflections from playing games. Instead, she uses the XPs earned in *World of Warcraft* and in 3D GameLab (rebranded as Rezzly, in mid-November 2015), a gamified learning management system.

Because Sheehy is in a community of practice of game-using teachers, she is privy to learning about best practices to using games in the classroom. "Most of the time the games that I used were used by colleagues, or The Tribe," she said. With the case of *World of Warcraft* or other games, she plays to grasp the appropriateness for her 6th grade class. "Sometimes, however, games are not the answer."

If a game incorporates elements of historical fiction, as in the *Civilization* series of commercial, off-the-shelf games, Sheehy integrates it by having her class research what was true in the game, comparing it to what was not. "I think this approach gives students independence to own the learning," she said. Sheehy later described the process of bringing games to her students:

> I love this and it is so much fun, but what does that do for my learning goals, what I want them to be able to do when they leave my room at the end of June? Number one: it's critical thinking, problem solving, logical thinking, systems thinking, and I make them write about it. So I can always pull an English language arts piece and say write a review. The other piece is the social science portion of my curriculum, which needs to be equally supported and respected.

Suffern Middle School, where Sheehy teachers, is a public suburban school. It serves students from grades 6 through 8. In 2013, there were 1,107 students in the school. Typically, Sheehy teaches approximately 50 6th grade humanities students at Suffern Middle School, in the Suffern Central School District in Rockland County, New York. Her class is evenly split by gender. New York's public school curriculum meets the Common Core State Standards, and Sheehy's *World of Warcraft* lessons are Common Core-aligned.

For the past decade, Peggy Sheehy had been using virtual worlds with middle school students. Her journey using avatars in instruction began when she started the first Teen Grid, or virtual island, in *Second Life* in 2005. In 2010, Sheehy began to use the MMO game *World of Warcraft* with her after-school club. Three years later, in 2013, Sheehy was moved from her position as a librarian and became the humanities teacher. Sheehy's story was the focus of an entire chapter in Toppo's (2015) book, *The Game Believes In You*. Toppo, *USA TODAY*'s education reporter, had visited her classroom several times, beginning in 2011. In 2016, TechnologyEd, an Australian-based magazine, featured Sheehy on its cover, next to the headline, "The Godmother of Educational Gaming." She hints that Greg Toppo was the possible originator of the nickname, and has embraced it, using it in slides at conferences.

Sheehy was a speaker at almost every game-based conference I attended in 2015 and 2016. She played *World of Lexica*, a tablet-based reading adventure game, with our then four-year-old son at an open house at Schell Games' studio during the Serious Play Conference, in Pittsburgh. My son was entranced by Sheehy's (then) blue-streaked hair. At the following Serious Play Conference, at the University of North Carolina, Chapel Hill, my wife and son were again in tow (conferences during the summer become mini-vacations for our family!). Our son insisted on sitting with Sheehy during lunch, and even engaged in playing the card game *Guillotine* with her. Also playing *Guillotine* was Lucas Gillispie, Steve Isaacs, and myself. Who better to game with than The Tribe!

Room 339: Home to Epic Learners

Because I had met Sheehy several times over the years, gaining access to her classroom wasn't too difficult. Also, several other researchers had observed her approach. A precedent existed.

I visited her on Thursday and Friday, November 5 and 6, 2015. Her classroom is located on the third floor in suburban-set Suffern Middle School. The campus is large, with several connected three-level, red brick buildings. The room was at the end of a long hallway; the door adorned by a large sign reading, "Danger: Ninjas, Pirates, Monsters & Zombies." The door had no window. A smaller sign, with Sheehy's photograph, read: "Shhhh ... Testing," with the word *Testing* crossed out. The word *Learning* was scrawled underneath. A similar sign underneath read: "Shhh ... Gaming." Another note read: "Room 339: Home to Epic Learners." There was also an outdoor-style welcome mat at the entrance. Inside, signs read: "Never let school interfere with your education"; "This is your classroom: It needs to represent you ... get on it!"; and "Figure out why you are here and tell me. Do not tell me what you think I want to hear. But instead, tell me what you believe."

The classroom had a spirit of being different than the rest of the school, or the system of formal schooling, in general. In addition to technology, her room had a refrigerator and a microwave oven. The room was rectangular, with warmly painted walls: purple on two sides and yellow on the front and rear of the room. There were framed movie and game posters around the walls (e.g., *Starcraft II*, *The Hobbit*), as well as a GLS Conference poster and news clippings that featured Sheehy.

Sheehy's desk was in a nook at the rear of the room. Along the wall were framed diplomas. Behind Sheehy's desk were large *World of Warcraft* posters. In front was a bookshelf of game-based learning texts, including: Sheldon's

(2012) *Multiplayer Classroom* and Gee's (2007) *What Video Games Have to Teach Us About Learning and Literacy*. Sheehy had several other books on her desk, along with speakers, her personal iPad, and her iPhone. Her wallet was often left out on the desk. A bookshelf near her desk created a separation from the student area.

A line of Mac desktop computers snaked around the room's perimeter. The computers were arranged in a way that Sheehy could see all of the students' screens. Computers had *World of Warcraft* bulk subscription member cards under the monitor stands. The computer areas afforded space for only keyboards and mice—there was no room for student binders or notebooks. Each computer had a headset. Most students sat on rolling, orange plastic chairs. There was little room between workstations. Students stored bags and binders under the rolling chairs. There was a row of computers jutting out from the wall; students there sat on different colored swivel stools.

In front of the interactive SMART Board was a ring of seven Yogibo brand, oblong beanbag chairs. Each was a different color: blue, red, purple, and green. In the center was a rug adorned with a world map surrounded by children holding hands. Two flat-panel televisions were mounted on each side of the SMART Board: one with Xbox 360 and one with a PlayStation 3. This area was known as "Circle" (see Figure 4.1). There was a sneaker bin for students in Circle.

Figure 4.1. Circle area in Sheehy's classroom. Source: Author.

There were a lot of items and furniture in the room, with items arranged in neat piles and furniture placed in an orderly fashion. There were numerous books in the class, including history textbooks; however, students used none while I was present. There were overflowing boxes and crates of fantasy-themed books and game guides. Student artifacts were also scattered around the room. One showed handwritten text with stages of the hero's journey from Joseph Campbell's (1949/2008) seminal book, *The Hero with a Thousand Faces*. Next to each stage of the hero's journey were descriptions from *The Hobbit*. Stars hung from the ceiling, each with an image of the student in the center and descriptive words on each point. Stars were attached to yarn, hung several feet down, rather low.

Teaching Her Heroes

Sheehy teaches two double periods of 6th grade humanities each day: Periods one and two (Humanities AM) and periods six and seven (Humanities PM). Each class was 1 hour and 50 minutes in duration. There was a 2 hour break between classes; the last period of the day also had no students. Sheehy advises the *World of Warcraft* in School (*WoWinSchool*) afterschool club, Mondays through Thursdays. Students addressed the teacher as "Miss Sheehy." Each time a student said, "Mrs. Sheehy," she responded, "*Mrs.* Sheehy is on the beach in Tahiti." Students were called by first name. Sometimes, the class was collectively called "Heroes."

On both days I was there, students in the Humanities AM class arrived about 10 minutes before the bell. They entered the room quietly, sat at computers, put on headphones, and launched applications without teacher direction. She was observed planning lessons or playing *World of Warcraft* at her desk as students arrived. Occasionally she would look up and said prompts like: "On task and academic" and "Headsets on." On the first visit, Sheehy turned to me and said, "My style is to interrupt." Sheehy never left the room during my visits.

Thursday

The classes on Thursday both started by reading through current events on the "Replica Edition" (school version) of the *New York Times* for 15 minutes. Students were quiet, each wearing headphones. Sheehy stated that headphones were used "in case a video on the *New York Times* website had volume." It was her tactic to "keep them focused—this is not a collaborative time of the day." Each student was assigned to write a reflection about an article they chose, which was posted on a Google Doc. Sheehy reminded students to start with

"I feel" or "I see" statements. She looked up from her screen and announced, "You know the drill." Students logged into the *New York Times* and Google Docs. As more students arrived, Sheehy said, "When you enter the room, take the lay of the land, adjust your voice and demeanor accordingly."

In the afternoon class, Sheehy told students that the newspaper's front page was where students would get a perspective of the world. She said, "It's a tilted perspective. What does that mean?" A girl said, "biased," which prompted Sheehy to ask whether the *New York Times* had a liberal or conservative bias. About 15–20 minutes into each class, Sheehy circulated through the class, correcting students as they worked.

During Circle each day, a student closed the door to the classroom. Every child, as if on cue, then chanted, "And we are safe, and we are valued, and we are powerful learners." On Monday morning, Sheehy responded, "And you take it to heart that each of you are safe, and you are valued, and are you are powerful learners—if you choose to be." Students' eyes were fixated on Sheehy, in the center of circle. She either sat higher up, on a swivel stool, or at the students' level, on a beanbag.

At Circle in both classes, Sheehy asked, "How many people enjoy the *New York Times*?" Most hands went up. One girl in the morning class said, "Sometimes it gets boring." Another girl said that the newspaper was "good at some topics, but not everything." Sheehy took a moment to explain how students could write a letter to the editor. She suggested, "Don't say it mean, but say it appropriately. Say why and back it up with factual information."

Sheehy then introduced a new "vocabulary acquisition" application, known as Membean. "Today we're going to look at something not quite a game and we are going to do it three times a week—whether you like it or not," she said. Sheehy explained that the website takes a "scientific approach to vocabulary acquisition." Next, she said, "Close your eyes. What word do you see when you hear acquisition?" One student answered, "accuracy"; another said, "position." Sheehy told students that "schema" is how they are guessing at words. Several students shaking fists, with thumbs and pinkies extended, was observed. Sheehy indicated that meant that other students had the same correct answer in mind.

Sheehy's afternoon explanation of the Membean vocabulary tool was nearly identical to the description that morning. In the afternoon, regarding vocabulary, Sheehy said, "Remember what I said about words? All the words in the universe are yours and you have permission to use them—just not all of them." Students were focused on Sheehy as she explained how the software makes associations and connections with visuals and words. She asked the morning class, "What's the first thing you do with new software? You take a test—the dirty word." One student asked, "How is that dirty?" Sheehy replied, "In my world, it's dirty. How many tests have you taken in this class this year? Zero." Next, referring to departmental benchmarks, Sheehy distanced herself stating, "Those other tests aren't my tests."

A quick transition sent students back to computer stations from Circle. "The software comes at you in different ways, with pictures, video," Sheehy said. "You'll see when you do it." Sheehy gave the website address and the class code to create accounts. She circulated the room, assisting individuals in need of further help. Sheehy next announced:

> Yes, why can you put your real, legitimate name? What does the *s* mean in *https*? It means *secure*. So you can put your last name. You are unique in the world. Capitalize your name, because you are a proper noun—you are special.

All observed students remained on-task in Membean. Sheehy directed students to "read everything on the page until you figure out what's going on." Next, she said, "See you in about a half an hour. Be honest, no one cares if you are right or wrong."

When a student appeared confused and a neighboring child tried to help, Sheehy said, "Stick to your own screens, he'll figure it out." When another student asked for help, Sheehy answered, "Use your best intuition without asking me. What do you think you should do now?" A few students shared the words in Membean with friends across the room. Sheehy reminded students look at their screens.

After 15 minutes of Membean, students were observed on 3D GameLab, either on a quest relating to *The Hobbit*, or on BrainPOP, watching short-form animated videos on geography topics. BrainPOP videos were embedded in the 3D GameLab quests. When one student launched *World of Warcraft*, Sheehy noticed immediately, said, "You have no business logging onto *WoW*." This was the only student observed off-task. The transition from the current events part of class to quests was seamless.

After the Membean assessment concluded for all students, in both Thursday classes, Sheehy looked up and said "Ago." Immediately, students responded "Ame." Ago and Ame is a call-and-response to signal a group's attention; it has Ghanian origins. Ago (pronounced "ahgoo") means "are you listening?" Ame (pronounced "ahmaaa") means "you have my attention." Next, Sheehy quietly said, "Circle," followed by "15 seconds, don't close anything [on your computer]—we're going back to it"; then, "10 and counting"; and finally, "and 5, 4, 3, 2, 1." Before Sheehy counted to one, all students were seated on beanbags around her in the circle area. Sheehy then said, "How much does my heart go thump, thump, thump when I see you all bring *The Hobbit* to Circle." One student responded "magical." Sheehy laughed.

During the morning class, Sheehy brought up the topic of literary devices and said that with "traditional teachers, if you get the words right, you get a lollipop. Instead, if you do really well, you will feel accomplished." Sheehy then said, "Metaphor? Every hand should be up." One student said, "The moon was a candle in the sky." Sheehy asked students to turn the phrase into a simile. A few students guessed wrong. Sheehy restated her question regarding similes and gave positive encouragement until the correct answer was offered.

The conversation at Circle changed to *The Hobbit*. In the morning Sheehy played a scene from a film adaptation of *The Hobbit*. Sheehy paused the video occasionally, asking questions like: "Watch his face. What is going on in Bilbo's head right now?" After the video clips, the topic of annotating *The Hobbit* with sticky notes came up. One boy then said, "I personally really suck at annotations." Sheehy immediately kneeled down at the student's level, on beanbags. "Do you want to talk about that?" she asked. "A big piece of annotating is why you play *World of Warcraft*. You're all really early in the game, some of you are stuck and then go back and read the quest again and then figure it out."

Sheehy explained that students were "deep reading" *World of Warcraft* and are doing the same with *The Hobbit*. She continued, "Read to understand, to predict, and to analyze." The student was advised to annotate with sticky notes on book pages and to use note-taking prompts, such as "I think" and "I wonder."

In each class, when about 40 minutes of time remained in the period, Sheehy instructed students to play *World of Warcraft*. In the morning, she said, "Just go right into play. Headsets on. Never ever, ever, ever play *WoW* without listening to it." She walked around computers and stated, "I love the fact that someone opened up to the reflection journal." Students logged in immediately and appeared engaged. Just like the scene viewed in *The Hobbit*, Sheehy stated that students would write and recite riddles in *World of Warcraft*.

When students had questions about the game, Sheehy often answered, "Ask three, then me." She shared technical advice, such as "professions are your priorities today." When a student told Sheehy that he had inventory issues with his game character, she assisted the student in trading items (e.g., rabbits' feet, gold to buy leather). When the class was louder during play, Sheehy looked up and said, "Hey, bring it down to a roar."

The lights were off during play. Some students had their journals open on Google Docs. Journal entries were dated and student work was visible on screens. One student had *World of Warcraft* on one window, and Google Docs open next to it. The document was titled "WoW Reflection." The page had a date and a sentence or two describing the day's activity. This day's entry read: "11/5/15: Today I did my first dungeon. It wasn't exactly fun (most likely because I didn't do anything yet)." Other observed reflections were brief in length. One observed student's screen showed a longer reflection on game play. This reflection detailed three quests. The student wrote:

> Yesterday on WoW i did 3 quests. The first quest was to show the Guy sword then i had to defeat 5 training targets. The last thing i had t do was to spar with 6 people. I spared with 2 people then i was looking for the third guy and I fell off the cliff i was like where am I. So I was running for about 3 or 4 minutes then I found some little creatures [and] they attacked me.

On Thursday afternoon, the following teacher–student exchange was observed:

Student:	Can you help me do the dungeon level?
Sheehy:	Here's what you do, honey. Click on this—on dungeon—then on random. Now listen to me, what are you?
Student:	Night Owl Hunter.
Sheehy:	Always stay way back from the wall. You never go close up to it. See I'm trying to level this guy up so we can do this together. Let me show you something.
Student:	I'm not used to *WoW*, it's not like other RPGs [role-playing games] I've played.
Sheehy:	Good! I'm glad it's not like other RPGs you've played. It's much more complex.

Sheehy continued to give game play advice to students. In the afternoon Sheehy told one student, "Remember you're going into a dungeon with five, six, or seven players. They're going to the dungeon for different reasons, some want to just power-up, or they may not do it all right, they may not talk." To another student, Sheehy asked, "What are you?" The student replied, "Pandarian Warrior." Sheehy then asked, "What level are you? Did you pick your specialization at level 10?" The student answered, "Yes. I don't know the name. The bloody one?" Other student questions pertained to game quests, dungeons, and overall strategy.

When Sheehy saw one student on another student's computer keyboard in the afternoon she said, "Never touch someone else's stuff." Students were overheard talking to themselves, saying: "This is terrifying" and "I found a cave!" Some children solved problems out loud, sharing their character's abilities and limitations (e.g., abilities unique to druids). Others shared location in game (e.g., "I'm in Duskwood."). Students helped each other. Since Circle, students were observed still wearing socks without shoes. When Sheehy asked the class on Thursday afternoon if they wanted the air conditioner on, she said, "This is your class."

Sheehy stated that the game could only be accessed from school. At the conclusion of the afternoon class, Sheehy reminded students to write reflections to "legitimize their learning" and to read and annotate *The Hobbit*.

Friday

Sheehy's teaching schedule on Friday was identical to the previous day. She sat at her desk as students arrived, either planning an upcoming River Valley Civilization lesson or playing *World of Warcraft* herself. The class worked without any prompting. In fact, students had a concerned look whenever Sheehy called a student by name, though this occurred very few times. She looked up to emphasize that Membean was not a graded test, but rather it was "an algorithm evaluating vocabulary skills." Later that morning, when a student was observed helping another to log in to Membean, Sheehy immediately looked up and said, "Don't do it for her. Tell her what to do." She then recited:

> If you give a man a fish, he will eat for one day. Teach a man to fish and he will eat for a lifetime. That's the same thing with teaching. If I do it for you you'll never learn to do it by yourself.

Sheehy then turned to me and said that there were four children in the afternoon class who had attention deficit hyperactive disorder (ADHD) and two who had individualized education plans (IEPs). Those students with IEPs attend self-contained classes during the day. Sheehy said to me that this was her favorite class.

After 15 minutes on Membean, students in the morning and afternoon classes entered their 3D GameLab quests. Some watched a BrainPOP movie; others worked on a teacher-created Google Doc chart on *The Hobbit*. The chart included directions for students to complete a list of vocabulary words, to identify important characters, and to describe significant themes. Other parts of the chart were directions for students to describe Bilbo's (the book's protagonist) feelings and character development. This chart was part of a learning quest housed in 3D GameLab.

Sheehy mentioned that "The Weekly" packet, with the short story *The Cabin in the Woods* and accompanying questions, was due at the end of next week. Sheehy next told students that to "play whatever you want" after Membean. Upon hearing this, each class erupted in enthusiasm. Sheehy listed potential games to play: *Hearthstone*, games on iCivics, *World of Warcraft*, or *Guillotine*. Sheehy had suggested playing Xbox, PlayStation, or Wii, although the controllers were all missing.

In the morning class, one student turned from the computer screen to Sheehy and said, "Uh, Miss Sheehy, the *WoW* servers are offline; they're doing an update." Sheehy answered, "On a Friday? How can they do that to me? You know what, don't jump the gun. Did it say our servers are down or did it say rolling restarts?" A student read his screen out loud, stating, "Blizzard is performing a scheduled maintenance Friday, November 6 at 5:00 a.m. PST, and to expect severs back at 6:00 a.m. Follow on Twitter for updates." Sheehy replied, "There must have been something really buggy because they normally do updates only on Tuesdays." Another student mentioned the Pacific Time Zone.

Sheehy stood up from her desk and then began a whole class discussion on time zones. "Five o'clock California time is what time in New York?" she asked. "Raise your hands." No hands went up. "We know you studied time zones, think about it. What time do you think it is? Here's the logic: California is to the west of us, which way does the sun rise?" Most hands then went up.

Sheehy directed the morning class to check their progress in 3D GameLab. Regarding submitted work, she said, "Don't send me junk—I'll only send it back to you." Midmorning, Sheehy asked the class to search the word "armory" in WoW.net. She then asked students to search for their *World of Warcraft* character's name. All students searched. "Mine isn't coming up," one girl said. "This is me!" another exclaimed. Sheehy instructed students to take a screen shot showing if their character is at Level 10. She then walked around one cluster of students, saying, "I expect you to all be self-starters."

For the next few minutes, students freely explored the page. Some chatted with neighbors about games statistics and the names of guilds on the page. Students were also reviewing the results of "Search the legacy" on WoW.net, as well as the Sisters of Elune server. Sheehy next asked students to look up difference between "alliance" and "horde." "They are playing as an alliance now and will be playing in a horde later in the school year," she quietly said to me.

Soon enough most students were reviewing *World of Warcraft* statistics; three students returned to 3D GameLab. Seeing this Sheehy announced that students should go to iCivics.org while they waited for the *WoW* server. Two girls audibly said, "Yay!" Six students went to iCivics, three to 3D GameLab, and the remaining students to their *The Hobbit* chart on Google Docs. Sheehy asked the class what their favorite game was on iCivics. Several students enthusiastically responded *Win the White House* "because it was impossible to win." One student said, "I got so close."

Sheehy then looked up from a student's terminal and announced, "If you don't want to go to the *WoW* forums, the wiki might be a good place to look." Then Sheehy asked the class to check the servers again. From there—at student level, in the center of room in front of circle—she led a discussion on the reliability of wikis. "Wikipedia," she began. "Who can tell me what it is?" Two students answered incorrectly. "Both of you, thank you for guessing." The following exchange then took place:

Sheehy:	Why is a wiki different than the Encyclopedia Britannica?
Student:	Anyone can edit it.
Sheehy:	Does it make it more or less reliable?
Student:	It depends.
Sheehy:	Guess what? There was a study that showed that there were more errors in a print encyclopedia than Wikipedia. Why? If you're passionate enough to edit it, you're probably right. If not 500 million people are. Does anyone know how an article in encyclopedia works? Could articles in print be biased?
Student:	What does bias mean?

Sheehy continued, explaining what bias means. All students appeared engaged in wiki discussion. Sheehy suggested students should add a "Sisters of Elune" article to Wikipedia. Then, a student quietly stood up and closed the door. Immediately everyone chanted, "And we are safe, and we are valued, and we are powerful learners."

Just minutes later, Sheehy announced that the *World of Warcraft* server was back online. When students spoke loudly to one another, Sheehy reminded to "use guild chat to have private conversations and to invite people into your group."

The second halves of the morning and afternoon double periods were "free choice." One student went directly to the PlayStation 3 and asked another, "Do we want to play *Journey*?" Sheehy unlocked a cabinet and gave students two PlayStation 3 games: *Little Big Planet* and *Infamous*. She gave students in both classes her personal iPad to play *Hearthstone*, a *World of Warcraft* trading card game. It was around then when she realized that the all of the console controllers were missing. She spent about 10 minutes searching the room. Sheehy then said, "Ago." Students responded, "Ame." Sheehy said, "If they [the controllers] just show up, I won't ask any questions. If you have extra controllers at home, bring them in. I really want you to treat this as your second home."

Sheehy allowed three girls to set up the Wii console system on an older rear projection television, even though Sheehy made it known that there were no controllers available to use. "We'll just set it up and play!" the girls enthused. Sheehy was visibly excited that the girls decided to figure it out themselves.

In that morning class, five boys sat on beanbags and looked through at different game disc cases. Five girls stayed at their desks, two playing games on *Win the White House* on iCivics, three playing *World of Warcraft*. One student asked Sheehy about playing *Minecraft*. Sheehy said that he could play; he did not. Soon after, two boys played *Kinect Adventure* on Xbox, which did not require a controller. Instead, the boys waved their hands back-and-forth, which caused balls on the flat panel mounted television to be swatted from a net. A group of boys congregated to watch them play. "This is so much fun!" one of the boys playing exclaimed. Sheehy commented to me that she was happy about student problem solving by using the Kinect as an interface. Later, when the class got loud, Sheehy announced, "Stop having fun!"

Sheehy announced to the room, "Okay, I have a game." She handed *Guillotine*, a card game, to a boy. He read the back of the box, and then gave it to a girl, who left it unopened on a table. Some students were observed rolling in the beanbags. One girl was virtually whitewater rafting in Kinect with a boy. Two girls launched Photobooth on Mac and selected the animated roller coaster background. Sheehy asked the students, "How are you going to write a reflection on it." Three boys and one girl were playing Rock-Paper-Scissors.

In the afternoon class, at free choice during the second half of class, Sheehy organized a *Guillotine* card game at Circle with several students. Sheehy sat on a beanbag in Circle, surrounded by seven girls and one boy. Sheehy sounded unsure of some of the rules, even though she has played it prior. Students appeared engaged playing *Guillotine*, looking at their hand of cards as the game went on. When students played a hand, Sheehy would read the card's action out loud.

In the corner of room, by the door, three boys and two girls were playing *World of Warcraft*. Students spoke out loud, coordinating locations so they could go on the same quest. One child talked as he played, saying, "Don't attack me ... you're going to lose." Later he said, "This is too easy, I'm leveling up too easily." One student playing *World of Warcraft* then turned from his computer and said, "Miss Sheehy, I leveled up! How do I do dungeons?" Sheehy, in Circle playing *Guillotine*, did not answer his question. The student figured out a solution. Soon later, one student stood up, across the room, and asked another student, "Do you want to do a dungeon together?" Then he asked another, "What quest are you doing? I'll help you." A few other students walked around the room to see where others were in the virtual world of Pandaria in *World of Warcraft*. In the section of the room near the door, two girls played *LawCraft* and *Responsibility Launcher* on iCivics.

Sheehy continued *Guillotine*; she was the card dealer. Then Sheehy told the group, "I need you to be quiet. I'm going to teach you something." Sheehy demonstrated how and why the dealers cut cards. "This is so much fun," one student said. Sheehy remarked to another boy, "You like this [game]. It's competitive." Then she addressed the group: "In Circle, when I sit among you, I am one of you, not higher than you." Sheehy then asked the group if they knew who Marie Antoinette was (the game is set during the French Revolution). One girl responded that she had once read a book about her.

The *Guillotine* group consisted mostly of girls. They were smiling a lot, and were social. The *World of Warcraft* players were much quieter than students playing *Guillotine*. Sheehy chose which students would play the next *Guillotine* game. She announced, "If you played the last round, you're not playing—but you can help." This time, the game was entirely student facilitated.

Much was going on in Sheehy's classroom that early afternoon. In a corner of the classroom, one girl asked Sheehy if she could complete *The Cabin in the Woods* homework now. Sheehy said, "Of course!" Then two boys were heard speaking about their *World of Warcraft* quest. One had his Google Doc reflection screen open. Some *World of Warcraft* players spoke out loud, across the room. One said, "I found one of the things we were supposed to find." "I found something cool," another answered. "Do you need it?"

When one student announced to the class that there were three minutes remaining in class, Sheehy was observed playing *World of Warcraft* with students. The *Guillotine* group began to count their scores and cleaned up. The *World of Warcraft* continued playing, as did Sheehy. Three students stayed in *World of Warcraft* after the bell. One student said that he did not "want to abandon the dungeon." Sheehy said, "Tell people there [other remote players in the dungeon], 'Sorry, got to go.'" The student told his friend, "I feel bad saying that; I feel much shame." Sheehy then said, "First thing on Monday, we'll do another dungeon." Sheehy continued playing *World of Warcraft* with one student as all students left the room, without looking up from her screen. Five students were late to their next classes. Sheehy helped the remaining student for 11 minutes into the next class period, showing him how to trade and craft items. She wrote him a late pass, and quietly instructed him to not tell his next teacher that he was gaming.

References

Campbell, J. (2008). *The hero with a thousand faces* (3rd ed.). Novato, CA: New World Library (Original work published 1949).

Gee, J. P. (2007). *What video games have to teach us about learning and literacy* (rev. ed.). New York, NY: Palgrave Macmillan.

Sheldon, L. (2012). *The multiplayer classroom: Designing coursework as a game*. Boston, MA: Course Technology/Cengage Learning.

Toppo, G. (2015). *The game believes in you: How digital play can make our kids smarter*. New York, NY: Palgrave Macmillan Trade.

· 5 ·
"FOR THE NEXT 3 HOURS, YOU HAVE A LICENSE TO SNOOP AROUND THE HOUSE"

Paul Darvasi is an English and media studies teacher at Royal St. George's College in Toronto, Canada. Royal St. George's College is an all-boys private school for students in grades 3 through 12. The school is affiliated with the Anglican Church and is situated in an urban setting, in Toronto, Ontario, Canada. Almost 500 boys attend the school. Darvasi's students are all male high school seniors.

As a transformational leader in game-based learning, Darvasi has spoken at several international conferences about his use of games to teach. Darvasi wrote a two-page case study reflection on his use of the video game *Gone Home* in the publication, *Learning, Education, and Games* (Schrier, 2014). He is, along with game-based learning journalist Katrina Schwartz and academic Katie Salen, included in the *MindShift Guide to Digital Games + Learning* (Shapiro, 2014). In spring 2016, Darvasi was a panelist at the SXSWedu conference, along with Peggy Sheehy and Greg Toppo.

In addition to teaching with digital games, Darvasi has designed pervasive games for his students, which are games that take place both in the virtual world and in the real world. *The Ward Game* is his game-based approach to teach Ken Kesey's (1963) novel *One Flew Over the Cuckoo's Nest* to his high school seniors. Darvasi also codesigned *Blind Protocol*, "an inter-school

Alternate Reality Game (ARG) that instructs on privacy and surveillance" (Schrier, 2014, pp. 9–10). He is currently completing a PhD at York University's Language, Culture, and Teaching program, with a focus on pervasive games. Darvasi's work "explores the instructional possibilities offered by the intersection of narrative, games and literature" (Schrier, 2014, pp. 9–10).

A visit was arranged to observe Darvasi use the video game *Gone Home* in his grade 12 English classes. The game, which is focused "on character development through environmental storytelling naturally lends itself to a consideration of the setting, characters, perspectives and nonlinear narrative structure—concepts relevant to any secondary school literature class" (Darvasi as cited in Schrier, 2014, p. 201). The unit is typically eight 75-minute classes. Three sections, totaling approximately 45 students, take part.

The school uses the Ontario Ministry of Education's Secondary English Curriculum. Teachers conduct assessments in grades 11 and 12 English according to an Achievement Chart. The Achievement Chart rubric is a "standard province-wide guide" for teachers to assess knowledge and skill in a content discipline (Ontario Curriculum Grades 11 and 12, 2007). Teachers are required to report on student progress on a Provincial Report Card (Ontario Curriculum Grades 11 and 12, 2007). There is no national Canadian set of core content standards (Ontario Curriculum Grades 11 and 12, 2007). There are no standardized tests in Ontario.

Gone Home

Paul Darvasi adopted *Gone Home* in 2013. He wrote several blog posts on his lessons, sharing about what worked and what did not. Prior to my visit, Darvasi contacted York University researcher Jennifer Jensen and invited her to his class, and they copresented a panel on the unit at the Games Learning Society Conference in 2014. Regarding meeting the curriculum with the game, Darvasi (2014) wrote in his blog:

> Fortunately, both the Ontario Ministry of Education and my school grant a great deal of flexibility in regard to choosing texts for English classes. The government emphasizes the practical communication skills of listening, speaking, writing and reading, and trust teachers to select texts and material that best suit their unique school cultures. ("Pushing It Through")

Darvasi and I had first met in summer 2014 at the Games in Education Symposium, in Troy, New York. The Speakers' Dinner was at Dinosaur BBQ, and I was seated next to Darvasi. Around the table was a veritable who's who of game-based learning educators: Peggy Sheehy, Steve Isaacs, [game design professor] Scott Nicholson, and John Fallon, amongst many others. During the meal, Darvasi was talking about his "discovery" of the canceled cable sci-fi drama *Battlestar Galactica*. Nicholson, a tabletop game expert, happened to have the eponymous board game adaptation of the show at the hotel where everyone was staying. Darvasi, along with other educators, played it prior to reviewing his *Gone Home*-themed slides for the keynote presentation he led at the conference.

I had previously interviewed Darvasi about his adoption of the video game into his teaching shortly after the conference. That fall, I read an article he submitted to MindShift, an educational gaming blog from KQED (San Francisco's PBS affiliate). I then sent him an email asking who his MindShift contact was, so I could similarly write a game-based learning post. Then, in late 2014, the lead editor of MindShift replied, asking me to interview Darvasi about his use of *Gone Home*. That article was published in January 2015.

To prepare for the MindShift article, in late 2014, I spoke with Aleksander Husøy, an English teacher at Nordahl Grieg Secondary School in Bergen, Norway. He codelivered the second iteration of the Gone Home unit. I also interviewed Steve Gaynor of Fullbright Games, the publisher of the game. Gaynor explained the nonlinear narrative as the central core mechanic of the game, stating: "*Gone Home* is a clear demonstration of how much the narrative process happens in your head, as opposed to on the page or on the screen" (Farber, 2015). It is groundbreaking because it lacks components traditional in video games, like a score or even a win or loss state.

Gone Home is a commercial, off-the-shelf game that has won several awards, including recognition from *Entertainment Weekly*, *USA TODAY*, *Polygon*, and *PC Gamer*. The game is a single player, "interactive exploration simulator," set in 1995 (Gone Home, 2014). *Gone Home* includes a simple point-and-click interface, similar to the computer games played during that time period (e.g., Myst). The game's narrative begins in the middle of the night, during a storm. Players take the role of Katie Greenbriar, who returned home from a year backpacking in Europe. She is greeted with a note on a locked front door. Once inside, the house appears suddenly abandoned—frozen in time, all family members nowhere to be seen. What follows is a deep exploration of the house, piece together clues about the whereabouts of the Greenbriar family. With the mood and tone of a horror game, the story is actually about a family's dysfunction.

In the structured interview that followed my field observations, Darvasi explained further details about the unit. He stated that he had no "set formula" to bring *Gone Home* into his English class. *Gone Home* was focus of study—the "central text"—in my observed lessons; it became the text in of itself. Initally, the first step Darvasi took was to find a game that "suited [his] curricular objective." Next, he had to create assessments that "would be in line with the typical high school lit class—but with some adjustments to honor, or to acknowledge, the fact that it is a game, and not a work of literature." Darvasi described the assessments he designed as "game-like."

The School

Darvasi was visited on Monday, November 16, and Tuesday, November 17, 2015. Royal St. George's Main Office is a renovated white building, in the style of the homes in The Annex district. It was a white structure with a green door and green trim. This building blended in with the Annex neighborhood's bay-and-gable homes. One could easily forget that the campus was only blocks away from Bloor Street, a busy urban thoroughfare. This neighborhood was tree-lined and quiet.

Students hail from different neighborhoods around Toronto. Jane Jacobs (1961/1992), the famed author of *The Death and Life of American Cities* had moved to this neighborhood, residing there until her death in 2006. Darvasi was proud that this district was where a critic of urban life chose to live. He remarked that houses in the area were not gentrified; rather, there was a mix of lower rental income to million dollar homes surrounding the school.

Upon arrival each day, I signed in at the school's main office. The receptionist was cheerful and welcoming. There was a fire burning in the fireplace in the adjoining room, which was the Headmaster's office. When I arrived on the first day, the same time as prospective parents who were on a tour. The visitor's room in the main office building had cookies, water, and coffee set on a grand piano for both the parents and students. There were red couches around a coffee table, and a rug on a hardwood floor. Near the entrance were stairs leading up. There was a large trophy case on one end of the room, and a flat panel television on the adjacent wall. The television scrolled through a slideshow of students playing on iPads, participating in archery tournaments, hiking, and acting in a drama class. On the opposite wall, class photographs hung; a pair of ceremonial swords displayed in the middle. The lampshade in the room was adorned with a map of the London Underground. Adding to the

"British feel"—reminiscent of a Harry Potter book—the school was divided into a house system, populated by students in mixed grades: Canterbury, Westminster, York, and Winchester. The house system gamified the entire school: every year, in September, there is a "terry cloth" run in the park, in which students compete, earning points for their house.

Prospective students arrived with parents. The Parent Ambassador greeted them in the visitor's room. The Ambassador explained that grades 6 and 7 students often took the subway together back and forth to school. One parent shared that he was a Royal St. George alumnus. An 8th grade student then led the prospective parents on a school tour. The tour began in the chapel. Students at Royal St. Georges College all wore white shirts and blazers adorned with the school's crest. Teachers were addressed formally as *Sir* or *Ma'am*. There was a block period schedule: four periods per day, which included a daily short meeting in the school's Anglican chapel at mid-morning and lunch.

Darvasi led me on a tour of the grounds. The school had been recently expanded, so there were older buildings mixed in with newer ones. The expansion included excavating under the school, and the addition of a new theater and new buildings. The visitor building was the oldest, aside from the chapel. While the campus itself was not large—it fit within a city block—it snaked around, like a labyrinth. Outside, there was a small grassy field with a sign acknowledging its benefactor: the McCain Foods family.

The school, which has an Anglican affiliation, had students from many religious and cultural backgrounds. For example, a Sikh boy wearing a Patka and a Jewish boy wearing a Yarmulke were observed. When introduced to the school's chapel minister, I was told he preferred the word *acceptance* to the word *tolerance*. To the minister, tolerance implied that a person did not agree with someone, but rather "puts up with someone."

Observing *Gone Home* in the Classroom

Three class periods were observed, each lasting 1 hour and 15 minutes in duration. On Monday, the first period began at 11:15 a.m., followed another at 1:25 p.m. that afternoon. The second observation was on Tuesday, at 9:35 a.m. Royal St. George's has a 4-day rotating schedule; each class was unique. The unit will take Darvasi about eight class meetings, which could last several weeks based on the school scheduling system. Unlike previous years' *Gone Home* units, this year included both Swedish and Norwegian student counterparts. Darvasi arranged to have his students work asynchronously with two other classrooms on student blog posts and in presentations relating to the game.

Each observed class began with Darvasi taking attendance from his MacBook as students sat down. There did not appear to be assigned seats. All classes met in a classroom shared by multiple teachers; there were no personal artifacts (e.g., family photographs) on teacher desks. The classrooms were new, clean, and bright. In both rooms where observations took place, student desks were arranged in a horseshoe formation, along the side and back wall of the classroom. The laptop screens faced the wall, out of sight from the teacher. Students faced the center of the horseshoe.

Monday's classroom featured a bookcase along the back wall with World War II propaganda posters lined up on the top shelf. The class had a lectern, which was not used. The classroom used on Tuesday had no teacher desk; Darvasi sat on one end of the horseshoe. The back wall of the room had small posters along it with literary devices such as tone, setting, theme, and mood. One corner of the room had signs written in French. The rest of the room was bare. The cinderblock walls were painted beige; the floor was linoleum.

Darvasi had a comfortable rapport with the boys in his class. Whenever a student spoke out of turn, Darvasi simply stopped his direct instruction until they quieted. This approach was successful. Students almost always addressed Darvasi as *Sir*. A total of 45 students were observed: 30 on Monday with 15 boys in each of the first and second periods, and 15 boys playing *Gone Home* on Tuesday. (Darvasi's other class block on Tuesday was a media studies course, which involved a research lesson taught by the media specialist.)

The entire unit was hosted on Haiku Learning, the school's learning management system. In Monday's classes, Darvasi used a SMART Board to lead a tour of the main page for the unit, which included a trailer for *Gone Home*. Darvasi described the trailer as "quite moving." Also on the main page was a link to the lesson's Word document, and technical tips for students, such as how to take screenshots as "textual evidence." Darvasi explained that subsequent classes would include time for free and unrestricted game play. During free play, students would be gathering evidence by taking in-game screenshots. The unit's culminating activity would be student presentations on subtopics, including character tracking; 1995 archeology; video game references; and *riot grrrl* references—which prompted students "to consider why Sam [the protagonist] was drawn to a west-coast feminist punk movement" (Darvasi, 2014). Each day's lesson also included traditional formative assessments, like completion of charts and answers to open-ended questions.

After attendance was taken, Darvasi took a moment to introduce me to students. He asked students to briefly close their computers, and asked for a "warm, Georgian welcome to the researcher," which was followed by light applause. Darvasi then spoke to students about how he knew me from various game-based learning conferences. He told students that I was "exploring possibilities to use games to make education a more interesting thing."

Darvasi wore a jacket and tie every day. Students brought their own MacBook to class. They were to have the game already installed and to bring along headphones and mouse controllers. For those who did not preinstall, Darvasi had download codes readily available. The class was highly engaged and eager to play. No one interrupted the teacher.

To the Monday morning class Darvasi announced, "Today is one of those things that you do something that you would think would never happen: you get to play a video game in English class." The students erupted in exuberance. This was typical in other observed class sections. While Darvasi is a high-end user of games for teaching, at this early point in the school year, *Gone Home* represented the first of several game-based units. What follows in the spring are pervasive games (games set in the real world).

In each observed class, Darvasi spoke about the story of the Fullbright Company, publisher of *Gone Home*. He explained that the game came out in 2013 and how the Fullbright Company was comprised of four individuals, all of whom had designed commercial and critical successes, such as the *Bioshock* titles. Darvasi detailed how the team rented a house together in Portland, Oregon, and then spent 2 years designing this game. He said, "They took what they learned in *Bioshock* about storytelling, and then they left out the ostensible shooting and violence. This game [*Gone Home*] has a creepy quality to it, but I won't say too much about that."

The game's mood and tone—including ominous music, nighttime rainfall, and the open staircase in the house entrance—suggested horror. One student in the Monday afternoon section asked, "Sir, how creepy is this game?" Darvasi replied, "Pretty creepy. The game's biggest secret is ultra-creepy. You may get through this whole game without realizing its deepest secret. It's under your nose the whole time."

In all classes, Darvasi read the *Gone Home's* description from the Haiku LMS page: *Gone Home* is a first-person interactive video game. He also mentioned the critique that some people have said *Gone Home* was not, by certain definitions, a game at all. One student in the Monday afternoon class asked, "Sir, can you die in this game?" Darvasi replied that he did not "want to answer." Darvasi explained the goal of the game to each class: find items and put the story together. In the Monday morning class Darvasi said:

> The whole fun of the game is that you have freedom to make a choice. The problem with a game in an educational setting is that I start telling you what I want you to find, or how to play. Then it gets boring at that point; you're not as engaged; you want have your own decision making process. You will have the freedom to do whatever you want to do in this game. You can go home and play the entire game, if you want. You may have played the whole game this past weekend—even though I asked you to not. It's entirely up to you.

Similarly, Darvasi directed the Monday afternoon class:

> Typically, the beauty of video games is the freedom to do what you want. This is why sandbox games and open world games are so popular. You can just wander around. There's a great engagement in that. For most of this unit, you will have free and open access to the game. You are arriving at the front porch of the house. You are Katie Greenbriar, an 18-year-old girl, and you came back from backpacking for a year. For the next 3 hours, you have a license to snoop around the house.

Darvasi told students that the game was actually self-paced. He warned not to "run through" the game because it would be "like fast-fowarding through a film." He told students to be patient, to explore rooms thoroughly, and to closely read all found documents "to see how the story gets richer." Just for today, he instructed students not to leave the foyer. He said on Tuesday afternoon, "Much like a symphony is summarized in an overture, an opening paragraph in essay, or a prologue in Shakespeare—the entire family is introduced in the foyer." Darvasi expressed his concern to keep students in the foyer on day one to ensure that everyone grasped the game's interface and storytelling devices: found artifacts. As he told the Monday morning class:

> Ultimately you're in control of your own destiny. If you run through, it will ruin your experience. You want to savor it, like a good meal. Does that guarantee that you'll love this game? No, some of you might hate this game. Let's wait till we get to that point before we get to that decision. Keeping you in the foyer teaches you the pace at which to explore.

Darvasi set up a series of assignments that take place in the foyer, which was "the hub of the story" (see Figure 5.1). The document included directions for students to provide the full name of each family member, accompanied by a screenshot as evidence. Under the chart were two open-ended questions about Sam. Students were instructed to respond with a 150- to 300-word blog post predicting if their character, Katie, was in danger, as well as what they think happened to Katie's sister, Sam. The blog post would ultimately be shared with the Swedish and Norwegian student counterparts. In Tuesday's iteration of the lesson, Darvasi suggested to "predict whether you think the family was murdered, whether aliens came down and abducted them. What you think happened." Then he stated, "You'll all help out each other as you discover things."

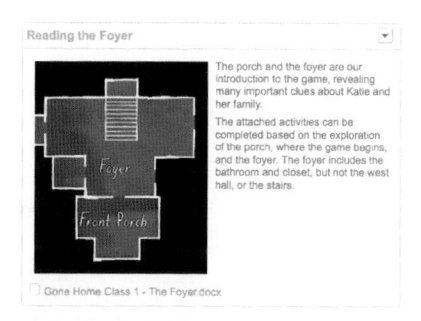

Figure 5.1. Screenshot from Darvasi's Haiku page.

During the Tuesday class, the SMART Board was malfunctioning and all directions were given orally. Darvasi continued, "The way we go through a text in English is we find citations from the text. In this case, our citations are screenshots. We've got to learn how to do that." The screenshot keys on a Mac operating system were the same as "hot key commands" in the game, which presented a technical conflict (e.g., the keys associated with screenshots might pause the game). Because Darvasi foresaw this from previous iterations of the unit, instructions were prepared and posted on the Haiku page.

Darvasi also emphasized the unit assignment to collaborate with the Swedish and Norwegian students. One student Monday morning stated that he had already had a videoconference; however, because of time zone difference, it was difficult to coordinate. Darvasi replied to the Monday afternoon students his expectations: "Get the ball rolling—or at least make a plan—with your group." No hands went up regarding using Skype to videoconference, just yet. Six hands went up when Darvasi asked if arrangements were made. One student, later in that class, remarked that his female counterpart "looked like a Swedish supermodel." Another boy stated, "She's a goddess." Darvasi then jokingly chided the students, asking why they had not yet all contacted the

88 GAME-BASED LEARNING IN ACTION

partner students. After the Skype assignment was reviewed, the conversation switched to university entrances essays, and how student's English essay scores could bring down their marks. In Canada, grade 12 grades are a major factor in university admissions.

Each class, Darvasi led a mini-lesson on the chart he prepared for the class (see Figure 5.2). "To answer the questions in the chart, find things in the foyer," he said. "For example, what is the father's name? Put a screenshot

Annotating The Foyer

As you explore the mansion's foyer, collect the information requested in the chart below. For each response, take a screenshot to show where you discovered the requested information.

The Foyer

Description	Response	Screenshot evidence
(Example) Avatar's name	(Example) Kaitlin Greenbriar	(Example) 
Father's full name		
Mother's full name		
Family's prior address		
Family's current address		
Mom's college roommate		
How long does it take mom to get to work?		
Where does mom work?		

Timeline

Combining evidence from both the porch and the foyer, fill in the appropriate date and corresponding screenshot in the spaces provided.

Event	Exact Date	Screenshot Evidence
Katie leaves for Europe		
Family moves to new house		
Katie returns from Europe		

Sam

What item triggers Sam's journal entry entitled "At the New House"? Does this sort of voiceover affect the realism of the story? How?

Write 5 point-form notes discussing anything your know about Sam based on what you have discovered in the porch and in the foyer.

Figure 5.2. Screenshot of blank game evidence chart.

of the found items—in this case, a packing slip—as evidence." He provided a connection, declaring, "It's like a scavenger hunt." Darvasi mentioned the "greater objective," which would involve using today's screenshots for a later part of the project. The details of the culminating assignment were not yet revealed.

About 10 minutes into each class, students were able to play freely. Students had no observed issues with the game's point-and-click interface. There is a white dot in the center of the screen. When lined up on objects, like a door, the player is prompted with words on a screen to make an action (open door, pick up object, play cassette tape). To the Tuesday afternoon class, Darvasi announced, "Enjoy the game and get to work. Let me know if you need anything."

During student exploration of the game, Darvasi would return to his laptop, grading the remainder of the essays assigned the previous week. He would usually remain seated for the entire period as students were playing. Without teacher instruction, students simply helped one another to find objects. Darvasi stated that collaboration occurred more "naturally" in this unit, than with other lessons.

Students talked quietly to themselves and to one another as they played, progressing from the porch to the foyer (see Figure 5.3). Darvasi would inquire about leaving the lights all off, which the students overwhelmingly preferred. One student on Tuesday remarked, "This is really dark and ominous." Darvasi had given little background on the game's story. One student in the Monday afternoon class said that the game "looked like terror." Darvasi replied, "More terror will come."

Figure 5.3. Foyer of the Greenbriar house. Source: Steve Gaynor, manager of Fullbright Games.

Students mostly stayed on-task during each of the three observed classes. Once in game, students spoke quietly to one another about discovering items, such as a wooden duck. When students discovered something on the porch, they announced phrases such as: "Look! The house key." Students were also observed closely reading the note on the house's front door. To advance into the house, certain information had to be read in detail.

Darvasi did not correct chatting students, nor did he answer basic questions already covered in the lesson, such as "Can I leave the porch?" Some students were observed being stuck on the opening screen because graphics settings were not set to low. One student on Tuesday required clarification about the differences between a foyer and the porch. Darvasi was clearly knowledgeable about the intricacies of the game. He stated that there were only three objects to find on the porch. He also suggested that some students could collect items and put them in a pile in the foyer.

On Tuesday, one student told Darvasi that his computer was restarting every time he attempted to play the game, and that his computer had been doing that lately. The student restarted his computer. Darvasi suggested that the student "play along" on a neighbor's computer until the school's technologist could remedy the problem. The student having problems with the game and had to keep restarting was observed texting on his phone. He told Darvasi that he kept trying to open the game. He hypothesized that it may be because he updated his MacBook's operating system recently. He did not follow Darvasi's suggestion to play along with a neighboring student.

Students were whispering, helping one another nearby to adjust settings. Students all brought their own headphones. Very few had brought their own mouse controllers. A few students were observed adjusting the settings on the game so it would not interfere with taking screenshots. It took each class about 10 minutes to figure out how to enter the house and begin exploration of the foyer. Several students asked technical questions in the Monday classes, such as how to take a screenshot if an audio journal is found. Darvasi explained that once collected, a visual is later available in the game's inventory. Only two students that day required teacher intervention. On Tuesday, Darvasi explained screenshots of archived audio artifacts upfront, before play.

Early in the Tuesday class, a student asked Darvasi if it was "weird" that he did not yet find the key to the house. Upon overhearing this, another student said where the key was located. Then, another student, in a scolding tone said, "Why'd you tell him that? He needs to figure it out on his own."

Darvasi occasionally looked up from his laptop and provided game advice. For example, he suggested that students look for a manila folder in the game.

Students were visibly engaged as they discovered items. When done exploring the foyer, students would sometimes ask, "Sir, where can we go now?" Students would often progress in the game without yet taking screenshots or completing the chart. Other students would assist each other quietly. A few students were observed with a headphone in just one ear. Darvasi occasionally informed students that he could not prevent them from entering the rooms when they were done with the foyer; he just "preferred" that they did not.

A few students were observed each class fretting over an upcoming math test. During the Monday morning class, at 11:54 a.m., one student was overheard discussing a math equation with a classmate. Darvasi corrected the students, saying, "That sounds a lot like math, guys." The students quickly went back on-task. At 1:47 p.m. on Monday afternoon, Darvasi jokingly said, "Stop doing your math homework and start playing video games!" The students quietly joked about gaming in class. At 10:34 a.m. on Tuesday, Darvasi said that, because students had a math test in the following class, they could "choose how they managed their time," completing the *Gone Home* paragraph from home, studying now for math test. Two students in that class studied for math, taking out math notes.

There was tension in the room regarding the potential for someone to reveal, or "spoil," the ending. At 12:10 p.m. on Monday, one student announced a "spoiler." A few students sounded angry at this announcement. Darvasi warned not to spoil the story in the game, "the same way you would not do that with a novel." One student then whispered to another, "Why are you raging about *Gone Home*?" Shortly thereafter, Darvasi stated that students in previous years had found a "flaw in the game," in which players could open a wood panel in the wall by the foyer and "do a speed run" to the conclusion of the game's story. Darvasi said it was "more of an issue" because students were playing simultaneously in the same room.

I continued to observe students in the class activity. Students were organizing screenshots from the game into a newly created folder on their computer desktops. All students seemed to know how to take screenshots on a Mac operating system. One student read the open-ended questions about Sam, the female protagonist in the game, out loud. Darvasi reminded students to complete the prediction paragraph. When a student asked if the paragraph was to be completed in class, Darvasi answered, "If it is done in class, then you have no homework." He also advised them to screenshot often in case they could not return to a location.

One student during the Monday morning class confessed that he had played the game already, a few years ago. His brother was in Darvasi's class.

The student said he was cautious not to spoil the story's ending. Darvasi advised that he replay the game, and to not share the ending with the class.

Students were focused on the game, and politely spoke to one another. One student Monday afternoon remarked, "I like the fact that you can hear the rain from in the house." Another replied, "Yeah. It's pretty ominous, right?" A student that morning asked, "Sir, do we get to fight anything?" Darvasi joked, "Something will jump out at you." Then he reminded them to be patient. In fact, in each class, a question regarding "jump scares" arose from students.

One student on Tuesday inquired out loud if the missing family was actually hiding in the attic. Darvasi played along, agreeing, and then adding that the killer was also there. This prompted another student to ask, "Are there any jump scares?" Darvasi joked, saying that Master Chief, from the video game *Halo*, will jump out.

At 10:04 a.m. on Tuesday, one student was heard correcting another, saying, "You're not allowed to go upstairs." Darvasi agreed, saying that, technically he could not prevent further exploration, but "ideally" he wanted students to remain in the foyer. Students continued playing at a whisper-volume. Students seemed interested in the game. There were not a lot of smiling students; the class exhibited determination from game exploration, akin to reading a book. Students spoke to themselves as they explored, saying phrases out loud, like: "Find the light." Students were on-task, picking up objects, observing them by spinning them around. Two students were observed peering over at other's screen. Darvasi asked if that student went upstairs; he replied, "No." By 10:12 a.m., Darvasi announced, "The whole thing about not leaving the foyer—I'm just asking you not to. It is by design of the lesson."

During play, Darvasi continued to offer technical advice. One student had to "force quit" the game. Another took a while to start. This was because settings for graphics needed to be reset to low. When a question arose, students were very polite to the teacher. Darvasi took time during the middle of the class to briefly walk around room, making sure all students were set up and on task.

At 12:12 p.m. on Monday, Darvasi announced, "Can everyone stop what you are doing and take a break. Please look up." Then he said:

> For the next class, turn in your charts with screenshots and information. You have to write that paragraph and you should make time to engage with counterparts [in Norway and Sweden]. Come back next class with either an exact time set or that you have already spoken [to your counterpart]. If you have any questions, please write me and I will clarify whatever the problem is.

Students listened intently. Then Darvasi switched the lights back off, and sat back at his desk to grade papers.

Students continued to talk quietly among themselves. A few asked if they were "allowed" to go upstairs. At 2:07 p.m. on Tuesday, Darvasi asked, "Is everyone doing okay?" Most students were, and continued to work quietly. Darvasi then made a joke insinuating that the students could simply hide in a closet in the game for 2 hours. He had a comfortable rapport with students, talking to them as peers. Around that time, one student corrected another who was confused by Sam's gender, saying, "Sam was a girl because it's a girl's voice when she is reading her journal." At 2:09 p.m., a student said Sam's mother's name out loud, which generated a response from a peer: "Hey, don't spoil it."

One student asked if they could "LAN [local area network] this game," making it multiplayer, rather than single player. The class was usually near silent. Most were completing the chart by the halfway point of class. Some asked classmates questions about the assignment such as, "Where do we put this blog post?" One student then said he was trying to find a cassette tape. Another asked what floor he was on.

At 2:13 p.m. on Monday, a student asked, "Sir, when we fill up the table, what do we do?" Darvasi asked if he had completed the paragraph; the student had not. Darvasi said to complete the paragraph, and then to exit the game. Students were reviewing their inventory in the game, exploring the foyer, or completing the chart in Word. At 2:19 p.m., a student asked, "How many words do you want the paragraph to be?" Darvasi did not reply. A few minutes later, one student said that he could not find the family's previous address for the chart. Another student helped, pointing out where to look, without explicitly showing exactly where the answer was. Darvasi continued to grade essays on paper and his MacBook as students completed today's assignment.

At 10:40 a.m. on Tuesday, Darvasi suddenly asked the room if anyone knew what the Hawthorne Effect was. One student replied, "It is when behavior changes because someone is being observed." The student then spoke about a film with a prisoner experiment.

Student predictions about the characters in *Gone Home* were observed. One question in a student chart was, "What item triggers Sam's journal entry entitled, 'At the New House?' Does this sort of voiceover affect the realism of the story? How?" A student during the Tuesday class was observed typing, "The invoice regarding the moving company. I think it maintains its theatrical atmosphere either way, doesn't particularly break the immersion."

Another prompt in the chart read: "Write 5 jot notes discussing anything you know about Sam based on what you discovered in the porch and in the foyer." The same student on Tuesday was observed writing, "She is somewhat sassy and rebellious. She has a possibly strained relationship with her mother. The lack of trophies involving her may suggest that she is the less favored child."

During the three class observations, two students left to use the bathroom or to get water. Very few students spoke off-topic. Almost all students closed cabinets and doors, switched lights back off, and returned objects after inspection in the virtual house. Students first play the game, casually looking for items in the chart, and then retrace their steps, completing the chart. Students did not question the morality of snooping through items in house. One student showed Darvasi his screen. He started a collection of objects found in the foyer and piled them on the rug. Another student said, "Why are there so many tissue boxes?"

When class ended, Darvasi reminded students to use Turn It In, an online plagiarism checker, for homework. Darvasi told students that the game "autosaves" (automatically saves the player's location). Throughout the classes, students were very polite. Students put their blazers on, closed their MacBooks, and exited.

References

Darvasi, P. (2014). *Prologue: A video game's epic-ish journey to a high school English class*. Retrieved from http://www.ludiclearning.org/2014/03/05/gone-home-in-education/

Farber, M. (2015). *Gone Home: A video game as a tool for teaching critical thinking skills*. Retrieved from KQED/MindShift website: http://ww2.kqed.org/mindshift/2015/01/16/gone-home-a-video-game-as-a-tool-for-teaching-critical-thinking/

Gone Home. (2014). Retrieved from http://www.gonehomegame.com/

Jacobs, J. (1992). *The death and life of great American cities* (Vintage Books ed.). New York, NY: Vintage Books (Original work published 1961).

Kesey, K. (1963). *One Flew Over the Cuckoo's Nest*. Berkeley, CA: Signet.

Ontario Ministry of Education. (2007). *Ontario Curriculum: Grades 11 and 12 English*. Retrieved from http://www.edu.gov.on.ca/eng/curriculum/secondary/english1112currb.pdf

Schrier, K. (2014) *Learning, education and games: Curricular and design considerations* (Vol. 1). Retrieved from http://press.etc.cmu.edu/files/Learning-Education-Games_Schreier-etal-web.pdf

Shapiro, J. (2014). *MindShift guide to digital games + learning*. Retrieved from MindShift website: http://www.kqed.org/assets/pdf/news/MindShift-GuidetoDigitalGamesandLearning.pdf

· 6 ·
"LIFE JUST GOT EPIC!"

Steve Isaacs is a teacher of video game design and development at William Annin Middle School, in suburban Basking Ridge, New Jersey. William Annin Middle School (WAMS) is a public school with students from grades 6 through 8. In 2013, there were 1,409 students attending the school. New Jersey's public school curriculum aligns to the Common Core State Standards.

Isaacs' teaching was featured in a 2012 Joan Ganz Cooney Center and BrainPOP video case study series about video games in the classroom. He has written about the difference between game-based learning and gamification for ASCD In-Service, the blogging portal for the Association for Supervision and Curriculum Development (ASCD). In 2014, Isaacs was one of Code.org's Teachers of the Month. Code.org is a nonprofit organization that advocates for computer science in the classroom.

Isaacs teaches about 120 8th grade students per year, meeting with a cycle of 60 per semester. The 7th grade has about 300 total students, of which 25 are in Isaacs class per 6-week cycle. The mix of genders in grade 7 is relatively even; however, in grade 8, there are usually more boys than girls enrolled. Because the 7th grade class cycle switched during observations—and because those students were primarily writing about, rather than playing, games—they were not observed. Data on the three grade 8 sections were collected.

Isaacs was observed for 2 nonconsecutive days, over a 2-week time span. William Annin Middle School's campus is comprised of several wings, each one story tall, connected by hallways. During the scheduled dates to collect data, the 7th grade cycle changed. The 7th grade students were not always learning in a game-based setting; some were reviewing course requirements or finishing projects. Therefore, the 7th grade was not included in the study. Data was collected for the three 8th grade class sections, which were the same students for both visits. The 8th grade class is called Video Game Design and Development, an elective course.

Room 322: Iterative Design and Student Choice

Isaacs is in a computer lab: Room 322. His desk was at the front of the back-to-back student desks. The room had two doors: one from the hallway and one leading directly into the school library. The walls were concrete blocks painted white. The floor was linoleum tile and the ceiling was tiled, with hanging florescent light fixtures. The rear of the room had two flat panel televisions, one attached to an Xbox 360 console, the other to the newer iteration, the Xbox One. Near the Xbox One was an unlocked iPad cart. The front of the room, near the hallway door, had a third, mounted flat panel television. It was connected to a PlayStation 4, which sat on a table under the screen. Near it was a box of *Disney Infinity* figurines and a laser printer. Under the table was a drum kit from the video game *RockBand*. There were two blank dry-erase whiteboards on each of the walls.

There was a bulletin board by the front door with pictures of Isaacs' family. Nearby, there was another bulletin board, which was adorned with six Hour of Code posters. Across the room, a sign titled "Using the Iterative Process" hung on the white board. Underneath was a circle with the phrase "The Video Game Design Loop," scrawled in the center. Around the circle was a cartoon depicting design in different stages: start; brainstorming; design; implement; play test; suggestions for redesign. Next to the sign hung several badges from conferences Isaacs attended.

Students used one of 29 Dell desktop computers, arranged around the left and right sides of room. The computer screens faced the center of the room, in view of teacher (see Figure 6.1). In the center of the room was a row of desks arranged back-to-back, also with student screens facing outward, in view of Isaacs. There was an Oculus Rift virtual reality headset on Isaacs' desk, as well as Raspberry Pi kits.

Figure 6.1. Isaacs' classroom. Source: Author.

Day 1

I first arrived on Tuesday, December 1, 2015, which coincided with what Isaacs dubbed: "#20PercentTuesday"—a day set aside weekly for student choice projects. In the interview that followed field observations, Isaacs explained how the idea was inspired from corporations that found innovations when employees were given free time for personal projects. Isaacs noted one famous example: 3M's "accidental" invention of Post-It notes. Similarly, Isaacs' goal was to design "student-interest, passion-driven" lessons.

In period one, 8th grade, there were 16 students: 14 boys and two girls. Students arrived as Isaacs worked from his desk. His laptop was open to a Google Sheet page, with the student attendance listed alongside each child's current project. Isaacs was organized digitally, as evidenced by the spreadsheets and lesson quests he prepared, and in the physical classroom, which was orderly.

Isaacs took attendance, followed by self-reported progress on individual student projects. Students called out their individual projects, which included working on the second level in a game; making graphical sprites; adding gravity to a game; designing GameMaker: Studio using a Raspberry Pi kit; proposing a project to be funded on DonorsChoose; authoring *Minecraft* design document; making an Xbox game using Project Spark; and designing in the *Disney Infinity* sandbox. One student asked a question about a reflection on a design document. "Be specific, like I'm working on getting the boss to attack my player in Project Spark, or something like that," Isaacs advised.

Isaacs offered suggestions as he called around the room. For example, he suggested that a student take a picture for a blog post. Isaacs also asked students to be specific in their project reports. When a student answered in general terms (e.g., "I'm working in *Disney Infinity*"), he would ask, "What exactly are you creating?" When one student responded "GameMaker," Isaacs followed up, asking about what the student was trying to do with it. When another student replied that he was going to use the Makey Makey kit, Isaacs inquired, "For what?" The student replied that he was mapping the arrow keys for a game he designed in GameMaker: Studio.

Assessing where students were in their 20% projects took about 10 minutes. Isaacs was supportive and asked if anyone needed help. He mentioned a board for students to add their names if help was needed. No one used the board in the first observed day.

The topic of homework came up during period one, after a pithy introduction to me, as the observing researcher. Isaacs asked the class if they ever "have homework." The students all replied no. Then Isaacs asked the class if they "do work at home." Some of the students answered that they did. When asked why, several responded, "Because it was fun" and that they "wanted to."

Students worked on their projects for the remainder of the period. Many spoke at a conversational volume to neighbors. Isaacs circulated, answering individual questions. None of the students had books. All work was done digitally, on computers. Students were focused. There were no lesson objectives on board; it was personalized based on individualized learning quests and 20% choice.

One student was observed on the littleBits webpage. He was creating a DonorsChoose crowdfunding campaign to purchase the kit for the class. Isaacs stated that corporate sponsors would match half of all student-authored DonorsChoose campaigns. Isaacs next explained bitCraft to the student. Bit-Craft is an external computer that works with the digital game *Minecraft*. Isaacs stated that he and his wife saw bitCraft in use at another teacher's maker lab.

Isaacs then sat next to the student who was on the DonorsChoose page. He gave the student advice about online retailers who participated in the funds matching program. Isaacs also advised the student to use certain phrases in his pledge campaign, such as the phrase, "physical computing." The boy was focused on completing the DonorsChoose campaign. On the student's screen was a Google Doc titled, "DonorsChoose Student Led Project." Next was a teacher's prompt that read:

> How will you—with your teacher's help—be a leader in bringing this project to life? (Usually, teachers are in charge of classroom materials and school projects. Not

today! Your awesome teacher is encouraging you to take the lead. Explain how you'll make this project happen.)

The student responded:

> With some help, and experience, I think that we can show people how valuable game design is and how the games can help the students in our classroom learn, and better our knowledge and education for brighter futures. I think that I can help make this project work because I can come up with ways to persuade people to donate and I can make our project fun and interesting!

At the bottom of the student's screen was a second teacher prompt: "Why is this project important to you and your school community?" The student's written answer read:

> This project is important because everyday the world advances in technology. But how? Well the answer to that is the people that create new ways of thinking and make new creations. The students of the world we live in are the future. The students now will make incredible advances through technology everyday. But we need your help! What better way to empower students?

The pledge goal on DonorsChoose was set at $1,792. One girl in period three merged her DonorsChoose campaign for *Mario Maker*, the Nintendo Wii U *Super Mario Bros.* level editor, with the period one student's campaign. Isaacs had suggested it. Isaacs and his students eventually authored the final, published campaign page. Isaacs wrote, "The Empowering Learners project is intended to truly put the learning in the students' hands, so it was important for them to engage in the entire process. This project is the culmination of their collaboration." Within 2 weeks, 16 donors fully funded the project.

Students were observed on different projects, including writing a blog post on the Medium website; editing a song for a game; creating game art with Piskel; watching an instructional video on building castles in *Disney Infinity*; creating "room properties" in GameMaker: Studio; adjusting a side-scrolling game; and testing how aluminum foil interacted with Makey Makey's alligator clips when attached to a virtual computer keyboard. During this time, one student was observed creating a puzzle on the *Zoombinis* iPad application. He had a design document open to Google Docs, which described his puzzle. Another student was observed revising a design document. There were notes about GameMaker: Studio, along with a screenshot of the game he designed. The paragraph was titled, "Jumping!" and was a written reflection on how the mechanic works. The student wore headphones as he typed. A student's 3D GameLab task was observed, which read:

> To submit this quest you can simply respond to this quest for 10XP or submit a blog post or YouTube video and receive a bonus 10XP. If you submit a video or blog post please do not include your complete name or personal information. Please do the following:

- What product/tool are you working with?
- Share what you have learned so far through the experience.
- What progress have you made so far?
- What is your plan for moving forward (next steps and bug plans)?
- Interesting or a-ha moments you have had through the experience of taking ownership of your learning.

The student wrote the following in the box under the prompt:

> We are using the toybox in *Disney Infinity*. I have learned how to make a battle areana by placing blocks togeather and I have also learned how to spawn in enemies. We have made the battle areana and are working on aesthetics and we are trying different enemy combinations to make it balanced.

Most students were observed collaborating with other students. One student asked Isaacs a question pertaining to the "if-then" logic in his programming code. The student could not work out his game's virtual gravity. Isaacs moved to that student's chair and reviewed the design document and written code. Isaacs discussed debugging with the student.

Shortly after, another student posed a question to Isaacs: "How do I spawn in Creative [mode] in *Minecraft*." Isaacs did not know the answer; instead, another student walked over and switched the game's setting to "Peaceful," which resolved the issue. At the end of class, Isaacs helped with the Donors-Choose campaign.

When the period bell sounded, ending the class, Isaacs phoned the Donors-Choose student's social studies teacher to say that the student would be a few minutes late. The student stayed through the entire next period, missing his next class. Isaacs called the teacher's room again to notify the teacher of the student's whereabouts.

As in the first period, the next class period of 8th graders saw students arriving and working on their projects without prompting from Isaacs. Most sat at a Dell desktop computer; one sat at the PlayStation 4 near the front of the room, and launched *Disney Infinity*. Very few students had questions about projects for the teacher. There were 20 students in this period: 17 boys, three girls.

As soon as the bell rang, Isaacs announced from his desk that he was going to take attendance. He said, "When I call you for attendance, tell me *exactly* what you are working on today—*specifically* for 20% time." As in the earlier class, Isaacs took attendance and gathered update reports on student projects. When one girl replied, "Project Spark," Isaacs asked her to be more specific. She replied that she was "remaking a game." Isaacs then asked if it was "like the 'Watch It, Build It' site." He also asked her if she was going to submit it to him early so he could play it. The next student mentioned that he was coding; Isaacs mentioned "GitHub" and "Choose to Code" as an option for the student (both are portals in which programmers collaborate on open source coding projects).

Similar responses from Isaacs were observed from other students. He would ask, "What are you working on *specifically* today?" Student responses included: GameMaker: Studio; the website Choose to Code; and coding in HTML5 and JavaScript, for students intending to host websites. Isaacs sometimes followed up with technical questions (e.g., "What server will you use?"). Regarding the students on the PlayStation 4 console, Isaacs asked, "What are you doing in *Disney Infinity*, guys? Is that going to be your regular game [for 20% Tuesday]? Are you writing a design document? You're going to need to do that." Another student was then observed on *Disney Infinity* at the rear of room. At the time, students were playing the game, not building using the sandbox feature.

Students worked independently. Two boys were designing a virtual racetrack in the *Disney Infinity's* sandbox. The game was in split screen mode, enabling both to work. One boy was observed testing a modified version of the game *Flappy Bird*.

Isaacs briefly checked if anyone needed help. No one did. Several students were observed with their Game Design Google Doc open. One student was in his 3D GameLab page. The assignment was as follows:

> In order to complete this quest, please provide a screencast (video) or screenshots that show your creation. You can post them in the legacy gaming community on Edmodo. If you created a video please link to it. You should maintain a YouTube channel or blog to showcase your class work for the entire world to see! In addition, please provide a description of what you created. Reflect upon the experience in your post. Did you encounter certain challenges? Was it easy to replicate?

The girl on the class Xbox One was observed reviewing a menu of options in Project Spark with her game controller. Because she worked on a large, flat panel television, the entire class could observe her progress. She did not appear to mind.

Students were designing more than playing. The students were talkative, but not overly so; there were no disruptive students. At one point, the student designing on *Disney Infinity* in the front of the classroom room had his feet up on a chair. He continued to work independently. He then asked a friend for help.

Students continued independently. One student called Isaacs over to show code he wrote and the server he was uploading to. Isaacs then went to the girl working on Project Spark on the class Xbox One. Isaacs took an iPhone photo of the girl with her Project Spark project. He then put the photo on Twitter, adding: "#20percentTuesday making games with @disneyinfinity @proj_spark @keith_guarino @fabhistory." In the accompanying Twitter photograph, only the backs of students' heads were visible; the girl designing on Project Spark displayed the peace sign with her fingers (see Figure 6.2).

Figure 6.2. Students designing with Project Spark and Disney Infinity. Source: Author.

Ten minutes later, Isaacs sat on rolling chair by another student. Students stayed on-task and were focused and engaged. Toward the end of class, there were two clusters of student—one with three students and one with four students—off-task and socializing. Then the bell rang. Isaacs told students to have a good day as they left the room. Isaacs remained seated next to a girl on DonorsChoose when the bell rang. After 5 minutes passed, Isaacs wrote her a late pass.

The final 8th grade class began just before lunch. Similar to the other morning classes, students arrived and sat down before bell to begin their "20%

Tuesday" projects. There were 18 students: 15 boys and three girls. From his desk, Isaacs announced, "Folks, in a moment I will take attendance." Again, he recorded specifics in Google Sheets about where each student was in their 20% project.

As with the other classes, the answers were diverse. One girl replied that she was on Project Spark. Two boys were observed creating command "Redstone" blocks [bricks in the game that can act like electrical circuitry] on *Minecraft*, and then writing a guide about it for the website SnapGuide. One girl informed Isaacs that she began using MIT App Inventor. Isaacs then asked if she "made an app that worked." The student replied that she had. She was creating a mobile application with an accelerometer set to pace how fast the holder of the device was running. Isaacs then told her, "Part of the process is the design process, which can include sketches, and ideas about how it would work." Isaacs next asked if anyone wanted to figure out how to code for the Oculus Rift. There was audible enthusiasm.

One student reported issues installing the Unreal Engine, a professional game design platform. He was observed viewing instructional videos on the installation, as well as its use. Several students watched "Watch It, Build It" online tutorial videos. Two students were viewing videos on the Makey Makey webpage. Isaacs then uploaded an image of the student project on Twitter, which included the Makey Makey kit attached to several alligator clips (see Figure 6.3). The tweet read: "Student created #makeymakey tinfoil game controller works with original #gamemaker game @yoyogames #20PercentTuesday."

Figure 6.3. Student-designed Makey Makey controller. Source: Author.

Students were observed working throughout the period. One student had a complex concept map on the website Popplet. He had a similar map on Twine, the authoring tool to write and share interactive fiction stories. Two other students were on *Minecraft*. One student was observed still reading through the Unreal Engine website. Several other students were in the sprite editor in GameMaker: Studio.

The students were on-task, working independently. Three wore headphones. Four were observed next to one another helping with projects. When a student had a technical issue, Isaacs suggested that the student view his personal blog as a resource. Isaacs advised a student in GameMaker: Studio on how to "code variables for health, lives, and scoring mechanisms." He explained how each "came standard and are actually all mechanisms for scoring." A few minutes later, Isaacs answered a student's question about creating variables for game sprites. Then, a student entered Isaacs' class; she had left her other class early and wanted to continue a project.

Students were designing, rather than playing, games. Examples included *Minecraft*; Twine, the interactive story engine; GameMaker: Studio; SketchUp, the 3D object application; MIT's App Maker; and the *Disney Infinity* toybox. Students occasionally collaborated with one another. Some were observed talking and singing to themselves. When they helped each other, there was some socializing, but not enough to be considered off-task.

Isaacs took several iPhone pictures of students and shared on Twitter. In the course of this class period, like the two that proceeded, almost no students left the room to use the bathroom or to get water. Then, one student asked, "Could someone help me test my multiplayer game?" A student came over and he explained how to play. The game was in GameMaker: Studio. A few students tried it. When a student discovered a bug in the code, he said, "I'm glad we playtested this."

Isaacs announced an upcoming "Skype-a-Thon speaker" that he arranged to videoconference with the class. Then, he helped a girl code a variable in GameMaker: Studio until the bell sounded. This was the last class of Isaacs' day.

Day 2

My second visit was during Computer Science Education Week's Hour of Code. The class period times were different because there was a character education morning meeting, which takes place twice a month, for 20 minutes just after homeroom.

The students in each of the three observed classes entered the room and sat down at computers stations within minutes of the bell ringing. Most launched GameMaker: Studio. For period one, there were 17 students in attendance: 15 boys and two girls. In period three, which began at 10:21 a.m., Isaacs played a *Mario Maker* game walkthrough from YouTube on all three flat panel televisions. Isaacs pointed out that the project was close to being funded on the student's DonorsChoose page. There were 19 students in period three: 17 boys, three girls. Period five had 20 students: 17 boys, and three girls, all of whom sat together. Period three was social and occasionally off-task, whereas period five was more focused on the lesson. Period five students were more cheerful, too. For example, a student at the start of period five asked Isaacs if she could write an anime [Japanese-style cartoon] review instead of a game review. When he replied that she could, she exclaimed, "Life just got epic!"

At the start of each observed class, Isaacs stood at one of the whiteboards, or in front of the students, and led a whole class discussion. He wrote on the board with an orange dry erase marker as he spoke. In the first period, Isaacs said:

> I'm pretty sure it's what you call workflow—what we're doing for the next couple of days. What are the things you are supposed to be doing that you haven't done yet. Or, for the next few days [what] should you be accomplishing?

When a student replied that they should peer-review games, Isaacs reminded them to first submit the game link onto a shared Google Form. Next, Isaacs reviewed file types. He explained how ".exe" can be executed to run on any computer. Alternately, a game's work-in-progress could be saved as a ".gmz" file, which required GameMaker: Studio to be installed on a machine to launch effectively. Isaacs asked open-ended questions such as, "What are the two formats?"; "How do you make the .gmz?"; "What's the benefit of .exe?"; and "Why do we use it?"

Isaacs explained that he could review the code in a .gmz file, which can enable him to offer substantive teacher feedback. "How many games should you be reviewing?" he asked. Most students responded, "Two." Isaacs reminded everyone to use Google Form. "That's a quest you should be submitting," he continued. "After reviewing two games, what do you do? How do you decide what edits to make?" Students replied that they needed to edit their games.

The discussion moved to testing games. "After editing your game, you want people to look at it," Isaacs continued. "What's another way to get feedback on that game?" Several students responded that they should get people to come to their computers and play it. "Why?" Isaacs asked. "What happens when you watch someone else play your game?" Most responded that they would have immediate feedback. Isaacs reworded the question, leading students to the answer he was looking for: students would be able to see player reactions. He continued:

> It helps you to better understand the user experience. It's one thing to see that every time I go left I fall into a pit of lava. Maybe there's a wall here and the designer didn't understand that the player would see an invisible wall. The conferencing and feedback is important. How should you observe? You should be doing what? Probably not speaking so much. If it is [a student's] game, he should not tell you what to do. You benefit as a developer seeing your game through someone else's eyes. Then iterate. These are our more pressing points today. This is what we're focusing on today—unless it is your 20% day.

At this point, 20 minutes into the class period, students began independent work. At times, students in period three seemed to frustrate Isaacs; several went off-task. When reviewing workflow, one student got up to get headphones from the closet. Isaacs admonished the student. "Sit down," he said. "You don't need to get headphones when I'm talking." During the whole-class instruction, when most of student's eyes were on the teacher, one student was observed clicking his computer mouse. Isaacs corrected him. "Stop what you're doing, please." Isaacs then said to the class, "Okay folks. Settle in."

Isaacs' direct instruction in periods three and five emphasized issues he had observed in period one. Regarding submitting games to the class' Google Sheet, he said to the period three class, "People in period one thought they needed a done game, basically, you need some functionality in your game. Part of the iterative design process is to just create your design document and an alpha version, which you did." He pointed out that many neglected to "flesh out game storylines."

In period three, when Isaacs was visibly frustrated by off-task responses, he offered an analogy: "When I buy a game at GameStop, do they ever send the guy who designed the game home with you? Have any of you had that experience? That's why the feedback is valuable." Isaacs finally reviewed what students should be doing. "That will take us through today, tomorrow, maybe Monday," he said. "By the time we leave for winter break, I need a playable prototype, not a completed game, the mechanics work and I can give good feedback." Isaacs also told the period class that animations were not important. "The game could be a circle and a square with the boss a bigger square. Please don't get caught up in the graphical part. Get to work everybody!"

When Isaacs told the class to get to work, about three students throughout the day wrote their names on the whiteboard, indicating that teacher intervention was needed. Isaacs walked around room and asked if everyone was testing games. He asked a girl if she needed help. She needed to create a spreadsheet about ninjas she added to a game. Isaacs reviewed how many images per row and what to change. He stood near her and helped resolve the issue. "You're getting the idea, right?" he asked. He then showed her how to copy-and-paste images. Then she had another question about how to control the sprite's movement. Isaacs explained to make a new sprite, then walked on to make sure students stayed on task. Some were observed off-task, not playing or reviewing games.

Isaacs did not saying anything to specific students who were laughing or talking at a loud volume. Isaacs was often on his personal iPhone, which served as his mobile device, as he walked the room. Occasionally, a student with a question flagged him down. He would answer, "Look in the notes, it's all in the notes."

The period three class remained talkative, louder than periods one or five. At one point Isaacs said, "I need you to not be so loud." When the noise level continued, Isaacs announced, "I'm setting a clock. For three minutes, I want no talking. Remember, no talking. The timer is going for three minutes now. We're going to enjoy some game-like, Zen playtesting." There was a countdown clock visible on Isaacs' laptop (on Google), not on the screens in view of the students. There was some talking, which Isaacs corrected. Isaacs remained seated at his desk on his laptop. When the alarm beeped, Isaacs reset the clock for another 3 minutes. He joked that he "would make it like jail" if necessary. Although students in period three were sociable, no one was overtly disrespectful.

Students were observed entering information to a Google Form. The fields that required data responses included the game to be evaluated, the student's real name, and the student's 3D GameLab "gamertag" nickname. Next, the form had the following: "Storyline/narrative: All games should have a rich story to guide the gameplay. Provide feedback on the storyline/narrative of the game you are testing." Under that was a scale, from one to five: "1 = doesn't exist; 5 = storyline truly immerses player in the game." The next field was "Gameplay: Is it fun? Are the controls good? Is it overly buggy?" That was followed by a scale from one to five: "1 = very buggy, difficult to play; 5 = fun and engaging gameplay." "Difficulty ramp" was next, asking the student to assess each other's level design. It read: "Level of challenge should increase appropriately to keep the player engaged and provide high replayability. How does this game measure up?" The scale which followed included, "1 = lack of attention to ramp of difficulty (too easy, too hard, inconsistent); 5 = game becomes increasingly challenging at an appropriate pace." The final question on Isaacs' form was, "What did you like about the game?" One student response was observed: "I like how the game mechanics work and how the sprite moves differently."

The students were asked to provide their game's "storyline," which "should include 2–3 paragraphs describing the background story to provide context. Include information related to plot, conflict, and goal." One student response read, "Seagulls had a peaceful life of eating small creatures of the sea." Under that field was, "Characters-Include name and detailed description of characters. Character description should give reader a good about who the character/enemy/boss/NPC [non-playable character] is, what their abilities are, what they look like, etc." The student wrote the following: "Playable (Characters): Antonio the seagull. Enemies: Clown that try to grab you. Boss(es): A shark." Finally, the students were required to describe each level in their game. This field was more specific:

> Levels—Describe how each level is different from the last. This should include the look and feel of each level (i.e., if a level takes place in a desert, describe the desert environment, etc.). Also discuss how each level will increase in difficulty (i.e., Does the level have a boss, certain monsters, sprites, etc.).

The observed student answered:

Level 1:	This will be a simple Bombing on the clowns.
Level 2:	Then you bomb the whole boardwalk.
Level 3:	When you go to the towel there will be a shark in your way that you need to defeat (Boss Battle).

Isaacs' questions were about objects in the game ("items that you encountered in the game, i.e. power-ups, weapons, coins, armor, etc.") and the scoring mechanisms. He reminded the whole class, "Remember, you need that Google Form open because you're evaluating a game based on three important questions: What did you like? What would you improve? What would you add? Answers should be simple and concrete."

Teacher-designed quests on 3D GameLab were also observed. Next to each quest were the XPs a student could earn, followed by the approximate time required for completion, the type of learning (e.g., social media, coding), and a due date, which often was "no end date." Quests included: #Games4Ed

Twitter chat Thursdays 8 p.m. ET; 20% Tuesday reflections; Creating a text-based adventure: Plan the story; Create your own text based adventure; GameMaker: Prepare your game to receive feedback; GameMaker: Creating moving enemies in your game; GameMaker Language (GML): Adding background and sounds; Hour of Code challenge: The maze; Skyblock: Cobblestone generator in *Minecraft*; and *Zoombinis*: Initial impressions.

The remainder of the classes was spent playing and reviewing games. Students had a choice about the quests to complete, even though Isaacs presented the workflow of the lesson. Isaacs continued to provide individual attention to students requiring specific help. For example, Isaacs had to "unaccept" a submitted student game that was prematurely shared on a Google Sheet. One morning student noticed that Windows detected all .exe files as possible malware. Finished GameMaker: Studio games use this file type to run. Occasionally, Isaacs sat in student chairs to help resolve coding issues or glitches. While most students used GameMaker: Studio, there were two students creating an Xbox One console game using Project Spark in back of the classroom.

For the most part, students in period one were independent. Many helped each other. One student was called by another to "judge a song" for his game. Another asked a classmate, "Which direction is left? When I rotate, is it 90 degrees or 180?" Then he asked the teacher: "Mr. Isaacs, I need help with shooting. It's not shooting right when I'm pressing space." Isaacs reviewed the mathematical coordinates in the game. He helped student with variables, asking Socratic-style questions. "This is going to be what?" he asked. "Ninety degrees," the student replied. "No," Isaacs responded. "Ninety degrees is up."

Isaacs resolved individual problems quickly and got students back on track. He would often return to his laptop at his desk to review 3D GameLab or shared work on Google. Students worked at their terminals, with the occasional students rolling a chair to see another's game, or chatting amongst themselves. Conversations were generally project-related. Every student had his or her own project.

Period five was on-task; all students were observed on GameMaker: Studio. When one student was on SnapGuide authoring a *Minecraft* gold sword step-by-step guide, Isaacs reminded him to review games, not work on 20% Time projects. One girl expressed an issue opening a GameMaker: Studio file. Isaacs intervened. Shortly after, a student said, "Mr. Isaacs, there's something wrong with this level." Isaacs went to the student's terminal and sat in his chair and helped resolve the issue.

Several students required teacher intervention simultaneously. Isaacs asked students to wait while he was resolving technical issues with other students. "You don't need to keep your hand up," he said. "I know to help you, when I can." Isaacs aided students in reviewing "sprite packs"—graphical components of game worlds. He then announced, "Folks, every day, you should export a back-up version of your game on Google Drive." After two more brief student questions were tended to, Isaacs returned to his desk. The room in period five was quiet. Typing on keyboards was audibly louder than students speaking.

About half of students were in Google Forms writing their game reviews and completing the template. The remainder of the class played games or changed properties to their games, all in GameMaker: Studio. At this time, Isaacs was observed standing over a student's computer helping him set coordinates for the game's sprite. Then Isaacs returned to his desk and checked his email. He laughed at some comments amongst students. The class was engaged.

Toward the end of each of the three classes, Isaacs walked the room to see who tested or submitted their games. Because of the schedule change, students did not seem aware of when the period ended. In the first period, when it was announced that 5 minutes remained, the class and Isaacs audibly groaned. By the conclusion of the morning classes, students submitted work on 3D GameLab and on Google Drive. Several students in each class requested lunch and study hall passes. Isaacs said they could have them, but they needed to be quiet because some people were recording.

References

Isaacs, S. (2015a). *Empowering learners in the maker age: Take 3*. Retrieved from DonorsChoose website: http://www.donorschoose.org/project/empowering-learners-in-the-maker-age-ta/1804714/?rf=email-system-2015-12-proposal_approve-teacher_1420407&challengeid=384761&utm_source=dc&utm_medium=email&utm_campaign=proposal_approve&utm_swu=4258

Isaacs, S. [mr_isaacs]. (2015b, December 1). *#20percentTuesday making games with @disneyinfinity @proj_spark @keith_guarino @fabhistory* [Tweet]. Retrieved from https://twitter.com/mr_isaacs/status/671679613442084864

Isaacs, S. [mr_isaacs]. (2015d, December 1). *Student created #makeymakey tinfoil game controller works with original #gamemaker game @yoyogames #20PercentTuesday* [Tweet]. Retrieved from https://twitter.com/mr_isaacs/status/671716232551399424

PART III
"GO WHERE THE GAME TAKES YOU!"

Peggy Sheehy, Paul Darvasi, and Steve Isaacs tended to seek open-ended games with affordances for playfulness and gamefulness. Students had a sense of identity play and agency over their learning. These playful conditions brought students to their zone of proximal development in a self-directed way.

Part III of this book starts with a reflection on the observations I made during the previous three chapters. It is a discussion about how teachers in The Tribe are not just practitioners delivering lessons, they are designers of meaningful experiences for their students. Games are used as high-quality curriculum, adapted to meet learning goals. As Tribe member Zack Gilbert once told me, "When teaching with games, you must be ready to go where the game takes you!"

· 7 ·

PLAYFUL LEARNING

Why are playful affordances so ubiquitous in The Tribe's teaching praxis? What is it about play that is so important to learning? Perhaps it is because playfulness—the act of playing—creates the zone of proximal development for children (Bodrova, Germeroth, & Leong, 2013; Vygotsky, 1978). The zone of proximal development is "the distance between the [child's] actual development level as determined by independent problem solving and the level of potential development as determined through problem solving under adult guidance or in collaboration with more capable peers" (Vygotsky, 1978, p. 86). As games increase in difficulty and complexity, new knowledge is distributed or scaffolded (Bodrova et al., 2013; Csikszentmihalyi, 1990; Koster, 2014; Vygotsky, 1978). Play is a social activity that occurs within the construct of a game (Salen & Zimmerman, 2003). Play "drives learning" (Squire, 2011, pp. 138–139).

"Any time a student is playing, they are also learning," Mark Suter told me, early in 2017. "Play, in my mind, is something someone chooses to do. It's not necessarily playing a game—it's a mindset." Suter's computer technology classroom engages students with playful game design tools, like GameMaker: Studio. "When I am playing with computer code, I am experiencing what I cobbled together to make a simple game or app." He continued:

> Play is almost the same thing as saying passion or engagement. When I see a student playing hard, it's hard work—but it's also fun. When I see that, I ask students to spin that off to become their project. Play drives curriculum because I encourage students to tap into something they like.

This chapter opens with a discussion of how those in The Tribe apply play theory. These experts were adept at being able to toe the line between free and structured play. Montessorian approaches to game-based learning were evident in classrooms, too.

Play Theory

Play is ambiguous, or difficult to define (Sutton-Smith, 1997). Brian Sutton-Smith (1997) included seven "rhetorics" to describe play. Sutton-Smith's work is seminal and influential, serving as a critique of the exactness of defining the boundaries of play. He listed seven rhetorics to describe play as including the following:

1. *Progress*—how people grow and learn from playing;
2. *Fate*—luck and chance in contests;
3. *Power*—competition to be the hero in a game or sport;
4. *Identity*—playing together at social events, including family gatherings;
5. *Imagination*—creative play;
6. *Self*—hobbies and personal activities; and
7. *Frivolity*—silly or foolish play. (Sutton-Smith, 1997)

Children play for more reasons than to achieve psychological growth (Sutton-Smith, 1997). Sutton-Smith's rhetorics are the result of several hundred observations, including children engaged in make-believe and rough-and-tumble play. Rhetorics describe play, and change based on one's perspective (Sutton-Smith, 1997). Play does not unfold linearly, like in a taxonomy; rather, it is cyclical, organized in a way that also helps to enforce, or regulate, social skills (Eberle, 2014).

Piaget's (1962) view was that games enable children to assimilate information. Sutton-Smith (1966) published a criticism of Piaget, stating that play is not merely a function of intellectualism. He disagreed that imitation play existed to enable children to assimilate new knowledge (Sutton-Smith, 1966). Unlike Piaget's view of play as a function of assimilation, Sutton-Smith's opinion was that play has more to do with the accommodation of knowledge (Sutton-Smith, 1966). To Sutton-Smith (1966), play "distorts" reality and is not truly imitative (p. 109).

Play Theory in Practice

The overall observed learning environment in Paul Darvasi, Peggy Sheehy, and Steve Isaacs' classrooms espoused a playful culture positioned to be at odds with the way students were taught in other classes throughout their day. Instead of being passive learners receiving information directly from their teachers, students were actively engaged in learning from experiences. For example, Sheehy's call-and-response mantras and signage indicated that her room was like a refuge from the testing regime her students encounter during the remainder of their school day. Darvasi's students were audibly enthused at the prospect of playing a video game in class. Regarding Darvasi's school, its house system gamified the students' overall school experience with in-school competition.

When I surveyed Sheehy's students, of 42 responses, 21 used the word "fun" to describe the games played in the lessons observed. Many respondents desired more freedom to play. Perhaps elements of the game were mastered, putting students outside the flow channel (Csikszentmihalyi, 1990; Koster, 2014). Two students wrote that the games were "boring" and two described the games as too "challenging." One student used the word *fun*, but then said, "not a lot of fun for me." The responses for what students wanted the games to do varied. Some wanted more abilities—from flying to running faster in *World of Warcraft* to the freedom to customize pets. One wanted the game to be more like *The Hobbit*; another wanted the map of the game world to be smaller. Regarding learning, students stated that they learned about content, such as how the government functions (from iCivics games), and skills, such as independent learning and how to persist at solving problems. One student—an outlier—responded, "Honestly I don't think that video games in the classroom teach you anything."

Sheehy had students play from a menu of pre-selected multitude of games (e.g., iCivics' games, *World of Warcraft*). She was encouraging her students to be "active and critical, not passive" learners (Gee, 2007, p. 221). *World of Warcraft*, the centerpiece of the WoWinSchools Curriculum, was played daily. Student players were rewarded with "experience points" (XPs) for achievements in the game, as well as in their 3D GameLab quests. To "level up" student avatars (digital, onscreen representations), the rhetoric of power had to be demonstrated through win states (Sutton-Smith, 1997). The crafting mechanic in *World of Warcraft*, in which found items could be combined and upgraded, represented the rhetoric of imaginary play, as did the game itself, a role-play hero's journey (Sutton-Smith, 1997).

In Isaacs' classroom, students were on personalized quests. He designed a series of challenges, each meaningful based on student interest. His students demonstrated the ability to "appreciate design and design principles" (Gee, 2007, p. 221). Many were engaged in authentic activities, their content published online (e.g., DonorsChoose employs gamification mechanics in its crowdfunding pages), embodying Vygotsky's (1997) notion of playing games "as preparation for his life in the future" (p. 93).

Gone Home, the primary game observed in Darvasi's classes, challenged several definitions of what games are. You don't "win" *Gone Home*; you explore the story. Similarly, you don't win by reaching the end of a novel. Or do you? There is a feeling of accomplishment when reaching the conclusion of a story. *Gone Home* lacked the rhetoric of play as fate, stemming from luck, or the rhetoric of play as power (Sutton-Smith, 1997). But like reading a compelling novel, the narrative of the nonlinear story drove engagement. The fun of the experience was dependent on the rhetoric of play as progress—intrinsic satisfaction from discovery (Sutton-Smith, 1997). To further enhance student engagement, Darvasi added in the rhetoric of frivolity, suggesting that students could collect items in the house and then pile them all in the foyer. The point-and-click interface embodied Vygotskian sociodramatic play: Players follow a set of rules based on the role they play (Bodrova et al., 2013, p. 374). Engagement may be rooted in the freedom one has to explore while role-playing as Katie Greenbriar. He also engaged students in social collaborations with other classes.

Expectations regarding what Darvasi's students wanted *Gone Home* to do, as free play, was reflected in the open-ended responses to my survey questions. Many wanted more freedom to explore. Some wondered what was outside the house, while others wanted to engage actions associated with different genres of video games (e.g., running, jumping). Responses pertaining to learning a nonlinear narrative story in a free play and open-ended environment varied. Nine students responded that it was too soon in the game to comment on what they have learned thus far. Of the students, 13 expressed an appreciation of the storytelling techniques in *Gone Home*. One response was, "It's hard to identify what exactly I learned, but it's very refreshing to study a video game." Another wrote, "i dont think i learned anything new but that's not unusual when it comes to small projects in school. This felt like a regular class assignment but more interesting." One responded, "I would like to be able to listen to all documents as I am an oral learner and have a nonverbal learning disability."

When asked about what video games could teach effectively, students in Darvasi's classes used phrases such as *critical thinking* and *problem solving*. From the students' perspective, they understood the potential that video games have to promote "active critical learning" in "all aspects of the learning environment" (Gee, 2007, p. 221). One student wrote, "Problem solving and piecing together evidence are practiced in *Gone Home*, I also think that the interactive quality of games is better at capturing the interests of students."

I observed the third yearly iteration of the *Gone Home*. "The unit, thus far, was generally effective in its intent to familiarize them [students] with the game, the content of the game and various game play features in it," Darvasi said in November 2015. "I feel like we meet all of those objectives by the end of the lesson. The only changes were adding counterparts from Norway and Sweden." The codelivery of the unit with foreign counterparts was intended to apply a system of apprenticeship learning to the game's epistemics: Each student brings his or her expertise to the unit's outcome (Barab, Downton, & Siyahhan, 2010).

Husøy—who simultaneously taught *Gone Home* with Darvasi—is in a high school with classroom spaces that are relatively devoid of playful affordances. Nordahl Grieg Upper Secondary School is a glass-and-concrete structure. "My classroom space is really boring," Husøy said, in December 2016. Husøy and Tobias Staaby—both game-based learning teachers—share the same workstation. "Our classrooms aren't really playful—but we adapt. We move desks and chairs around when we need to. Most of our play is within the digital sphere."

I asked Sheehy, Isaacs, and Darvasi's students what they thought video games could teach in school. In Sheehy's class, one student responded, "There are many different types of video games, and I think that different games could be used to teach different subjects, for instance, *Minecraft* can be used to teach architecture." Another wrote, "I think video games should be teached in school because I found out that I learned more with a video game than siting and listening to the teacher." In Isaacs' class, answers ranged from coding skills to storytelling. Engagement and critical thinking was a common thread in Darvasi's student responses. Several remarked on how exploration mechanics can be effective in teaching problem solving and nonlinear storytelling. One responded, "I think video games teach the same thing as books, but I actually enjoy it. It brings a nice balance to our course load. I wouldn't want to play video games for every unit."

Playful learning experiences with games are often personalized, and the goals change based on student choice and the identities taken on during play. Spanish teacher Glen Irvin spoke to me in November 2016 about the challenges of designing for meaningful experiences. Upon hearing how I observed Sheehy, Isaacs, and Darvasi—whether intentional, or not—incorporated affordances for playfulness into their lessons, Irvin asked me to forward him Sutton-Smith's (1997) list of rhetorics. To him, adding in invitations for students to view learning through playful lenses seemed like a natural lesson plan addition. Rhetorics of play can be another way to differentiate instruction to drive engagement. If Irvin is differentiating based on Gardner's (1983) theory of multiple intelligences, or on Bartle's (1996) Player Types Model, then why not also include considerations for Sutton-Smith's (1997) rhetorics of play?

Balancing Play and Game

There exists a "very fine balance" between play and game (DeKoven, 1978, p. 40). Free play is when "children learn to make their own decisions, solve their own problems, create and abide by rules, and get along with others as equals rather than as obedient or rebellious subordinates" (Gray, 2014, p. 18). Free play is sandlot baseball, whereas Little League represents an organized activity, often planned by outside forces (e.g., adults; Gray, 2014; Sutton-Smith, 1997).

There is an inherent issue when bringing play and games into compulsory education. Teacher cannot assign a child to play a game; rather, teachers can create conditions for student choice and invitations to play (Bodrova & Leong, 2007). Play is a "voluntary" activity (Huizinga, 1938/1955, p. 28).

Play freedoms enable players to fail, experiment, fashion ideas, change degree of effort, and interpret activities (Klopfer, Osterweil, & Salen, 2009). In most cases, students in The Tribe's classes were assessed based on written reflections; how well students played was not assessed. Thoughtful care was taken to ensure that the play within the structure of games was "child-initiated," and as free as possible (Bodrova et al., 2013, p. 53).

Free play is "an illusory freedom" (Vygotsky, 1967, p. 10), with "no agenda" (Klopfer et al., 2009, p. 5). Free play is "self-chosen and self-directed; intrinsically motivated; guided by rules; imaginative; and conducted in an active, alert, but relatively non-stressed frame of mind" (Gray, 2015, p. 125). Gee (2017) embraces "mucking around as a form of play" that allows for risk-taking and exploration in low-stakes settings (p. 34). Play requires "a combination of curiosity, imagination, and experimentation" (Resnick, 2017, p. 127).

Play observed in The Tribe's classrooms occurred in a "fixed" place or "magic circle" (Huizinga, 1938/1955, p. 10). In the magic circle, the player is safe and free from actualizing real-life "material consequences" from game actions (Huizinga, 1938/1955, p. 10). The magic circle can be a gym, a field, a living room, or a game board (Salen & Zimmerman, 2003; Schell, 2008). Play in the context of a game requires players to agree on a space and then "restrict this territory with respect to rule-binding criteria for adaptation and interaction" (Walther, 2003, "The Form Logic of Play and Games"). Although there is usually a physical space in which one plays, it could also be said that play actually happens in the minds of the players, not out in the real world (Walther, 2003).

The Tribe's students often played games on computer screens. But they also were put in playful situations within the confines of the geography of classrooms. Games tended to be open-ended and nonlinear, giving students choice on quests to take and levels to master (e.g., *World of Warcraft*). Isaacs' students moved from console to computer. Sheehy's students selected which *World of Warcraft* quest to take, and which iCivics game to play. Darvasi's students explored *Gone Home* on their own volition. He "suggested" that students stay in the foyer for the first day; they were told that they would be free to explore in subsequent lessons. As a result, in "the prescribed space of a game," students exhibited "all of the freedoms of unstructured play" (Klopfer et al., 2009, p. 5). Darvasi then "gave permission" for his students to snoop around, open medicine cabinets, and read game characters' mail. Interestingly, given these constraints, students were observed switching off lights and closing doors as they exited rooms in the virtual house.

Free play can be tricky when students play open-ended games that have affordances which invite exploration of virtual environments. Husøy, who codelivered the *Gone Home* unit I observed in Darvasi's class, restricted students early on to only explore the first couple of rooms, basically the porch and the foyer. "The reason for this is because we want the discussion that the students have among themselves to revolve around their shared experience of having limited knowledge of the plot and theme that will later be revealed in the game," Husøy said, in late 2016.

This approach is similar if students are reading a novel. If some of the class read halfway through a book while some only read the first two chapters, a discussion of the story and content would not be on the same terms. Student experiences would differ. "Basically, they wouldn't be able to speculate on equal grounds based upon what we read and experienced so far," Husøy continued. "By restricting the class, you lay the framework for more interesting discussion where the discussion is based on all students having access to the same amount of information."

C. Ross Flatt, of the Institute of Play, spoke to me about free play in game-based classrooms in December 2016. "I want students to follow the rules, because if they don't, it is going to change the outcome," he began. "I wouldn't give students *Survive and Thrive* [a Columbian Exchange-themed board game] and just let them go and be free with it. There are things I'm looking for when they're playing the game."

If a student is not following the rules a game, then the game is no longer the same. For example, if a group pools their letter tiles together in *Scrabble* and then play cooperatively, is it still *Scrabble*? Is it okay to play a game wrong? Flatt continued:

> If I want students to experiment with the concepts of the Columbian Exchange, or to design a tool to aid them on their quest about the Columbian Exchange—or even to pretend to be Christopher Columbus encountering natives—well, that's going to be a little more playful. That's where I would step back and let them be and try something. Then we would talk about what happened afterwards. Play is lower risk and it's not as worried about the final goal, but rather with the experience that is happening. With a game you have to be more concerned with the final outcome because games have a win-state and goal, play doesn't have to. Play is led by the person experiencing it.

Games are highly systematic, and play is less so. Not all game-based learning classrooms involved actually playing games with rules. Giving students opportunities to tinker with something, or to having students be able to design or make something, is a playful activity. Tinkering is "at the intersection of playing and making" (Resnick, 2017, p. 136).

I spoke with researcher Sande Chen in December 2016 about how game design can be a playful act. "To design a game, you need you understand how parts interact and form a system," she said. "In higher education, we see systems in sciences and economics. It is a view of the world—or whatever it is you are trying to model—as a system."

The skills Isaacs' students learned from the iterative cycle of designing a game go beyond science, math and even computer science skills. His students learn problem solving and systems thinking. A systems thinking framework teaches students to look at patterns and systems around them. "How do things interact?" Chen continued. "How do I debug? Students need this in the 21st century. Is there a system of how people interact? They become be keyed in to a community, to learn outside the classroom, to ignite their passions and to learn peer-to-peer."

Montessorian, by Design

Maria Montessori (1912/2012) wrote that children have an innate ability, an appetite to learn. The instructional dynamic observed in The Tribe's classrooms were Montessorian, supporting the idea that "the Montessori system provides a model of what a game-based learning system should look like" (Squire, 2011, p. 49). The Montessori method is a teaching strategy that pertains to how children learn from playing freely. Through uninterrupted play, new information is discovered individually.

The games used by those in The Tribe were also Montessorian in design. Games gave immediate feedback, and they did not "insist by repeating the lesson" (Montessori, 1912/2012, p. 62). Negative feedback did not "make the child feel like he has made a mistake" (Montessori, 1912/2012, p. 62).

A Montessori-like approach was also observed in how games were contextualized to students. "Brevity" is how Montessori (1912/2012, p. 61) described how long an explanation should take before students engage in a learning activity. More time was reserved for students to play with the affordances and constraints in game's systems (Bogost, 2008; Norman, 2013). In Sheehy's and Darvasi's classes, students were given brief mini-lessons on the background of the games, as well as the interface. In Isaacs' class, the game design tools students used were constructivist.

Observed teachers seldom, if ever, interrupted a child during play. When needed, only technical advice was offered to students; they shied away from intervening with processes of students figuring something out. Students in each observed classroom were handed over ownership of the experiences afforded by the games. The teachers were often working on his or her computer, planning upcoming lessons, or grading submitted student work. If a student had a question about how to resolve a problem within the game itself, he or she was usually directed to solve it without teacher assistance.

This approach afforded students an opportunity to play within the system of games used. Darvasi's students were observed remarking that they should let classmates "figure it out on his own." Sheehy's students similarly were advised to work completely independent from one another. Isaacs' students were driven by affinity group affiliation guided by students' personal interests (Gee, 2007).

Playful Learning Environments

Robert Kalman is a middle school computer technology teacher. We have spoken on occasion, and have met at the 2016 Games in Education Symposium, in Troy, New York, where he led a presentation on the game design toy *Bloxels*, from Pixel Press. To play, plastic color-coded cubes are placed into a 13-by-13 board. Then, using a tablet camera and the *Bloxels Builder* application, the cubes are translated to become game components. Gold cubes can represent gold coins, and green cubes may be digital grass.

While he represents *Bloxels* in teacher forums, he does not work at the Pixel Press office. Kalman teaches in Ramsey, New Jersey, and his primary career role is in the classroom. He and I spoke March 2017.

"It's awesome to head to the Games in Education Symposium, the ISTE Conference, and to connect with likeminded educators," Kalman began. Next, he mentioned Isaacs, who stewarded him through The Tribe as community of practice. "I never met someone who taught entirely game design until Steve. In his district, he created that curriculum."

This was Kalman's fourth year in the middle school; he had been a 5th grade teacher for two years prior. He was moved to the middle school based on his passion for educational technology. Kalman has freedom and agency to experiment with new ideas, and he helps to write curriculum. "They trust me to use this class, and it fits with [the school's] exploratory model to inspire kids," he said.

Kalman teaches digital design to grades 6 through 8. "It is computer science, web design, game design, VR [virtual reality], and AR [augmented reality]—all innovative educational technologies." All students used to cycle through for a "little 6-week snippet." But in 2017 his class becomes an elective. "So, I have kids for longer, but with fewer total students. It's not a mastery-based model. It gets kids interested and exposed and excited about innovative technologies."

A year ago, Kalman reached out directly to the team at Pixel Press, maker of *Bloxels*. "I started using *Floors* with my 6th grade classes," he recalled. "I thought it was really awesome." *Floors* is an application where users draw game levels on graph paper, and then they scan the pictures with a tablet camera. It was the starting point to what is now *Bloxels*. Kalman used *Floors* during an administrator's teacher observation of him. "I could tell a lot of educators were interested in their product, but Pixel Press wasn't a traditional educational company. I was already interested in their technologies and could help them bridge the gap to the educational market." Kalman became *Bloxels* educator-in-residence, leading Pixel Press' educational ambassador program.

When we spoke, Kalman was working on his master's thesis on learning environments. He was researching the physical space of classrooms. "The term learning environment is thrown around a lot," he said. "And the teacher's pedagogy plays a role. My thesis is specifically focused on the physical aspect. I break it down to things like furniture, layout, and technology."

When Kalman was moved to the middle school, he had the opportunity to redesign the computer lab. He received a $10,000 grant from the Ramsey Public Education Foundation to renovate his classroom. "I was in a traditional computer lab that was designed in the late 1980s and early 1990s. It was a typing and word processing classroom."

Early on in Kalman's transition into his new role, his principal and he agreed that this was not the learning environment for the type of classroom he envisioned leading. With the grant, he was able to fully replace all of the furniture. He also acquired 20 laptops and 10 desktop computers. This was in addition to the fact that his middle school is a 1:1 iPad district. "The classroom went from the 'sage on the stage'—the Word Document up front—to a much more playful environment." Kalman tries to lead a classroom based on student choice, excitement, and enjoyment. He continued:

> As I crafted my master's thesis, my hypothesis was the student mindset when entering a classroom—and physical space plays a part in that. My room is a huge contrast from what it was to what it is now. The room contrasts the students' other classrooms very much. When you combine that with the kind of activities we are doing—like using *Bloxels*, coding and using playful innovative tools—it becomes a great complement to their other classes. It is different, but the kids seem to enjoy it a lot.

Part of Kalman's research included interviewing students. He asked whether other classes should consider making changes to me more like his. "It was so clear from interviewing them that they see my class like a different species than other classes," he said. "They don't understand that a math class doesn't have to be drill-and-kill. They don't know that it is even possible."

Sheehy's classroom was similar: a refuge from the poor game that school can be. Kalman was clear to not indict other teachers, and he empathized with their pressures from standardized tests. In a math class there is pressure to try to figure out how to get a wide range of ability levels to learn the same concept. He also noted the issues that an open and playful classroom may have, like being prone to behavioral issues. "There needs to be more of an understanding of how the classroom works. Students have been trained and ingrained that certain subjects run a certain way."

Kalman's teaching places an emphasis on experimentation. "I try to avoid giving students answers, and I don't want them to be so concerned with right and wrong," he continued. "I try to encourage them to take risks and not be failure avoidant. A lot of activities we do encourage students to try things out, to experiment."

Because Kalman introduces 6th grade students to so many new technologies, he provides has more structure to his lessons. "When they get choices they sometimes try to find the easiest thing," he explained. Students may choose to use iMovie on iPad simply because they already know how to use it. But Kalman is tasked with teaching students to learn different technologies. "I have to monitor their choice to things they may not already know how to do something. I tell them, 'This is not the class for that.'"

In Kalman's classroom, some students are "outwardly fearful to make a mistake." He spends time encouraging students to try new things out. "The ways I learned new technologies was by using them, and by trying and creating things," he said. "There is nothing wrong with going to a tutorial or to YouTube for guidance, or asking a friend or a teacher. Students have been trained that mistakes are a bad thing."

Chapter Summary

The playful affordances within the structure of a game can create conditions in which learning occurs. Games, as designed experiences, can potentially bring equity to student access to a prescribed curriculum. Students were observed participating in a personalized environment in which challenges adapted to the their abilities. This was often based on the freedom to explore game worlds, and it served to engage learning. The trial-and-error of game play, as well as the iterative process extolled in Isaacs' game design classroom, were effective in encouraging children to learn from failing.

References

Barab, S. A., Downton, M. P., & Siyahhan, S. (2010). Using activity theory to understand intergenerational play: The case of family quest. *International Journal of Computer-Supported Collaborative Learning*, 5(4), 415–432.

Bartle, R. (1996, April). *Hearts, clubs, diamonds, spades: Players who suit MUDs*. Retrieved January 11, 2017 from http://www.mud.co.uk/richard/hcds.htm

Bodrova, E., Germeroth, C., & Leong, D. J. (2013). Play and self-regulation: Lessons from Vygotsky. *American Journal of Play*, 6(1), 111–123.

Bodrova, E., & Leong, D. J. (2007). *Tools of the mind: The Vygotskian approach to early childhood education* (2nd ed.). Columbus, OH: Merrill/Prentice Hall.

Bogost, I. (2008). The rhetoric of video games. In K. Salen (Ed.), *The ecology of games: Connecting youth, games, and learning* (pp. 117–140). *The John D. and Catherine T. MacArthur foundation series on digital media and learning*. Cambridge, MA: MIT Press. doi:10.1162/dmal.9780262693646.117

Csikszentmihalyi, M. (1990). *Flow: The psychology of optimal experience*. New York, NY: Harper & Row.

DeKoven, B. (1978). *Well-played game: A player's philosophy*. Cambridge, MA: The MIT Press.

Eberle, S. G. (2014). The elements of play: Toward a philosophy and a definition of play. *American Journal of Play*, 6(2), 214–233.

Gardner, H. (1983). *Frames of mind: The theory of multiple intelligences*. New York, NY: Basic Books.

Gee, J. P. (2007). *What video games have to teach us about learning and literacy* (rev. ed.). New York, NY: Palgrave Macmillan.

Gee, J. P. (2017). *Teaching, learning, literacy in our high-risk high-tech world: A framework for becoming human*. New York, NY: Teachers College Press.

Gray, P. (2014). *Free to learn: Why unleashing the instinct to play will make our children happier, more self-reliant, and better students for life*. New York, NY: Basic Books.

Gray, P. (2015). Studying play without calling it that: Humanistic and positive psychology. In J. Johnson, S. Eberle, T. Henricks, & D. Kuschner (Eds.), *The handbook of the study of play* (pp. 124–127). New York, NY: Rowman & Littlefield.

Huizinga, J. (1955). *Homo Ludens: A study of the play-element in culture*. Boston, MA: Beacon Press (Original work published 1938).

Klopfer, E., Osterweil, S., & Salen, K. (2009). *Moving learning games forward*. Retrieved from MIT Education Arcade website: http://education.mit.edu/wp-content/uploads/2015/01/MovingLearningGamesForward_EdArcade.pdf

Koster, R. (2014). *A theory of fun for game design* (2nd ed.). Sebastopol, CA: O'Reilly Media.

Montessori, M. (2012). *The Montessori method*. New York, NY: Renaissance Classics (Original work published 1912).

Norman, D. A. (2013). *The design of everyday things* (rev. and expanded ed.). New York, NY: Basic Books.

Piaget, J. (1962). *Play, dreams and imitation in childhood*. New York, NY: Norton Library.

Resnick, M. (2017). *Lifelong kindergarten: Cultivating creativity through projects, passion, peers, and play*. Cambridge, MA: MIT Press.

Salen, K., & Zimmerman, E. (2003). *Rules of play: Game design fundamentals*. Cambridge, MA: MIT Press.

Schell, J. (2008). *The art of game design: A book of lenses*. Amsterdam, The Netherlands: Elsevier/Morgan Kaufmann.

Squire, K. (2011). *Video games and learning: Teaching and participatory culture in the digital age.* New York, NY: Teachers College Press.

Sutton-Smith, B. (1966). Piaget on play: A critique. *Psychological Review, 73*(1), 104–110. doi:10.1037/h0022601

Sutton-Smith, B. (1997). *The ambiguity of play.* Cambridge, MA: Harvard University Press.

Vygotsky, L. S. (1967). Play and its role in the mental development of the child. *Soviet Psychology, 5*(3), 6–18.

Vygotsky, L. S. (1978). *Mind in society: The development of higher psychological processes.* Cambridge, MA: Harvard University Press.

Vygotsky, L. S. (1997). *Educational psychology* (R. J. Silverman, Trans.). Boca Raton, FL: St. Lucie Press.

Walther, B. K. (2003, May). *Playing and gaming reflections and classifications.* Retrieved from Game Studies website: http://www.gamestudies.org/0301/walther/

· 8 ·

GAMEFUL LEARNING

Filament Games produced the election simulator *Win the White House* for iCivics. Anecdotally, I knew my 7th grade social studies students loved it. Often, the day after playing in a class period—it can take about 30 minutes to complete—students requested to play again the following day. (Take that, worksheets!) Louise Dubé and Carrie Ray-Hill of iCivics shared insight in a (2016) blog post about the design decisions embedded in the game that encourage replay. They wrote:

> We also wanted to make sure that the game was replayable. Students have multiple opportunities for customization. They can select their party, they can select different issues within that party and even run as a maverick! Within the game, they can also choose to run more positive or negative ads, and try different state strategies. Multiple plays not only provide more practice at the game, it allows for greater exposure to content and strategy. (Dubé & Ray-Hill, 2016, para. 16)

In *Win the White House*, the goal is to win by scoring at least 270 votes on the Electoral College map. Student are not asked quiz questions about the election process; rather, they *become* presidential candidates.

The game presents a series of meaningful choices. Meaningful play in a game is defined as "the relationship between action and outcome" in the game as a designed system (Salen & Zimmerman, 2003, p. 34). If a game experience is meaningful enough, it may warrant replay. Paul Darvasi remarked on how *Gone Home* was unexpectedly engaging to play through a second—and even a third—time. He wrote:

> In all honesty, I wasn't thrilled at the idea of retreading every inch of the big ol' Greenbriar mansion. I'd already played twice, but I thought this third forensic run would be a bit painstaking and laborious. Happily, I was wrong. The time flew by, the developers' commentary was extremely engaging, and I discovered many new details that I'd missed the first two times around. I was reminded of a quote by one of my favorite writers—Jorge Luis Borges—"rereading, not reading, is what counts." (Darvasi, 2016, p. 124)

So, what exactly is the secret formula to making games—and learning, for that matter—replayable? What drive players to want to play over and over again? And—more importantly—in a classroom, how can teachers make learning replayable? This chapter opens with an analysis of gameful learning. Good games are gameful, which makes them replayable. Members of The Tribe also apply elements of self-determination theory to their designed lessons.

Gameful Learning Practices

Students in The Tribe's classrooms are asked to consider how game roles informed decisions. Via the core mechanics of *Gone Home*, Paul Darvasi gave students permission to "snoop around" an empty house without fear of reprimand. Darvasi's students were no longer boys in a high school English classroom; they became 21-year-old Kaitlin Greenbriar. Similarly, when Sheehy's students played *World of Warcraft*, they became druids or mages—they were no longer 6th grade humanities students.

Remi Kalir (neé Holden) coauthored a (2014) paper on gameful learning. An assistant professor of information and learning technologies at the University of Colorado, Denver, Kalir emanated from the University of Wisconsin, Madison's Games Learning Society (GLS) program. We spoke about gameful learning practices in November 2016.

Gameful learning focuses "attention on how attitude supports learning beyond the immediate time and space of game play" (Holden et al., 2014, p. 195). It is at the intersection of Bernard Suits' (1978) lusory attitude, identity play, and ignorance—or uncertainty—of that not knowing what will happen next (see Figure 8.1). In a good game, "there is an inherent motivation to accept constraints, and involuntary obstacles," Kalir began. "Lusory attitude is really critical to one's sense of gamefulness."

Gameful learning

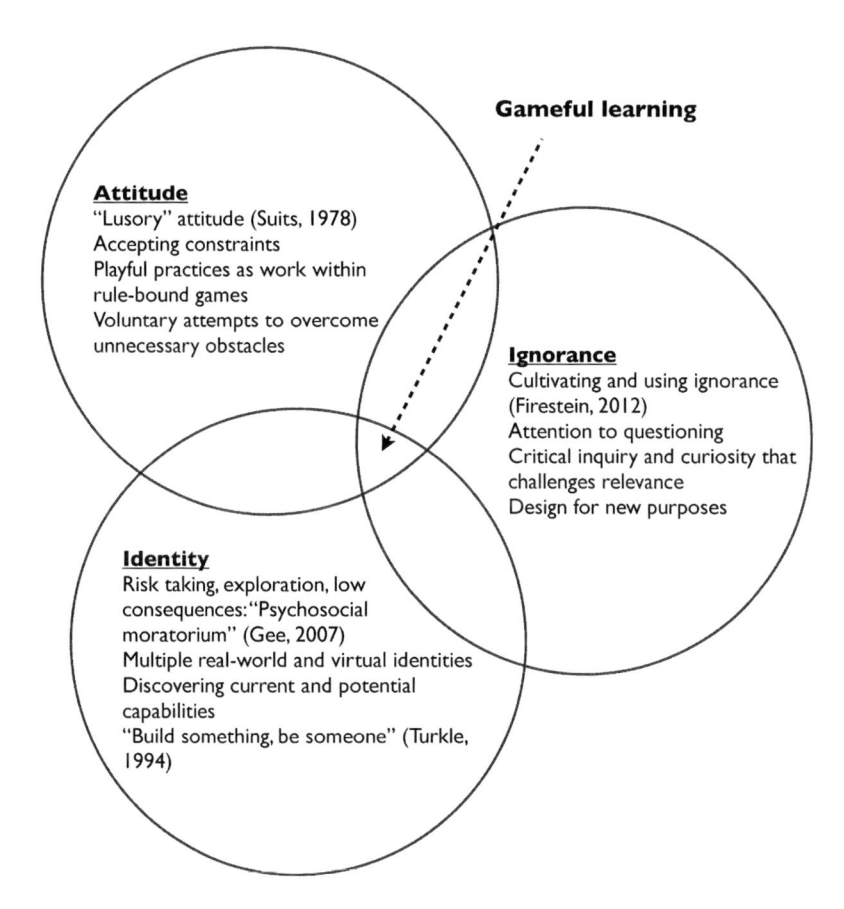

Attitude
"Lusory" attitude (Suits, 1978)
Accepting constraints
Playful practices as work within rule-bound games
Voluntary attempts to overcome unnecessary obstacles

Ignorance
Cultivating and using ignorance (Firestein, 2012)
Attention to questioning
Critical inquiry and curiosity that challenges relevance
Design for new purposes

Identity
Risk taking, exploration, low consequences: "Psychosocial moratorium" (Gee, 2007)
Multiple real-world and virtual identities
Discovering current and potential capabilities
"Build something, be someone" (Turkle, 1994)

Figure 8.1. Elements of gameful learning (Holden et al., 2014, p. 185).

A lusory attitude means that players willingly accept the challenges and obstacles in games (Suits, 1978). It is a playful mindset, and can extend to games without clearly defined goals. For example, playing through *Gone Home*, students embarked on an experience with a playful mindset—a lusory attitude. Nonetheless, playing a game requires students to voluntarily accept challenges and obstacles. To do so requires a lusory attitude. Suits (1978) wrote:

> To play a game is an attempt to achieve a specific state of affairs [prelusory goal], using only means permitted by rules [lusory means], where the rules prohibit use of more efficient in favor of less efficient means [constitutive rules], and where the rules are accepted just because they make possible such activity [lusory attitude]. (pp. 54–55)

During games, players willingly step out of their ordinary sense of being and are free to exercise imagination (Huizinga, 1938/1955). Learning through identity play gives students the "chance to play with ideas and take on new roles" (Barab & Gresalfi, 2011, p. 308). This notion harkens back to Brian Sutton-Smith's play lens—the "rhetoric of identity" (1997, p. 106). Sutton-Smith wrote, "The most important identity for players is typically the role that they are playing (first baseman, 'it,' trickster). Whatever else might be subserved by that identity is generally a secondary matter during the moments of play" (1997, p. 106). Regarding projective identifies, game-based learning scholar James Paul Gee wrote:

> Learning involves taking on and playing with identities in such a way that the learner has real choices (in developing the virtual identity) and ample opportunity to meditate on the relationship between new identities and old ones. There is a tripartite play of identities as learners relate, and reflect on, their multiple real-world identities, a virtual identity, and a projective identity. (2007, p. 208)

In addition to lusory attitudes and identity play, the third piece of gameful learning is ignorance. "Embracing what folks don't know, we argue for the embrace of high quality ignorance," Kalir continued. "That comes from scientific literature on the value of ignorance over knowledge. It was an argument for educator agency, combined with this idea of a lusory attitude with identity play with ignorance."

Ignorance speaks to the unpredictable nature of outcomes in some games. "In a game, you have to not know where it is going a little bit," researcher Benjamin Stokes told me in December 2016. "You can't know the outcome. This is a problem because a lot of overly didactic games have basically one right answer." It can be rare for educational games to acknowledge different pathways to a goal, or to offer multiple endings.

When a teacher uses a good learning game like *Win the White House*, or a commercial game like *World of Warcraft*, consequences of decisions made during play are inherently uncertain. When students finish playing gameful games, they are often left with a desire to play again, testing out other pathways or identities.

Making School Replayable

School is often presented to students more like a puzzle than a game. Puzzles are "fun problems" (Schell, 2014, p. 240). But because puzzles only have only one right answer, they are not as inherently replayable as the types of games that offer multiple pathways and solutions. Kalir (2016) wrote that when school is presented as a puzzle, it "has little replay value for students, whose repetitive schooling-as-puzzling is just that—confusing, irrelevant, and disconnected from everyday interests, or curiosities, or cultural heritages. Just as troubling, teaching—for many educators—has become both puzzle making and maintenance" (p. 362).

I spoke to Barry Fishman in March 2017 about how school can be more gameful. A professor of learning technologies at the University at Michigan, Fishman and Caitlin Holman created GradeCraft, a gameful learning management system. "For many students, school is a puzzle where the teacher knows the one right answer, and the students' job is to guess it," Fishman began. "This is inherently not replayable."

Gameful learning is the pedagogy behind much of Fishman's recent work. He referred to it as "meaningful gamification, or deep gamification." Beyond the extrinsic motivational factors "shallow" gamification can promote—like points, leaderboards, and badge accumulation—meaningful gamification is "the use of gameful and playful layers to help a user find personal connections that motivate engagement with a specific context for long-term change" (Nicholson, 2014, p. 1).

"Our starting point is that school is a game," Fishman said. Salen and Zimmerman (2003) defined games as "a system in which players engage in an artificial conflict, defined by rules, that results in a quantifiable outcome" (p. 80). This definition can be used to describe any organization or system, like a school. Fishman continued:

> But we think school is a terrible game. It has all the wrong features in it to get students to engage with the content, to work hard, and to be intrinsically motivated. When we talk about gameful learning, we're talking about changing key element of the system design that leads to that lusory attitude, and that leads to more intrinsic motivation.

So, how can school be gameful? First, elements of self-determination theory can be applied. Deci and Ryan (1985) theorized that people's actions towards achieving and goals are affected by intrinsic and extrinsic motivations. Intrinsic motivation refers to "doing something because it is inherently interesting or enjoyable" (Deci & Ryan, 2000, p. 55). Extrinsic motivation, however, are when outside factors drive engagement, and refer to "doing something because it leads to a separable outcome" (Deci & Ryan, 2000, p. 55). Extrinsic rewards, like stickers, can actually demotivate learners (Kohn, 1997; 1999).

Proponents of game-based learning note the intrinsic motivation from players have when playing good games (Kim, 2012; McGonigal, 2011). Amy Jo Kim (2012) wrote that good video games are "pleasurable learning engines" (para. 2). Players persist not for points or achievements, but for the overall experience. Play becomes meaningful when choices have consequences that intrinsically matter to players (Salen & Zimmerman, 2003).

Fishman reads self-determination theory as a set of guidelines for gameful teaching. In particular, he applies Deci and Ryan's (2000) three drivers of self-determination theory: "competence, autonomy, and relatedness" (p. 57). Each is an "innate psychological need" (Deci & Ryan, 2000, p. 57). In education, autonomy describes the agency—or control—students should have over how—and what—they learn. Agency is "the satisfying power to take meaningful action and see the results of our decision and choices" (Murray, 2017, p. 159).

In addition to autonomy, students should feel competent, and capable to perform (Deci & Ryan, 2000). Self-determination theory also includes affordances for students to have a sense of belongingness (Deci & Ryan, 2000). Fishman continued:

> Learning environments are always more engaging when they are designed for productive support of autonomy, competence, and relatedness—or belonging. Most motivation theories are descriptive—they describe the learner. Self-determination theory is almost like design guidance. It says, if you do these things in an environment, it will lead to a certain kind of outcome.

To Fishman, autonomy is the most important element of self-determination theory. "I think that students perform poorly in school is because there is a lack of autonomy," he said. "Students have no say in what they are learning, and how they are learning it. And nobody has ever explained why it's important. There is very little intrinsic motivation."

20% Time—or Genius Hour—is an affordance intended to maximize student autonomy. I observed Isaacs' students linger after class ended. Many asked to eat lunch in his room, continuing to work on projects that they proposed. "Students are finally asked what interests them, and are given agency to pursue that interest," Fishman continued. "That is replayable because they [students] are coming up with it."

Fishman cited Darvasi's alternate reality game, *The Ward Game*, as a model for gameful learning. *The Ward Game* is a real world-set game about Ken Kesey's (1963) novel *One Flew Over the Cuckoo's Nest*. Darvasi created it to inspire learner agency within the constraints of school. Fishman said:

> When Paul Darvasi teaches *One Flew Over the Cuckoo's Nest*, he knows what his learning objectives are. But he doesn't suppose the order in which students are going

to uncover them. He literally turns the asylum over to the inmates. He gives them lots of ways to experience a book, and to take the things they're reading and apply it to the learning environments he's carefully crafted and curated for them. Again, it's not infinite choice—it's curated choice. And it's infinitely replayable. Students can keep going. Eventually the game ends because they have to graduate. But it could go on forever. He has students design new missions when they complete the missions he designed for them. That is a brilliant model.

To play *The Ward Game*, students use Kesey's book to solve real world missions set at school. Students have control over which missions they want to complete, and achievements to pursue. Darvasi even dresses up as the tyrannical Nurse Ratchet! Describing *The Ward Game* in a chapter he contributed to Williams-Pierce's (2016) *Teacher Pioneers: Visions from the Edge of the Map*, Darvasi wrote, "I strove to design the game in such a way as to preserve the novel's oppressive atmosphere and narrative arc but also, paradoxically, to bestow my students with the freedom and agency to play as they saw fit" (2016, p. 71).

Self-determination theory can be thought of as a continuum. "In the absence of intrinsic motivation, [some teachers] provide a lot of extrinsic motivation to get students to do things," Fishman said. "Now what we have is more stick, and less carrot." Here is the conundrum of school as a poorly designed game. Students see a path of grades, standardized tests, college entrance, and, ultimately, jobs. "We show things that are down the road for students, and we turn school into this long slog. High school used to be preparation for college. High school now is preparation for applying to college."

Members in The Tribe were cognizant that their classrooms exist in the highly interconnected system of their schools. They spoke of learner agency to their classes like it was a feature, or highlight, of the students' school day. "When I talk about gameful learning, part of it is talking about what the individual teacher can do in the classroom," Fishman explained. "But the other part is talking to school leaders and politicians stating that we should do this to make school a better place to learn in." Fishman sees this agenda scaling up, as well as down to the individual child. "In a gameful learning environment students will regain autonomy that they have control over their outcomes."

Learner Agency

Paul Darvasi, Peggy Sheehy, and Steve Isaacs tended to use games that were open-ended and nonlinear; students then had a choice on quests to take and levels to master. Students were given agency to learn, guided by core mechanics, or actions of doing. Lessons gave students agency to "make choices, rely on their own strengths and styles of learning and problem solving, while exploring alternative styles" (Gee, 2007, p. 223). These experiences helped to situate students into their personalized zone of proximal development (Bodrova, Germeroth, & Leong, 2013; Vygotsky, 1978).

Students in these classrooms either had a choice of games to play or authoring tools with which to design games. In cases when an entire class played the same game (e.g., *Gone Home* in Darvasi's class), students had choice to select what the culminating activity or presentation would be. After play, students were led in whole class discussions in which shared experiences were unpacked and connected.

Choice, based on interest, kept students engaged in a state of flow (Csikszentmihalyi, 1990). When one is in the "flow channel," optimally involved in an experience, there is "a sense of discovery, a creative feeling of transporting the person to a new reality" (Csikszentmihalyi, 1990, p. 74). Once mastery of a play in a game occurs, boredom sets in; the game becomes no longer fun to play (Koster, 2014).

Isaacs' teaching goals were explicit: student-interest, passion-driven lessons. His curriculum afforded a lot of student choice. Students had many games and project outcomes to choose from. This arrangement may stem from the fact that his class was more skill-focused than content-based. He did not have to teach about literary devices or historical events. Instead, Isaacs taught his students iterative design as the focal point of instruction.

While there were different games and design tools observed, Isaacs' students were not free to openly select games and design tools; rather, they made decisions based on the learning quests posted in the 3D GameLab learning management system. (In the 2017-18 school year, Isaacs switched to Classcraft, which had just added a quest structure to its system.) The choices in each quest were mostly gameful. And the games played "offered intrinsic rewards from the beginning, customized to each learner's level, effort, and growing mastery and signaling the learner's ongoing achievement" (Gee, 2007, p. 223). When asked, "How would you describe the game(s) played this week to a friend?"; the word *fun* appeared in 16 of the 24 student responses.

I spoke to researcher Caro Williams-Pierce about how members of The Tribe design lessons to enable students invest in their own learning. "A really well-designed school is one in which kids don't feel like their lives are involuntarily controlled by outside forces," she said. Games used by The Tribe were part of a larger construct intended to give students a sense of agency, or control, over their own learning. Williams-Pierce concluded:

> Steve, Peggy, and Paul know how to build those structures. If we don't give student choice, the products they create won't have any investment beyond some random external pressures that may or may not be important, like grades. A valuable assessment is when you get a student to care intrinsically that they are butting up against the edges of their capability. Then you can assess where they are and design for the next opportunity to be just beyond where their capabilities are for learning.

Meaningful Role Play

At Quest to Learn, the New York City-based school the Institute of Play cofounded, students take part in "missions," which are weeks long units subdivided in to daily "quests." In the missions, students take on roles ranging from doctors to book publishers. C. Ross Flatt, of the Institute of Play, spoke to me about role-play in 2016. "They know that they are involved in make-believe scenarios, and that's what makes them playful," he said.

At Quest, Leah Hirsch codesigned a mission in which students had to rescue Dr. Smallz, a character who shrank himself into the body of his patient. "Leah's Dr. Smallz video [produced by the Institute of Play, and published as part of Edutopia's *Made with Play* series], has a line where she calls the concept 'completely ridiculous,'" Flatt recalled. Hirsch's students knew that it was ridiculous, but they also knew that the experience was intended to be playful. "It's just like when students are 8-years-old and pretend to be Batman or Ninja Turtles. Well, we're going to pretend that we're all going to rescue Dr. Smallz together. Or we're going to pretend to be forensic scientists and solve a murder."

To play a game, one often takes on a virtual identity as a lens to master increasingly complicated skills (Prensky, 2006). Role-play gives players agency over their virtual destiny (Fullerton, 2008). Meaningful role-play was often embedded and baked into The Tribe's teaching praxis.

Glen Irvin's high school Spanish students take on real world career roles in his "Commerce World"—a game he made within *Minecraft* where students manage virtual businesses. "I set up different roles for students to do and to be," Irvin began. We spoke in late 2016. "This may seem 'cheeseball,' but it gives them a chance to get together with others of a like mind. Whether they want to be soldiers, miners, farmers, ranchers, or vendors selling commerce."

Irvin gives his students agency to do different things in the game, to play out roles. In a sociocultural framework, this kind of role-play can prepare students "for participation in social life" (Squire, 2011, p. 162). *Minecraft* offers an illusion student choice; Irvin is really the game-master, guiding his students along. "I give different choices within this world I am creating," he continued. "You are pretending to be someone, and you are that person for the rest of the project."

When designing his *Minecraft* games, Irvin consults with his community of practice. "When I create something, I go to the experts and run my scenario and project through them," he explained. "It gets viewed in the lens of someone who knows games—like Garrett Zimmer." Zimmer is a *Minecraft* mentor, and he and Mark Grundel are the cofounders of the weekly "#MinecraftEDU" Twitter chat. He is also a YouTube content creator, and designer of educational *Minecraft* adventure maps. "I send him things, and he will destroy it all," Irvin said, laughing. "He says, 'You have no competition, or you are missing these elements. But here are some ideas.' I don't always follow his ideas, but I do tweak things. Identity is huge, as is a narrative element."

Zimmer recommended that Irvin include design considerations for Bartle's Player Type Model, a framework from game designer Richard Bartle. In it, Bartle (1996) proposed that people play games for different reasons, sometimes to explore, compete, socialize, or gain achievements (Bartle, 1996). "Within the game, students have different gaming styles and I want them to be able to apply that within the game, and still reach the outcomes," Irvin said. "You want to have an adventure, maybe a fight or conflict, cooperate with a couple of classmates. You might have to resolve a conflict with classmates."

Of course, not all students like building and constructing in *Minecraft*. For those students, Irvin allows for an analog, or traditional, way of demonstrating knowledge. Some students create poster presentations, using paper and pencil. "I give a variety platter with all of my projects," he said.

Dan Curcio similarly embraces meaningful role-play in his special education science classes. His students become scientists in biomes, solving inquiry-based problems. "I turned my chemistry class into Harry Potter houses," Curcio said, in January 2017. Like Darvasi playing Nurse Ratchet in *The Ward Game*, Curcio becomes Professor Severus Snape, Harry Potter's dubious potions class instructor.

Role-play carries over to Curcio's use of "teamification,"—the gamified way he groups students. "Any time we do a collaborative project, they assign a secretary position to report for the team, and an announcer to announce the team's results. The roles help with the collaborations on teams."

In *Minecraft*, students may self-select roles organically, during play. "It takes guidance, and I don't force it," Zack Gilbert said, in December 2016. His students start by identifying a project manager who "makes sure everyone is doing what they need to do. You find the kids who are good builders, and those who are creative. Some just do the research, making sure the build is historically accurate—and that they can prove it to me." Gilbert then assesses students based on the roles they take. Formative assessment questions include: Do the people in your village have roles? Explain those roles. How do those roles help your society? Compare and contrast what you did to what people actually did.

Scaffolding Student Choice

Seann Dikkers trains preservice teachers at Bethel University using a game-like approach. Scaffolding describes how he designs for student choice. On the first day of class, he places three different stacks of cards—each with a different homework assignment—in three different colors on a desk. He then instructs students to select any one of the three colored homework cards as they leave class.

"But I don't have enough of a whole color for the entire class," Dikkers said, in November 2016. "So, when the six blue cards run out, we're down to red and yellow." As a result, making a choice quickly gives students the most options; if a student takes too long to decide, options get eliminated. "The way I set it up is so a student would at least be able to choose. For those that struggle with making a choice, the choices actually got simpler—you're down to one or two. Even non-gamers understood that."

Some students aren't conditioned to making choices. They have become too good at the game of school, the endless loop of worksheets, lectures, and multiple-choice tests. "We have curated their existence as learners so much that they don't know how to make a choice," he said. "Even saying, 'You can pick this assignment or this assignment,' they lock up. Some of my students had to sit down and council with me over the class. I had to tell them, 'It's okay, life will go on, there are no wrong choices here.'"

Dikkers is preparing his students to be self-directed learners. Like a video game, he scaffolds by expanding options, making them more complex as the course goes on. "Really what I'm doing isn't my brilliance," he confessed. "I'm completely stealing this from the design of video games." He continued, explaining how his approach compares to games:

> In a video game, the thing we first thing we might teach is how to move forward and backwards and side-to-side, maybe teach them to jump. We really don't get into complex movement sequences in the first hour of play in any off-the-shelf video game. In my class I initially made a huge design mistake blitzing them with a unit's worth of choices. Students now feel confident when they make those small choices.

Dikkers' research and experience indicated that he needed to take the class on a journey from the traditional "you do the assignment with no choice classroom" to lots of choices. Choice became more important with projects than homework because of the time commitment required. Eventually, Dikkers unveils "the quest tree"—a branched course design. In a study of this approach, Dikkers concluded:

> Overall, this quest-based design of my courses shows clear promise that students can be more effectively motivated, engaged and challenged within a ZPD [zone of proximal development], as evidenced by their perception and approval of the learning model combined with increased and voluntary time-on-task outside of scheduled meeting times. Simply put quest-based learning is in it is infancy, or at least in the hands of too few educators, and is showing local results worth building on. (2016, pp. 68–69)

Soon enough, Dikkers' students realized that they weren't losing just because they didn't pick an option. "In 'gamerland,' we just replay the game," he continued. "I'll play it as this character this time, and if I really want to replay the game, I will play it as another character."

Like others in The Tribe, Dikkers observed students who preferred to not leave any choices behind. "One option I get is when a student asks, 'Can I do all of the options?' And my answer is, 'You can do as much of the work that you want to do.'" To remediate the likelihood that some students will attempt to complete everything and become overwhelmed, Dikkers adds enough options so that doing so is virtually impossible—"it's too much work." He explained:

> Those students tend to—when they get smaller choices building into bigger choices—see that coming. I still have those students, but it is unbalanced. They don't try for 100% anymore—they try for 80%. Largely that competitive thing that I saw in my earlier research still stays in place because students see that other students are doing more than they have to, and they start to respond to that over time.

There are some students who are really engaged by course content, and tend to do extra work. "They have time on the weekend, and they get together in little tribes, little groups, and they 'binge-quest' because there's no limit," he said.

Traditional teaching can message to students that when an assignment is complete, it is okay to cease working. "But learning isn't like that. Learning is when you keep going as hard and long as you can with as much time as you have." Some of Dikkers students completed 180% of the coursework required before they get to their final projects. "I saw that the first time I did choice-based learning, and all the way until now, after all of these iterations, I just keep seeing that trend. When students figure it out and realize that learning is on them, they learn as much as they want."

Dikkers gives instructions to students in a game-like way. This includes the use of rubrics to detail his expectations. Of course, the usefulness of a rubric is only as far as the student who reads it to figure out how to get the good grade. "They put a hyperfocus on understanding the rubric, and not understanding the ideas," he said. "I'm not anti-rubric. But when all students see is rubric after rubric after rubric, all they will do is what's on that rubric. So, when you tell them your expectations ahead of time—and I do think that's best practice—you're never going to be surprised as a teacher. They will do exactly what you tell them to."

In some cases, using rubrics is appropriate. "But when you teach obedience and compliance, you'll never get innovation," Dikkers said. He shifted away from rubrics, and adapted "*World of Warcraft*-style quest descriptions." He embraces "brevity"—how Montessori (1912/2012) described the amount of time that should be spent giving instructions (p. 61). Dikkers explained how he gives directions to those in his teacher education courses:

> A description might be to do a tour of a classroom and tell me what connects to the educational psychologists that we've studied. I give a really short 140-word description. This is also the direction games went into. Quests used to be more elaborate, like in [the role-playing game] *Baldurs' Gate*. They [the designers] found that within these role-playing games, people weren't reading the quest descriptions—they would just do the work once they thought they understood the quest. I think the same might be true in classrooms. We think the students are reading all of these details, and when they don't, we punish them.

If students don't follow instructions, Dikkers meets with them and has them redo the work, like in a game. "The point of playing a game is to play—it's not to study the rulebook for 10 hours."

There are unintended benefits of student choice. Rather than grading the same essay prompts over and over, teachers have a variety of work to score. "I can't even tell you how less stressful that is for me," Dikkers confessed. "I taught for 22 years as a middle school teacher. Moving to choice-based now means that I am not grading the same work. I pull up work, and it's actually interesting." He now grades student work in his spare time, even on evenings and weekends. "I just don't mind it now. I used to dread grading. Students are so excited about sharing their work with me. To me that makes all the difference in the world!"

Designing Branched Quests

Chris Haskell and Lisa Dawley created 3D GameLab, which is "powered by Rezzly." It uses game mechanics, like digital badges and XP (experience points), in place of grades. It also is nonlinear, designed to encourage self-directed learning. Lucas Gillispie was an early adopter of 3D GameLab, and he was the person who put the *WoWinSchools Curriculum* on the platform.

Curious about how to convert traditional lessons into branched quests, I contacted Gillispie in December 2016. "When I was a science teacher, there was a very linear path you took to teach the curriculum," he explained. "I didn't realize there were other ways to do it because that was all I ever experienced. Taking a curriculum like *World of Warcraft* and treating it differently—not so linearly—was something I knew I wanted to do, but I wasn't sure how I wanted to do that."

In the downloadable guide—which Sheehy was observed using—Gillispie and Craig Lawson, his partner in the project, designed lessons about the hero's journey monomyth, a topic often covered in English language arts classes. "I thought, I want this to mirror the experience of *World of Warcraft*, where you can choose whether to take a quest and see where it goes. Or—if you do have an end goal—what are the multiple ways to get to it?"

Gillispie enjoys planning quests because he gets to apply his instructional design background. "I use something called chunking," he explained. "I break up what I want people to learn into small units of learning, which are successive. It is modeled after quest chains in *World of Warcraft*." Quest chains lead to a digital badge, or micro-credential. "There are a variety of pathways you choose to get you there. I usually start out with some, basic fundamental information. And then I create a chain. Students choose which way to go, all of which lead to a same end point."

First, Gillispie takes his ideas and writes them on Post-it notes. He then sticks the Post-its on a wall, arranging them in a branched structure, like an upside down tree. "You have to do this one before you do this one, but you don't necessarily have to do this one before you do that one," he explained.

He will also use online mindmapping tools like Popplet (which I observed Sheehy using to plan her Ancient River Civilization quests) or Bubbl.us to think about how to arrange learning.

When he and Lawson first attempted to make digital quests based on the *WoWinSchools Curriculum*, they used Moodle, an open source learning management system. But then they ran into systematic and entrenched issues. In a progress report, you can't tell a parent, "Your child earned 2,400 experience points out of 5,000. Congratulations, they are a now knight lieutenant!" So Gillispie and Lawson asked themselves, "Why do we grade? What's the purpose of a grade? Can we get away from that? And if we try to get away from that, what barriers are we going to run into?"

Gillispie shared their challenges on his blog. "That's when Lisa Dawley and Chris Haskell reached out to me with 3D GameLab," he said. "I jumped into the tools and was hooked right off the bat. It automated many of the things we were trying to do." That was in 2012, just as 3D GameLab was released to the market.

Haskell recruited several members of The Tribe to design exemplar quests for their nascent platform. Mark Suter was the first to design quests. "I let it slip once that we were building this thing, and he wanted in," Haskell recalled, in November 2016. He continued:

> I let a couple of people into the alpha version and, as soon as the beta version online, we decided that we were going to bring in "the cool people." We were going to have them create content and teacher workshops for us. Lucas and Peg were invited, and Steve, too. It was a way of building out expert content, and inviting people whom we like.

Nowadays Gillispie designs teacher professional development using the 3D GameLab. "My goal is to make instruction game-like, to incorporate as many elements of games as I can," he said.

Chapter Summary

The Tribe's classrooms are at the intersection of being a lusory experience with identity play. The teachers and students also embrace ignorance of the outcomes of using games, thus creating affordances for gameful learning (Holden et al., 2014). This included an embrace of sociodramatic role-play. While more common in earlier grades, role-play is often found in digital and tabletop games. Students were also afforded agency and choice. Students then navigated a series of meaningful choices in the games based on the roles they took on.

References

Barab, S., & Gresalfi, M. (2011). Learning for a reason: Supporting forms of engagement by designing tasks and orchestrating environments. *Theory Into Practice, 50*(4), 300–310. doi:10.1080/00405841.2011.607391

Bartle, R. (1996, April). *Hearts, clubs, diamonds, spades: Players who suit MUDs.* Retrieved January 11, 2017 from http://www.mud.co.uk/richard/hcds.htm

Bodrova, E., Germeroth, C., & Leong, D. J. (2013). Play and self-regulation: Lessons from Vygotsky. *American Journal of Play, 6*(1), 111–123.

Csikszentmihalyi, M. (1990). *Flow: The psychology of optimal experience.* New York, NY: Harper & Row.

Darvasi, P. (2016). Gone Home and the apocalypse of high school English. In C. Williams (Ed.), *Teacher pioneers: Visions from the edge of the map, Chapter 7.* Pittsburgh, PA: ETC Press.

Deci, E. L., & Ryan, R. M. (1985). *Intrinsic motivation and self-determination in human behavior.* New York, NY: Plenum.

Deci, E. L., & Ryan, R. M. (2000). Intrinsic and extrinsic motivations: Classic definitions and new directions. *Contemporary Educational Psychology, 25*(1), 54–67. doi:10.1006/ceps.1999.1020

Dikkers, S. M. (2016). Questing as learning: Iterative course design using game inspired elements. *On the Horizon, 24*(1), 55–70.

Dubé, L., & Ray-Hill, C. (2016, June). *Would a kid make a better president?* Retrieved from http://www.gettingsmart.com/2016/06/would-a-kid-make-a-better-president/

Firestein, S. (2012) *Ignorance: How it Drives Science,* Oxford University Press, New York, NY.

Fullerton, T. (2008). *Game design workshop: A playcentric approach to creating innovative games* (2nd ed.). Amsterdam, The Netherlands: Elsevier Morgan Kaufmann.

Gee, J. P. (2007). *What video games have to teach us about learning and literacy* (rev. ed.). New York, NY: Palgrave Macmillan.

Holden, J., Dorfman, A., Kupperman, J., MacKay, P., Pratt, A., & Saunders, T. (2014). Gameful learning as a way of being. *International Journal of Learning Technology, 9*(2), 181–201.

Huizinga, J. (1955). *Homo Ludens: A study of the play-element in culture.* Boston, MA: Beacon Press (Original work published 1938).

Kalir, J. (2016). Good game: On the limitations of puzzles and possibilities for gameful learning. In C. Williams (Ed.), *Teacher Pioneers: Visions from the edge of the map, Conclusion.* Pittsburgh, PA: ETC Press.

Kesey, K. (1963). *One flew over the cuckoo's nest.* Berkeley, CA: Signet.

Kim, A. J. (2012, September 14). *The player's journey: Designing over time* [Blog post]. Retrieved December 29, 2013 from Amy Jo Kim website: http://amyjokim.com/2012/09/14/the-players-journey-designing-over-time/

Kohn, A. (1997). Why incentive plans cannot work. In S. Kerr (Ed.), *Ultimate rewards: What really motivates people to achieve* (pp. 15–24). Boston, MA: Harvard Business School Press.

Kohn, A. (1999). *Punished by rewards: The trouble with gold stars, incentive plans, A's, praise, and other bribes.* Boston, MA: Houghton Mifflin.

Koster, R. (2014). *A theory of fun for game design* (2nd ed.). Sebastopol, CA: O'Reilly Media.

McGonigal, J. (2011). *Reality is broken: Why games make us better and how they can change the world.* New York, NY: Penguin Press.

Montessori, M. (2012). *The Montessori method.* New York, NY: Renaissance Classics (Original work published 1912).

Murray, J. H. (2017). *Hamlet on the holodeck: The future of narrative in cyberspace.* Cambridge, MA: MIT Press.

Nicholson, S. (2014). A RECIPE for meaningful gamification. In T. Reiners & L. C. Wood (Eds.), *Gamification in education and business* (pp. 1–20). Cham, Switzerland: Springer.

Prensky, M. (2006). *"Don't bother me Mom, I'm learning!": How computer and video games are preparing your kids for twenty-first century success and how you can help!* St. Paul, MN: Paragon House.

Salen, K., & Zimmerman, E. (2003). *Rules of play: Game design fundamentals.* Cambridge, MA: MIT Press.

Schell, J. (2014). *The art of game design: A book of lenses, second edition.* Amsterdam: A. K. Peters/CRC Press.

Squire, K. (2011). *Video games and learning: Teaching and participatory culture in the digital age.* New York, NY: Teachers College Press.

Suits, B. (1978). *The Grasshopper: Games, life and Utopia.* Ontario, CA: Broadview Press.

Sutton-Smith, B. (1997). *The ambiguity of play.* Cambridge, MA: Harvard University Press.

Turkle, S. (1994). 'Constructions and reconstructions of self in virtual reality: playing in the MUDs', *Mind, Culture, and Activity*, Vol. 1, No. 3, pp.158–167.

Vygotsky, L. S. (1978). *Mind in society: The development of higher psychological processes.* Cambridge, MA: Harvard University Press.

Williams-Pierce, C. (Ed.). (2016). *Teacher pioneers: Visions from the edge of the map.* Pittsburgh, PA: ETC Press.

· 9 ·
GAMES AS HIGH QUALITY CURRICULAR MATERIALS

Many view educational technology as a tool to support learning, not the focal point of instruction. The mantra of educational technology is that one should not teach PowerPoint; rather teach students how to lead presentations using tools like PowerPoint. A teacher may use iMovie to teach students digital storytelling or concepts relating to remixing media. The idea is that any technology could be substituted, such as Windows MovieMaker or any other video application.

Unlike most educational technology tools, members of The Tribe were observed using some games as the centerpiece for their instruction. In this sense, games—like books, videos, and film—became "high-quality curriculum materials," enabling students to access curriculum (Darling-Hammond, 2013, pp. 14–15). In other words, games were used as "digital texts" (Shaffer, Nash, & Ruis, 2015, p. 10). With digital texts, teachers continue "to play the role of tutor and explicator, helping students make sense of their mediated experiences, selecting additional experiences, and weaving together a coherent curriculum from an increasingly large array of choices" (Shaffer et al., 2015, p. 11).

I spoke to Mark Chen in March 2017 about how games can be read like books. Chen is a game developer, part-time lecturer at the University of Washington, Bothell, and he wrote the (2012) book *Leet Noobs: The Life and Death of an Expert Player Group in World of Warcraft*. Chen likens his attraction to playing games to his affinity for reading science fiction fantasy novels. He said:

> I view games as works of art, and they should be read in class. Just like with literature, there is a way to help students learn how to read critically, and deeply on whatever it is they are reading. Often there are multiple meanings of things going on in a passage, and that's true of games as well. One thing we do really poorly is to help people see games as more than just a frivolous activity.

Chen noted benefits to studying games as texts. Games can help people see new experiences. "If you think of your life as a game—an interconnected system that you can untangle and figure out—maybe that will be useful for you," he said. "That can only increase our empathy with each other. We read novels because it makes us connect with each other. Games can serve the same purpose."

My observations of Paul Darvasi, Steve Isaacs, and Peggy Sheehy's teaching practice—as well as the subsequent findings from interviewing other members of The Tribe—support the notion that some games can sit alongside works of literature. Darvasi used *Gone Home* in his English literature class in place of a traditional text. Sheehy harnessed the experiences in *World of Warcraft* to inform students' readings of *The Hobbit*.

This chapter reviews how games can be as curricular materials. It opens with a discussion of models and examples of how games can be utilized as the focal point of instruction, like books.

Video Games as Text

Classic novels are often used as a high-quality curricular material to enable students to meet curricular objectives (e.g., literary devices like symbolism and irony). When Darvasi decided to use *Gone Home* to replace a traditional text in his curriculum, he explained to me that he was "pretty judicious" in this decision. Initially, he wondered if games could be similarly used as a high-quality resource. "It really took me a long time to find a game that was really and truly suitable for a senior English class—a university-streamed, senior English class," he explained, in November 2015. Darvasi's use of a game in place of traditional text is discussed in in Williams-Pierce's (2016) *Teacher Pioneers: Visions from the Edge of the Map*. Darvasi concluded his chapter, entitled *Gone Home and the Apocalypse of High School English*, with the following sentiment:

English class can become a sort of theater where everybody pretends the texts are being read. The sheer abundance of communications alternatives is making it harder and harder to focus on reading as we once did. The quickly changing ecology of modern communication expands the notion of literacy to include nonalphabetical visual elements, interactive texts, and a renewed emphasis on orality (Skype, YouTube, Siri, anybody?). Our duty as educators is to design our courses to prepare students to think critically and succeed in their current communication context, as that is the environment where they must survive and, we hope, prosper. (Darvasi, 2016, p. 141)

When close reading *Gone Home* as a text, Darvasi's students were directed to take their time searching for objects, and then to analyze for evidentiary significance. Students characterized *Gone Home* as a mystery. Darvasi described the game as such: A cerebral undertaking, the game to be close read, like a book. In a student survey in Darvasi's class, one student questioned whether it was a game at all, stating that he "would almost consider it a movie instead of a game." In class students anticipated jump scares, in line with their schema's expectations from the affordances of the mood and theme of the house. While seven students described the game as "fun," two used the word *boring* in survey responses. Perhaps the point-and-click mechanic was too simple for some to learn and, therefore, easy to master.

Darvasi stated to me that games could be the focal point of learning. Or they could serve to support learning goals. He said:

> In my case, my use of the game [*Gone Home*] becomes the central text of my class, so it substitutes *Hamlet* or *Catcher in the Rye*. It becomes the text in of itself, so it is the focal point. But games could also assist in furthering subject matter, but not being the central object of study. One example comes to mind. I have a colleague who teaches about colonization. During one of the classes he allows his students to play a game by Sid Meier called *Colonization*, then he asks them to think critically comparing their game play experience versus the reality of the historical occurrences around that period which is really valuable. In that case, the game is not central to the lesson, but it enhances the lesson with an interesting critical thinking element.

Gone Home's engagement may be rooted in the freedom one has to explore while role-playing as Katie Greenbriar. Darvasi used assessment strategies typically found in an English literature classroom. Student play was not assessed; rather, he assessed learning the story. A deep understanding of the narrative indicated effectiveness. "Because I use a game as a substitute for a traditional literary text, I turn to assessment strategies that are actually fairly traditional, in the sense that they [students] write responses and give presentations," Darvasi said.

These methods speak to a teacher who has a deep understanding of pedagogical strategies. Darvasi does not use digital quizzes draped like games for rote review. He is presuming that other likeminded teachers would know what 21st century skills are, as well as how to engage students to be higher order thinkers. He also selected games for different reasons than some others in The Tribe. *Gone Home* was to be read like a text, an approach that was intended to directly meet his particular content curricular goals.

Like Darvasi, Isaacs referenced a Sid Meier-designed game: *Civilization*. This commercial video game has a decade-long history of being modified to meet social studies curricular objectives. *Civilization III* was used in Squire's (2004) study, in which students played as different nations, and then compared their decisions and resulting consequences to what actually occurred throughout history (Squire, 2011). Aside from contrasting the virtual world to the real world, Isaacs emphasized how games create a situated space for experiential learning. His students meet design thinking learning goals by making, and then testing games. Isaacs said:

> I think a game like *Civ* [*Civilization*] becomes the focal point because that's where the learning is taking place. I think it's about making connections with the content. Also, it brings me back to that idea that we don't need kids to memorize facts. If we're using a game to get us thinking of a system or a concept, and that leads to a discussion. It's almost like flipping the classroom. We play this game and then we have this frame of reference we all share, and then we all share it or apply it to the class assignment.

Sheehy similarly remarked how games situate her students' learning. Like a novel in English class, games are the central text analyzed by students. Actions taken in *World of Warcraft* are compared to the hero's journey taken by Bilbo Baggins in *The Hobbit*. Regarding games as high-quality curricular materials in the her lessons, Sheehy said:

> The kids are all about the game: getting into the game; playing the game; leveling up in the game; doing things together in the game. However, I think, in addition to what they are learning intrinsically or inherently from the game—they've got the next batch of learning tools, which is the quest that the teacher has designed to authentically coincide with the game. Then they've got the next batch of thing, what happens outside the game. They're playing a game, then they're writing about it. They're playing a game, and then they have to compare it to another game. To me, the game is the focal point. Absolutely.

When I pressed about where games fit into the system of her classroom, Sheehy responded that they are front-and-center; games are the nexus of her instruction.

Video Games and Literary Devices

Her Story is police procedural video game about a woman whose husband was murdered. Told in a nonlinear fashion, players review a database containing hours of recorded video footage.

I first spoke to John Fallon in December 2016 when he was in the unit's planning stages. Then I caught up him in the summer of 2017, after he ran the lessons. This was one week prior to Fallon leading a keynote talk at the Games in Education Symposium, in Albany, New York, on his students' experience playing the game.

As an English teacher, any kind of narrative game is something that interests Fallon. It helped that *Her Story* happened to fit into his school's English curriculum. "I heard the critical acclaim it got for being a narrative game," Fallon said. "I played through and thought about how this is essentially a close reading game. These are exactly the skills that I would be talking about if we were reading a short story or a novel."

Her Story is a text in the broadest sense of the word. "It's a very literary experience," Fallon explained. Here, game-based learning becomes a vehicle that can help emphasize, build, and challenge English language arts skills. Once Fallon made the curricular connection, he then dove in to see what he could build around it. "Is this going to be the center of the unit, or supplementary to it? It depends on the restrictions of the game itself, or the lessons, or maybe the time I have free in the year."

The unreliable narrator in *Her Story* was the theme that resonated with Fallon. (Spoiler alert!) "To me, it is a great hook, a mechanic of engagement to get my students to close read," he said. "All of a sudden they are in a battle with the narrator, to not feel tricked. When I read things like [Edgar Allan Poe's] *The Cask of Amontillado*, I was fascinated by that element. *Her Story* is completely that experience."

Fallon structured his unit around the literary device of texts with unreliable narrators, and how stories can have multiple interpretations. He presented the concept of an unreliable narrator to students in scaffolded steps. Level one began with a discussion of Heath Ledger's Joker in *The Dark Knight* film. Ledger's Joker completely lacked a consistent and coherent backstory. Then Fallon taught Poe's *Cask of the Amontillado*. Other works followed, including *In a Grove*, a Japanese story later adapted by Akira Kurosawa as the film *Rashomon*. In the samurai classic, there were multiple testimonies given by several warriors, each version slightly conflicting the other. *Her Story* was the unit's "boss level." By then, students understood the concept of an unreliable narrator. Fallon continued:

> I started with the idea of the unreliable narrator. I did some research about stories like that, and I picked ones I thought were the most interesting. I then researched unreliable narrator theory and criticism. I found a teacher who published an in-depth article about the mechanics on how to teach it, as well as teaching tools to give students a scaffold—which I adapted. I then categorized things into levels: the very obvious unreliable narrator; the narrator you are not sure if you can trust; or multiple narrators you aren't sure if you can trust.

After framing the literary device for his students, Fallon presented the game. First, he showed it to the entire class and, with the Montessori-like brevity Darvasi, Isaacs, and Sheehy exhibited, he gives an expeditious overview. Then he offered up a challenge: "Now you do it. If you guys think you are good at unreliable narrators, prove it. I briefly lay it out and do it 'hot seat-style,' asking them to figure out this mystery in just a couple of days."

The hot seat model Fallon is referencing meant that rather than 1:1 computers, like Darvasi did with *Gone Home*, students shared devices (*Her Story* is available for tablet, as well as PC). The one device became the center of gameplay as different students each day (the unit takes about 5 days) took turns controlling the computer. Students not working the computer suggested search queries. At the Games in Education keynote, Fallon reported that this social play became optimal to his students' learning styles.

While students played, they completed a "Narrator's Table," which was the notetaker included with the lessons. Students were then directed to track the game's timeline (video clips are timestamped), summarize collected facts, specify evidence supporting those facts, as well as note direct quotes. The goal was to further aid students' understanding of the narrative.

Fallon's only graded requirement was to fill out the table; grades were based on effort and completion, not accuracy or amount of notes taken. At his Games in Education keynote, Fallon told the audience about the pages and pages of notes students took. He recounted one student—a boy who often struggled reading traditional text—who excelled in this assignment. That student was found writing paragraph after paragraph, putting in extra effort to grapple with the text, thus supporting Steinkuehler's (2011) study. In it, boys demonstrated dramatic gains in ability to accurately read text above their grade levels—in this case, *World of Warcraft* wiki discussions—because of their interest in the material (Steinkuehler, 2011).

Fallon's students also wrote and published game reviews. They first read professional reviews to understand expectations. Another assessment was to write investigative report-style articles. This kept the assessment as authentic as the game itself. "The cold case genre of writing matched to the context of the game," Fallon said. "They put their interpretation of the events into a narrative journalistic form. I also have them look at a couple of different types of models, and have them explore the themes and storytelling of the game that way."

For Fallon, it is about the experiences he can create using a game, and what experiences games engender well. "I am not a 'games for games sake' teacher," he concluded. "I'm not going to do something unless I am going to think it is going to work. Fortunately, games create so many meaningful experiences, I can often use them as texts."

Humanities Games as "Standalone Pieces"

In February 2017, I spoke with Marc Ruppel, Senior Program Officer at the National Endowment for the Humanities (NEH), about games and learning. The NEH had funded *Mission US*, a series of history-based games from WNET, which is a member station of the Corporation for Public Broadcasting.

Prior to Ruppel's tenure, the NEH viewed games for learning as a way to supplement existing educational materials. Its first funded games related to museum exhibitions, "adding a small interactive element to an otherwise larger project, driving home some of the core issues that were in those particular projects." When Ruppel was brought on, the NEH developed a much wider range of game-related initiatives. Instead of creating games as support material, the NEH began to look at games as standalone pieces, to be the hub of learning in a classroom. From that hub, spokes move outward into related class content, as well as into informal learning settings, outside the classroom. "The way we conceived of this was to make games or to fund games that ostensibly had an educational component to them, with some real hooks that take place within that game space, either directly or tangentially."

Walden, a Game has a point-and-click exploration interface reminiscent of *Gone Home*. Produced by Tracy Fullerton at the University of Southern California, it is an adaptation of Henry David Thoreau's classic book as a first-person video game. And the NEH helped to fund it. Actor Emile Hirsch voiced Thoreau, and the experience is filled with encounters of primary source materials (i.e., Thoreau's letters, journals). "That game allowed us [the NEH] and Tracy Fullerton to make and form partnerships outside of the game space that bolstered some of the content," Ruppel explained. "The game can be used as this mechanism within the classroom, and can go out in multiple directions, with the game as the starting point. The core mechanics have extensibility and scalability far outside of the game itself."

In *Walden, a Game*, the player is both philosopher and scientific examiner—"which is how Thoreau saw himself. Through the mechanics of the game space, the player has to balance that." Ruppel continued:

> You are identifying different strains of plants, or following different animals through the woods, classifying them. At the same time, you have the artistic and humanistic dimensions of those as a philosopher. The split there was really natural with Thoreau himself. He saw the union of those ideas as something that was wholly endemic to his pursuit.

The educational content in *Walden, a Game* is built off of that split. STEM-aligned resources include classifying and observing of nature using scientific terminology. But at its core, *Walden, a Game* is a humanities game. One could easily envision a philosophy teacher using it to teach transcendentalism experientially. "We look at games as the centerpiece of the classroom—as a thing to model classroom strategies around," Ruppel said. "That's a big priority for us moving forward: the ability to use a game as a hub for a unit, or an entire semester's worth of learning. This is something teachers seem to be clamoring for."

Walden, a Game is a textured and layered experience that can be read like a book. "In some sense, sometimes the story is the easiest part to latch onto," Ruppel said. "But there are other aspects, too. What is it about our roles as players that allow us to explore deeper sorts of engagement—not just with games, but also with media as a whole?"

Humanities games center on two things. First are the causal loops in games, which are often explicit with cause-and-effect relationships: actions have immediate consequences. But perhaps more is this notion of contingency that make humanities games potentially vital in learning spaces. "It's this idea that history—and, in some ways historical thinking—relies on being able to get students to think through choices based on perspectives."

When a student plays *Civilization*, he or she may decide to invade a nation, or to maintain peace. This may or may not align with what actually happened in history. In *Civilization*, you always play as a world leader, like Gandhi or Napoleon. Ruppel envisions games where more perspectives can take part in making big decisions. He said:

> What that perspective means—in terms of understanding historical thinking and contingency—is still untapped in the game space. That's what the humanities really

does well, and that's what games really do well: they boundary a contextual space where thinking and learning can take place. Shifting that perspective ever so slightly can lead to different understandings.

I suggested that this approach was like historical fan fiction writing. He agreed, continuing, "You are boundarying that fan fiction." Perhaps students could add in a new goal that was not in the original game. A student could rewrite *Gone Home* in a series of diary entries from the perspective of Katie Greenbriar's father. "This boundarying is the patchwork fence of the game's rules, characters, and behaviors in a particular time period or series of events. When students learn those boundaries, they are not only learning historical and factual information, but also ways of applying it contextually towards that notion of contingency."

Ruppel's assertion is that humanities games support whole range of class discussions. This differs from STEM games. While *Angry Birds* is engaging to play and situates physics well, it may not inspire a lot of class conversation. "There is an opportunity to get more whole class involvement with a humanities-based game than with a STEM game because of what the mechanics offer up," Ruppel concluded. "Face-to-face and whole class roleplay seems to be the key. I don't think there is any good learning that simply looks at the game as something to be used in isolation from instructor or student interaction."

The Versatility of Humanities Games

Karen Schrier has long been fascinated by the creative ways teachers incorporate games into classrooms. Schrier is an associate professor of games and interactive media, director of the Play Innovation Lab, and director of the Games and Emerging Media program at Marist College. She was also a freelance designer/producer working with Electric Funstuff, the original maker of *Mission US: For Crown or Colony*, the first in NEH's aforementioned funded series of history games. In *Mission US: For Crown or Colony*, players take on the role of Nat Wheeler, a young apprentice in Boston just before the American Revolution. "As a designer, you never know how teachers in your audience—or students—are going to actually interact with it," she said, in late 2016.

After *Mission US: For Crown or Colony* was released in 2010, Schrier participated in a symposium where she talked about the game and its design aspects. The panel included classroom teachers, each of whom used the game in practice. Each teacher implemented *Mission US: For Crown or Colony* differently—"all in all very exciting ways," she recalled. One teacher focused on the events of the Boston Massacre, while another used the game as a shared experience that led to a whole class discussion about why the game has so many perspectives. For example, in the game, young Nat has tea with Constance, a loyalist. Why include a loyalist in the game? And why make her sympathetic?

Teachers assessed the game experience differently. Some had students write diaries based on in-game decisions, while others were asked to think about more about the lives of historic figures in the game. "Some students went into more depth to understand the non-playable characters (NPCs), like Paul Revere," Schrier said. "Being able to interact with those characters in the game gave a richness to the students' ability to understand the multiple histories of these different characters."

A lot of why teachers use *Mission US* differently depends on their specific curricular goals. "What's nice about games is that they are so versatile," she continued. *Mission US* is a "layered game," deep in content. Like a good novel, teachers can highlight what parts meet their specific needs. Schrier continued:

> For example, with a game like *Mission US*, you can focus on the historical events, such as the battles or treaties. But you can also focus on the cultural norms and values of that historic moment, and the social ramifications of different decisions or interpersonal interactions. You can analyze and compare historical accounts, and then talk about what was accurate, or less accurate, because it was being put into a game. Or students could design what would be the next step in that game, to create their own fan-based designs on the original game. Even thinking about the language used, *Mission US* has a vocabulary to learn in context. An English language arts teacher could incorporate that, as well.

In my former middle school social studies classroom, I had students play *Mission US: For Crown or Colony* to learn about the events that led to the American Revolution. After playing, students were then introduced to Twine—a free interactive fiction authoring tool. The stories were text-based and told from the second person perspective. It became an exercise in historical empathy. Thus, Twine enabled students to then become creators of content.

Turning Literature Into Role-Playing Games

When Kip Glazer began her doctorate coursework at Pepperdine University, she was skeptical of how games could be used to teach. "When I started, I was required to take a game-based learning class from Dr. Mark Chen," she recalled, in January 2017. "On the first day of class I said, 'I don't see the point of gaming.'"

She had felt that learning required academic rigor and seriousness. "And I was honest—I felt that game-based learning had a lot of fluff, so I expressed my ignorant views. But I was open to learning. He had to convince me that it was something useful and relevant." At the time, much of game-based learning had a connection to STEM education and computational thinking. "A lot of people talked about numeracy," Glazer recalled. "But having been an English teacher, I felt that literacy was more important than numeracy."

While at a conference, Glazer had the opportunity to attend a session Trent Hergenrader led on creative writing and game-based learning. Hergenrader is an assistant professor of English and creative writing at the Rochester Institute of Technology. After the talk, Glazer's view of game-based learning changed: games didn't just have to be about math and science. Game-based learning can also be about using certain core mechanics and narrative ideas in a playful sense. "He used role-play game creation to teach creative writing. I still felt that it was too 'pie in the sky' for me." Glazer taught high school at the time, and Hergenrader instructed college students. His students presumably already had the ability to read and write by the time they got to his class to pursue a degree in creative writing. "But what about my high school students who were still in the throes of learning and understanding great literature?"

Nevertheless, when Hergenrader spoke about role-playing game creation and creative writing, Glazer realized that she could do the same thing—only in a slightly different way. "I wanted my students to develop literacy—including multimedia literacy. From there, I had this idea to develop a pedagogical framework, or model, to leverage role-playing game creation as an instructional practice to help students learn a great piece of literature."

Eventually, Glazer's dissertation used *Fahrenheit 451* to argue that people understand reality only after imagination. "I talked about Jules Verne and science fiction writers who had the audacity to dream up scientific advancements," she said. "The scientists that came after them made it a reality. I wanted to make sure the game-based learning community does not neglect this. You can't go with pure science without the heart for it. I wanted to give a literature voice to the game-based learning community."

As detailed in Williams-Pierce's (2016) book, Glazer had students take *Beowulf* and turn it into role-playing games. Unexpectedly, she found herself defending her students' projects. She was informed that her students did not design "true role-playing games because it didn't follow the same balance as *Dungeons & Dragons*." She explained:

> I had a struggle with purists—game creators versus the teachers. Enthusiasts of the game have told me that I am bastardizing the system, and that calling it a role-playing game is offensive. I never portrayed myself as anything but a teacher. I use whatever is available to me to improve my students learning, and that's it.

Creating role-play games helped Glazer's students meet learning goals. It enabled them to immerse themselves in literature pieces, and to empathize by being the characters—the people. "By embodying the struggle of *Beowulf*, I can ask, 'What are the moral ambiguities and struggles?' To me that is meaningful role-play."

Reskinning Games

A. J. Webster has a tendency to collect card games. Light and portable, some are of the collectible and trading variety. "I've played *Magic: The Gathering* for a long time," he confessed. Webster and I spoke in December 2016.

Webster cofounded the Sycamore School in Malibu, California, and has copresented at the Games in Education Symposium. Prior to Sycamore, he taught at the short-lived PlayMaker School, in Los Angeles, which used game-based learning techniques.

At the Games in Education Symposium, he and Christy Durham led a workshop on modifying the commercial card game *Fluxx*, a game of changing rules and goals. The game has suits of cards, including Keeper cards which get combined to match up with Goal cards. But there are multiple Goal cards that can be played—hence the game is always in flux! Other suits include Action cards and Rule cards, which can also change the game's rules and outcomes. (I know, it sounds confusing—unless you've played!)

Fluxx was first published by Looney Labs in the late 1990s. As of this writing, nearly one dozen versions have been released, including *Monty Python Fluxx*, *Star Fluxx*, *Oz Fluxx*, and *Doctor Who Fluxx*. "There's a new set every three months, and I am constantly acquiring more," Webster said. "I have almost every set! Then it occurred to me that they [Looney Labs] could do a *Fluxx* with just about anything. And then that part of my teacher brain—the pedagogy—lit up. If they can do it with anything, I can do it with anything!"

In *Batman Fluxx*, if the Goal card combination in play is "The Joker Got Away," and you play the Joker and the Batmobile Keeper cards, you win. But that goal can change, depending on which Goal cards are in play.

Batman Fluxx is also a transmedia story about the Dark Knight. It remains consistent with themes from the comic book, television, video game, and film versions. Transmedia storytelling "represents a process where integral elements of a fiction get dispersed systematically across multiple delivery channels for the purpose of creating a unified and coordinated entertainment experience. Ideally, each medium makes its own unique contribution to the unfolding of the story" (Jenkins, 2007, para. 1).

Media expert Henry Jenkins has been a long proponent for using transmedia stories as a teaching tool. When I brought up the word "transmedia" to Jenkins in a 2014 interview, he corrected me. "The word 'transmedia' is an adjective—not a noun," he said. "It needs something to modify. In the case that I've written the most about, media entertainment, transmedia storytelling. [The 1999 film] *The Matrix* started at a corporate level, and spread outward."

Another example of transmedia storytelling is *The Walking Dead*. Based on the graphic novels by Robert Kirkman, Tony Moore, and Charlie Adlard, it is about survival in a post-zombie apocalyptic world. The stories spawned a TV series, several video games adaptations, and a large fan community.

Reskinning, or changing an existing game, can be transmedia storytelling. In design grammar parlance, the nouns of a game are its theme. Think of all the versions of *Monopoly* that exist. The game's core mechanics (or action verbs, like building hotels) remain intact—only the nouns, or theme, change. In my classroom, students reskinned the party game *HedBanz*, which is like charades. Students used blank index cards to create their own deck based on historical figures. The game's mechanics stayed the intact—guessing; just the nouns—or what is on the cards—changed.

Allowing for a lot of flexibility, card games can be more easily reskinned than their digital video game counterparts; all that is required are index cards and pencils. Webster's son's 5th grade class reskinned *Fluxx* for a unit on the Age of Exploration. "It was great," he said. "There were many different ways that kids saw that they could combine things. Some were better than others—but each was able to enter it in their own zone of proximal development. They were able to say, this is what I understand, and I am sharing what I understand."

Webster and Durham's Games in Education workshop was called *Skin It, Mod It: Altering Games to Teach Content*. Teacher participants, including members of The Tribe, made a deck of *Fluxx* for their area of content. Examples ranged from Harry Potter to Shakespeare.

"Just by playing *Fluxx*, you are increasing the STEM awareness of kids," Webster explained. "You build temporal awareness—thinking about things in time—spatial awareness, and foundational math literacy concepts, like optimization. A lot of what someone does in math is optimizing." In *Fluxx*, to optimize, student designers pore over content to create pithy descriptions for the Keeper and Goal cards. "There is no mistake that nerdy people who are good at math play games. There is a mutually reinforcing connection there."

In early 2017, Looney Labs released *Math Fluxx*. The goals were dependent on mathematical combinations.

In November 2016, I adapted the *Fluxx* lesson with my 6th grade classes. Student teams designed "Asian History *Fluxx*." Early on, I had small groups model how the commercial version plays (*Fluxx 5.0*, as the box reads). Students needed to understand how the game's system worked before they hacked it. After all, you wouldn't ask someone who has never read a book to then write a novel! A person new to how books function would need to know which direction to read the text, and how chapters and pages work.

During the unit, some students brought in their cultural identities; the textbook focused only on China, Japan, and India in its Asia chapters. Using Internet resources, a student of Korean descent discovered that the peninsula once had three kingdoms. Immediately she created three Keeper cards—one per kingdom—with the Goal card being the Korean peninsula.

My students were able to identify and align learning to the game as an interconnected system. Students were embodying content as core mechanics. "There is a lot of higher order thinking saying that there is this one thing and I can translate it into something else," Webster said. "As a teacher, you want a kid to see the purpose of the Great Wall of China, and then be able to abstract that into a game mechanic."

Taking something from history, and then applying that to some other scenario exemplifies higher-order thinking. It is also a demonstration of students as systems thinkers. Webster continued:

> I was a history major, and that was one of the key things: Why are we learning all of this stuff? It's not just so we can put all of these facts into a bag, and then pull them out at a party to impress someone because we remember the Great Wall of China. It's so we can ask, what's the function of borders and walls? And do these structures matter to our changing society?

The assessment of reskinning *Fluxx* is, therefore, embedded. My lessons concluded with a formative assessment prompt: Talk at your table and decide the one or two most imaginative cards in your deck today. "Family and royalty cards to get the goal card of dynasty," one student replied. Another answered, "caste system and no money for the poverty Creeper card." (Creeper cards are in some *Fluxx* decks, and have negative effects on a players' hand). Yet another said, "Shah Jahan and Agra are cards to match the Taj Mahal Goal card."

In one class, I overheard a student ask another about Creeper cards that would fit medieval Japan. The student's reply was, "The outside world." The Creeper card's action thus represented the island nation's long-standing policy of isolationism from the West.

Students should be able to demonstrate awareness of key concepts and features of Asia—the systemic relationships. With *Fluxx* you have to have the nouns, the things we study in Asia. You also have students creating relationships." Webster continued:

> When you think about the kinds of thinking and the skills you want from kids, to me, content is less important. The history you are teaching in 6th grade does not build on the content learned in 5th grade. That's not a condemnation; that's the structure of school. You start a new year and you get a different kind of history. We can ask adults about the history they did in 5th grade and none of them remember any of it. For me it's less about content than shaping the critical thinking and exploration, the understanding of the themes of history.

Chapter Summary

Games can be the focal point of a classroom, a model for students to study, critique, and sometimes change. Experts of game-based learning are agnostic to media bias. They do not treat good games as better or less valuable than traditional media (e.g., books, film). Whether playing a game, or designing games, good pedagogical practices persist: games are used by The Tribe to meet curricular objectives and learning goals.

References

Chen, M. (2012). *Leet noobs: The life and death of an expert player group in World of Warcraft.* New York, NY: Peter Lang.

Darling-Hammond, L. (2013). *Getting teacher evaluation right: What really matters for effectiveness and improvement.* New York, NY: Teachers College Press.

Darvasi, P. (2016). The ward game: How McMurphy, McLuhan, and Macgyver might free us from McEducation. In C. Williams (Ed.), *Teacher Pioneers: Visions from the edge of the map, Chapter 1*, Pittsburgh, PA: ETC Press.

Jenkins, H. (2006). *Convergence culture: Where old and new media collide.* New York, NY: New York University Press.

Jenkins, H. (2007, March 22). *Transmedia storytelling 101.* Retrieved from http://henryjenkins.org/2007/03/transmedia_storytelling_101.html

Shaffer, D. W., Nash, P., & Ruis, A. R. (2015). Technology and the new professionalization of teaching. *Teachers College Record, 117*(12), 1–30.

Squire, K. (2004). *Replaying history: Learning world history through playing "Civilization III."* Available from ProQuest Dissertations & Theses Global.

Squire, K. (2011). *Video games and learning: Teaching and participatory culture in the digital age.* New York, NY: Teachers College Press.

Steinkuehler, C. (2011). *The mismeasure of boys: Reading and online videogames* (WCER Working Paper No. 2011-3). Retrieved from University of Wisconsin–Madison, Wisconsin Center for Education Research website: http://www.wcer.wisc.edu/publications/workingPapers/papers.php

Williams-Pierce, C. (Ed.). (2016). *Teacher pioneers: Visions from the edge of the map.* Pittsburgh, PA: ETC Press.

· 1 0 ·
"HOW CAN I TWIST THIS GAME TO MY PURPOSES?"

Back when he was a high school teacher, Seann Dikkers used the video game *Civilization* in his classroom. Only he did so *without* a computer. He appropriated it to meet his curricular goals by stripping out the basic core mechanics of the game—trading, moving along a game board—and used it to inform his class instruction. Dikkers wrote, "All I needed to do was create a game based on the core elements of *Civilization*. More broadly, many other digital games can be deconstructed accordingly" (2015, p. 11).

Dikkers is an associate professor at Bethel University, and he has broken down different approaches from researching teachers who use games. "One approach is *adoption*, where you adopt the child [the game] that it is into your lesson plans," he said, late in 2016. To adopt a game outright is to use it exactly as it is, with no modification. *Mavis Beacon Teaches Typing* is an example. The game teaches typing right out of the box. "The other approach is *adaption*—when teachers adapt games to their purposes. And the third is *appropriation*, which is when parts of games are pulled out and used to drive instruction." Dikkers appropriated the core mechanics of *Civilization* to drive his instruction.

From what Dikkers observed, appropriation occurs more frequently with individual teachers than within communities of practice. "There isn't necessarily 'a tribe element' to that," he said. "But adaption and adoption often happen within communities. The more comfortable you are, the more likely you are to adapt things to your own purposes." If a teacher is not confident about games, he or she might be more likely to use a product someone else has made as it is.

Members of The Tribe tended to adapt and appropriate commercial, off-the-shelf (COTS) games, tailoring each to meet their curricular goals. A. J. Webster adapted *Fluxx* (Chapter 9) out of need. "There have been educational games almost as long as there have been personal computers, but they often suck—they're not fun," he said. "That's why I like using games that are designed to be games first, and then use my intelligence as an educator to put a lens on it. I ask, 'How can I twist this game to my purposes?'"

This notion of twisting games to meet learning goals resonated with me. I observed it in action when studying Paul Darvasi, Steve Isaacs, and Peggy Sheehy's praxis. It echoed true from interviews with other members of The Tribe, too—they almost never adopted a game wholesale without alteration.

"Every teacher has to repurpose a game, regardless of whether a game comes with lesson plans," researcher Sande Chen said, late in 2016. "It is their particular classroom and they know their students, their levels, and what applies." This chapter discusses how teachers in The Tribe repurpose and adapt games to meet specific learning goals. It opens with methods for adaption, referencing some of my field observations—including Sheehy's use of *World of Warcraft*, and how teachers tailor *Minecraft* to multiple contexts.

How *World of Warcraft* Became Sheehy's Curriculum

The *WoWinSchools: A Hero's Journey* was the curriculum guide I observed in action in Sheehy's class. The hero's journey, or monomyth, is based on Joseph Campbell's (1949/2008) work; it posits that heroes take in mythologies are all basically similar. The hero's journey is ubiquitous in popular culture, from *Star Wars* to *The Hunger Games*.

In *World of Warcraft*, thousands of online players organize into guilds. Then they go on raids, or attacks. But can a hero on a quest be appropriated into a game where there are other players simultaneously on their own journeys? "That can come from her [Peggy Sheehy's] interpretation of that particular game," Sande Chen said. "In an massive multiplayer online (MMO) game like *World of Warcraft*, you are the hero—yet there are a million of you. You could also use *The Lord of the Rings Online*, which has a narrative that makes you feel like a small player in this universe, and that you have to do something big with your life."

In MMO games, players may "never reaches a final outcome but only a temporary one when logging out of the game" (Juul, 2003, "After the Classic Game Model"). They are set in "persistent" virtual worlds, in which events continually occur—even when a player is not actively playing (Sheldon, 2012, p. 57). "With MMO games there's a problem because it's a never-ending story," Chen continued. "That makes it hard to come back for the elixir if the search is ongoing. An MMO game is for millions of players; we shouldn't think of it as a single player experience."

In the *WoWinSchools: A Hero's Journey* curriculum, coauthors Lucas Gillispie and Craig Lawson (n.d.) recommend that teachers read research, particularly the contributions of James Paul Gee. They also stated that teachers should consult informational technologists in their school district, take time to play games themselves, and look for curricular connections.

Gillispie is in The Tribe, and he serves as the director of academic and digital learning for Surry County schools in Northwest North Carolina. He has led workshops at the Games in Education Symposium, has has been invited to the White House with Steve Isaacs, and he is active in tabletop game communities of practice. An avid video game player since childhood, Gillispie brought that passion to his classroom. We spoke in December 2016.

Early on in his teaching career, Gillispie discovered that video games were a meaningful point of connection between he and his students. "A lot of students found that I had an interest in the games they were playing," he said. "My room became the hangout for those guys, a good safe place to talk and chat about all things game related."

In 2001, a student came to Gillispie to recommend the MMO game *EverQuest*. The student knew of Gillispie's affinity toward science fiction, fantasy literature, and video games—*EverQuest* seemed the perfect fit. "He told me a little about the game, how you play it online, and that it was sort of like [the tabletop role-playing game] *Dungeons & Dragons*—but in a virtual world," Gillispie recalled. "When I picked it up on the store shelves, I read the fine print on the back and saw that there was a $10-a-month subscription fee to play. That blew my mind. The game already cost 30 bucks! Why would somebody pay $10 a month to continue to play?"

But Gillispie did purchase the game, and he was instantly hooked. "I was blown away by the virtual space." He approached the student about playing together online. "He was more advanced in the game, and he took me under his wing." In this instance, the student became the mentor. Gillispie continued, "Then I saw this extra thing under their names, which I learned was a guild. So, I asked if he wanted to start a guild."

Before long, Gillispie had his students in an *EverQuest* guild. "I'm talking to these kids during breaks and lunch about what we did in the game." The boundaries between work and play overlapped. "I would say, 'Dude, you really shouldn't be going on this raid tonight, you've got a huge test tomorrow and you've got to study for it!'"

Playing games like *EverQuest* persisted throughout Gillispie's teaching career. First came *EverQuest*, followed by *Dark Age of Camelot*, and then *World of Warcraft*. After earning his master's degree, Gillispie became the instructional technologist for Pender County Schools, also in North Carolina. "It was then when I had some a-ha moments. I thought, 'Wouldn't it be cool if we could do this in a more formalized context?'"

Gillispie envisioned using *World of Warcraft* with kids who were at-risk, and he first incorporated it for an afterschool club. He worked with a teacher in an area middle school—Craig Lawson—who also happened to be in his *World of Warcraft* guild. "I came up with ways and ideas we could connect it to learning," Gillispie recalled. "We pitched it to my assistant superintendent, and she said, 'I don't have a clue about what you're talking about with the gaming, but it sounds like it's good for the kids, so go for it!'"

From there, Gillispie worked with the principal and Lawson to launch the afterschool program. "We called it *World of Warcraft* in Schools," he said. "And around that time I talked to Peggy Sheehy. She was a good friend of mine, and said, 'I want to do it too.'" Sheehy's afterschool students were soon playing together with Gillispie and Lawson's students. "It was awesome!"

Gillispie and Lawson next persuaded the principal—and parents—to come in to observe what was taking place. "The principal said that the students were exhibiting things not seen in a classroom during the regular school day, and asked what we had to do to take this to the next level?" They then decided to make it part of the regular school day, as an elective enrichment course framed around Gillispie and Lawson's coauthored *WoWinSchools: A Hero's Journey* curriculum. Gillispie continued:

> Craig and I spent the next year running the course just ahead of where we were in developing the curriculum for it. We were building the airplane while it was in the

air, so to speak. We wrote the entire yearlong curriculum, and aligned it to the Common Core Standards for middle school 7th grade language arts. Then we brought in digital citizenship and digital literacy, and wove them together. But it was all foundationally built into the experiences in *World of Warcraft*.

World of Warcraft had been "reverse engineered" by Gillispie and Lawson to fit learning goals. I wondered how a teacher could similarly appropriate other video games to align with curricular goals? "One of my top pieces of advice to teachers is to go and play a game," Gillispie said. "Don't think about teaching—just experience the game. And then, after you're done, reflect on it. What was the content? What are the connections to standards? Would this be beneficial in the classroom?"

Nearly any game can be connected to curriculum. Sports-themed video games can be used to teach statistics and math. Fantasy role-play games teach about characters and plotlines. When games abstract science or history, ask students to contrast that to the real world. Gillispie recommended, "Ask students where the game is a good model, and where does it break down? That will drive kids to critical thinking. Like in [the video game] *Civilization*: What if Gandhi became a nuclear tyrant? Who knows? Simply asking the question, 'Why is that not accurate history?' gets students thinking."

Contextual Transposition

Some teachers in The Tribe contextually transposed a game's core mechanics to meet learning goals. Chris Haskell—the self-described "linchpin of The Tribe"—coined the term. Slightly different than adaption or appropriation of games, *contextual transposition* "is when you take an environment intended for one thing and you co-opt it to become what you want it to be," Haskell began. "You change the context of the thing."

Haskell is a clinical professor at Boise State University, and we spoke in December 2016. Haskell's concept of contextual transposition came about after he spoke with game-based learning scholar James Paul Gee at a conference. "Jim Gee mentioned in a conversation that in commercial games, context is everything," he recalled. "I added in that we transpose it—a term I carried over from my days as a musician." Thus, contextual transposition: the repurposing of games to match learning goals. Again, referencing Gee, Haskell concluded, "On the coattails of giants!"

How does one contextually transpose a game? Haskell shared with me how he repurposed *Kerbal Space Program*, a rocket kit sandbox. The game situates Newtonian dynamic physics, and players learn about velocity and drag. Clearly the game is adept at teaching math, science, and physics principles. But Haskell suggested contextually transposing it to teach Cold War history. He explained:

> You change the context of that game in a classroom setting. You have two computers; you split the class into two groups. You put up a divider between the groups, and you tell them they are in a space race. The kids on each side take the roles of governments, assigned as NASA mission administration, a couple of students to build the rockets, and others to take charge of the media. Give each team slightly different considerations, and let them play against each other, using only two computers to do it. You give them a process so they can see what it was like to be in the Cold War. You can put a spy on each side. All of the elements of good Cold War dialogue into this experience and ask them, how does this feel? Why do you think this happened? How does this relate to our study of the Gemini mission?

The lesson was also detailed in Haskell's (2015) interactive iBook, *Play This, Learn That*, which included Steve Isaacs and Glen Irvin as contributors. In the book, Haskell and his family narrated some of the chapters. He continued:

> What we've done is taken a game designed for one thing and we've layered context onto it. It gives us the vehicle for a space race, even though it wasn't designed to do that. It does the one thing we need a game to do: to provide the environment. Rockets blowing up on the launch pad, mistakes in mission planning, stuff getting out to the other country, nationalism. These things become experiences, which are powerful.

The Malleability of *Minecraft*

Teachers have adapted *Minecraft* into a variety of classroom disciplines. Dikkers (2015) suggested that a *Minecraft* teacher's role "is to frame the lens through which players will look at, design in, and compose stories within a powerfully flexible space" (p. 107). Science teachers have students use the canvas to create models; language arts teachers have used the game in writing reflections. In social studies, entire historical worlds are sometimes created. "*Minecraft*, like typing paper, can be used to represent ideas effectively and in a 3D space that is exciting" (Dikkers, 2015, p. 101).

"I had played *Minecraft* consistently with my son, but never thought about using it for an educational purpose," Glen Irvin recalled, when we spoke in November 2016. At that time Irvin just began gamifying his classroom. He was also in an online games and simulation course at Boise State University. His professor: Chris Haskell.

Haskell assigned students to choose a commercial game, and to contextually transpose it. "Our big, epic boss battle was to apply a commercial game to something we are going to do in our teaching," Irvin said. "It's a lot harder than it seems! You would think you could do it because games, by their nature, draw you in."

To Irvin, Minecraft represented itself as one of the easiest games to adapt—and not just because of its potential as an open sandbox. He was drawn in by the ability to create non-playable characters (NPCs) that could respond to student interactions, as well as the ease it took to build worlds. "It's easier than other kinds of games because it is so malleable, so easy to manipulate," Irvin said. "I can say, here is what I want to teach, now I want them to apply it within this game."

When Irvin brought Minecraft into his high school Spanish class, he first asked himself how he could best utilize the game. So, he consulted the experts: his students. "A student and I talked about how Minecraft can be manipulated, to make it be whatever you want. Then we talked about other similar commercial games, like The Elder Scrolls V: Skyrim and Assassin's Creed, and how these games come with deep storylines."

Irvin now teaches what is basically a language immersion course. But it is not set in a Spanish-speaking nation; rather, students learn Spanish virtually in Minecraft through meaningful role-play. In a blog post for educational travel company Prométour, Irvin described one of his Minecraft-set worlds. Describing "El Mundo de Leyendas" ("The World of Legends"), he wrote:

> Every communication must take place in the Spanish language, either aloud or written and the students are responsible for "reflecting" on a weekly basis in Spanish about their adventures in the game. Instead of thematic vocabulary, the students drive the learning by creating community-based vocabulary that they deem necessary to complete the global tasks (Irvin, 2017, para. 12)

Similar to Irvin, Dan Curcio uses Minecraft to immerse his students. He first heard about the game several years ago from one of his special education science class students. "Immediately, he said I had to use it," Curcio recalled, in January 2017. "I didn't understand it, or how to use it yet—and it was still in beta [the early and unfinished version]."

Curcio needed to see how Minecraft applied to his special education science curriculum. "A lot of my success in this school is that I don't create the curriculum—it is really a blend between the students and myself. I try to give them a lot for choice." So, like Irvin, Curcio and his students brainstormed ideas about how it could work. "Besides the conferences and The Tribe, it has to come from the kids. That's where *Minecraft* came from. You've gotta be where the kids are, right?"

Cell Games

Jim Pike's background in games and education is a bit of an accident. Like most, he played video games as a child. Then he stopped. But, when he became a teacher, he unexpectedly found himself gaming again. We spoke in February 2017.

Pike teaches in southern California, and I know him—like others in The Tribe—from online communities of practice. He began his teaching career in the urban section of Los Angeles known as South Central. Many of his students were first generation Americans. After two years into his career, Pike went on an interview for a job at a summer camp. There, he first saw *Minecraft*. "Instantly, I saw how this can be used to teach math," he recalled. "I had used a lot of hands-on manipulatives with blocks. I knew I could run the same lessons, digitally. And then it hit me: if every kid in the world is addicted to this, then why not do this?"

After that summer, Pike asked his school supervisor if he could teach with *Minecraft*. "I realized I could turn houses into algebra," he said. (Incidently, Pike is featured in Haskell's (2015) interactive iBook, *Play This, Learn That*, in a chapter titled, "Algebra Building a House.")

Nowadays Pike teaches at the Sycamore School, the same school A. J. Webster cofounded. As it happened, Pike and Webster also both worked at GameDesk, creating lesson plans for the now-defunct PlayMaker School. Before Sycamore, Pike taught in Beverly Hills—but not like *90210* on TV. He described it as the most diverse school in that district. There, he taught almost all content disciplines in the blocky virtual world of *Minecraft*. "We read things, and then designed them in *Minecraft*," he said.

One *Minecraft* science unit was dubbed "Cell Games" by Pike. In it, students made mini-games about cellular biology by applying level design, and by coding command blocks (special blocks that can be programmed to perform tasks). Level design mirrored Vygotskian theories of scaffolding learning: as each level was mastered, players then moved through the zone of proximal development.

Representing how *Minecraft* blocks can stand in for organelles applied both design and systems thinking. Pike's students first tasked players to go through a cellular membrane. Each subsequent level was more challenging, featuring different organelles, and the microscopic organs inside living cells. The "boss level" was the fight against an invading virus on the nucleus. "You teach these bits about organelles as you go," Pike explained. "You put some videos up, and kids come up with different kinds of games they can play. Then I twist the story and game plots into the science that would match organelles."

The Cell Games unit began with short animations on YouTube about cells and organelles. Pike then gave his expectations as a broad overarching objective. "How they reach that gives them a lot of room for creativity," he said. Students turned in a list of five or six level ideas. Levels must begin with a "staging room," which is the student-created narrative about why one would play their game. Students write stories about the need to save a dog, a plant, or even the president. And they come up with a story of how the player shrunk to a microscopic size. The story is told on screen using blocks with messages that pop up.

Once students frame their game narrative, they research three to five facts about each organelle, including the function of what they do. Then Pike has students play games that other classes have made, "so they can get a feel for what other people have done. They learn different types of game design, like parkour [obstacle courses to run through], player versus environment, and maze games." Pike also asks about the purpose of the game at each level. He continued:

> In the case of the membrane, they talk about bilipid levels. One student's game included an "elytra"—which is a wing suit—to fly through the membrane. Don't hit the phospholipid tail, or you'll crash! They'll then tell me how to play their games. Messages pop up on the screen as you play. And you can push a command block lever to teleport to the next room, or level. You may next be in the cytoplasm and see the lysosome—which attacks things that don't belong in the cell—and a guardian attacks you. You have to code in water-breathing potions and some armor so you don't get killed too quickly.

There is a lot of writing involved with this project, especially about the functions of organelles. "I love assessing, but I hate grading," he confessed. Sometimes he brings students into the process. "In our *Pac-Man* lesson we—as a class—came up with a list. Is it playable? Is it too hard to complete? How does it look?" Then they collaborated on a quantifiable spreadsheet, playing all of the students' games, and discussed the results.

Pike's students worked in groups of four, "because a lot of work has to be done." One student was the "master of the world;" they took the world home to complete, if necessary. At the end of the project, students turned in the world on a flash drive as the final deliverable. Pike shared a YouTube video (https://youtu.be/tn4MJn8qdIA) of a student's final project on Facebook, tagging multiple members of The Tribe—including Steve Isaacs, Bron Stuckey, Zack Gilbert, Microsoft Education's Deirdre Quarnstrom, and myself.

I shared an anecdote with Pike about my 6th grade social studies classes. They built *Minecraft* worlds, and then took screenshots to be used as panels for graphic novels set in Medieval Europe. Some veered off task, jousting one another on a multiplayer server. How off task should I let them go? "What are you supposed to do, say no?" Pike remarked. "They're doing something amazing, even if it wasn't what you asked for."

It takes balance to use an open-ended game like *Minecraft* in the classroom. It can be a constant learning process for the teacher, who has to iterate, often on the fly. "Sometimes I think it's going to take a month to complete a project," Pike said. "Other times we're in a class and an idea hits a student, or it hits me. Then, it is, 'Alright guys, full steam ahead that way!'"

In my Medieval Europe project, I likely gave students too many days to complete their projects. When some finished early, I asked students to test out new ideas for me, like screen recording their worlds. Pike continued:

> I don't recommend this style for everybody—but it works for me. It lets a lot of creativity out. I'm always trying to find ways to design. The first time we did Cell Games, it probably took a week longer than it should have. Now I've got it consolidated. We've got to write our scripts before we do anything else; we're not going to build the game first. It's very free-forming. I know how much time I want to spend on it. When I notice things are getting a little too "helter-skelter," I'll pull back to a traditional lesson for a day or two, to get our minds straight again. Then we'll go back to our games.

Pike got the idea for Cell Games while teaching a level design class at a local out-of-school learning center. He realized that he could add just about any story to a game level. "I can take that template [Cell Games] and use it for history, too. Let's build a Mayan temple, find interesting facts, have an archaeologist or Maya character, and you guys write stories in there."

He still uses *Minecraft* to teach math, only now, it is more complex, situated in real world applications. He combines architectural theory and math together. "We input math into spreadsheets," Pike said. "They come to me with original formulas for their house. And the house has to look good! No cubes—that's for third grade." He has the class watch Grian on YouTube (https://www.youtube.com/user/Xelqua), and stops clips at each step, so they can do math along the way. "Then they learn how easy spreadsheets are."

Not all of his students are proficient in *Minecraft*. And many more may not even like the game. "This year all of my students liked *Minecraft*," Pike said. "I had one who didn't like it—but he flipped." Pike keeps a pile of cardboard that is used as a hands-on maker space. Students can then opt to build physical structures instead of digital ones. He once had a student use Hot Wheels cars to conduct physics experiments. "They may not want to go home and do it, but they do have fun playing *Minecraft* in school."

Much of Pike's successes are due to his involvement in The Tribe as a community of practice. "When I started doing this I felt like I was on an island doing this by myself," he said. "It's such a valuable resource to share ideas. Steve [Isaacs] is such an inspiration. I love how he is putting together this esports league, and communicating what we're doing. It's so nice to have an educator community." In 2016, Pike attended Minefaire, a *Minecraft* convention that Isaacs helped organize in Pennsylvania. Pike continued:

> Steve really got me into colearning. I was doing it without realizing I was doing it! But when Steve put a name on it, it really made me focus in. I tell the class that at this time we're all going to be teachers, or we're all going to be students. We flip the roles around. To see Steve Isaacs do it emboldened me to try it myself, and to run with it.

Minecraft is a game in which the students are likely more expert than the teacher. By turning over the reins of his class, Pike used *Minecraft* as a medium to transfer learning to students. Students became the teachers, and Pike became the student.

Applying the EPIC Framework

Karen Schrier developed the (2015) Ethics, Practice, and Implementation Categorization (EPIC) Framework for the use of use video games in ethics education, proposing seven educational goals, and 12 strategies for ethics games. For example, the video game *Journey* can help students to convey emotion and perspective, while iCivics' *Argument Wars* teaches the deliberation of real world issues. "The teacher needs to play the game and think about the maturity of the students and the goals they have," Schrier explained. We spoke in November 2016.

Games offer more to players than goals of winning. The experiences along the way may often present ethical challenges to players. The idea of the EPIC Framework is to be a tool for teachers to refer to when considering which games to use in classrooms. The goals and strategies were drawn from a literature review of vetted frameworks. Schrier continued:

I thought about the different types of goals a teacher might have in trying to teach ethics. Goals might be building ethical awareness, enhancing character, or helping students practice reflection. I also looked at 12 different strategies that might be used in ethics education, things like role-play or modeling of behavior, simulating scenarios or issues. I used it to help teachers understand the appropriate game to meet their own goals and strategies.

A teacher might want a game that teaches students about practicing ethical reasoning skills or empathy. "What is the best match for the teacher's classroom?" she continued. "The context and goals of the classroom need to be at the forefront. You can't just drop in [the US History game] *Mission US*, or [the immigration game] *The Migrant Trail* without thinking through the kinds of strategies and goals you want to meet."

Members of The Tribe used games as a safe space for students to experiment with identity. Using *Gone Home*, Darvasi and Husøy engaged students in discussions about a game's mood and tone. Sheehy asked her students about their hero's journey through adolescence. These were among Schrier's (2015) list of strategies, as was the use of open-ended assessments for student reflections. The EPIC Framework suggests that students' choices and consequences during play can be written about in a diary, or charted on grid.

The way students interact with games is different. "Everybody is different," Schrier concluded. "We [as designers] might go in thinking we're making this great educational game. But games, like people, are complex. Not everyone will respond to every game the same way."

Using *The Walking Dead* to Teach Ethics

Norwegian-based high school teacher Tobias Staaby appropriated the core mechanics of Telltale Games' *The Walking Dead* to his religion and ethics class. *The Walking Dead* is narrative-driven, told over a series of episodes. Players are given multiple dialogue choices after extended animated sequences. It is similar to an interactive film, and some choices are more difficult to make than others. Staaby and I spoke in December 2016.

"We play the whole of episode one because it is a worthwhile investment into the characters and the setting," Staaby began. "If students don't get emotionally involved, then the decisions and dilemmas are not as impactful. It is important to be emotionally involved, and that takes a little bit of time. But it is worth investing that time."

Staaby brings his own laptop to school, and hooks it up to the classroom projector. He also brings my own wireless PlayStation 4 controller. "I hand it to students to play, but many don't want to play," he said. "Many are content sitting and watching. They are afraid that they might make a mistake while the whole class watches."

But there is always someone who wants the controller. "When we come to a dilemma, I pause the game, and give them a short introduction on the dilemma's consequential ethics, and the ethics of virtue," Staaby continued. "We have a discussion about solutions and consequential imperatives."

After a discussion, students vote on what to do in the game. "Whichever decision gets the most votes, we do that, and then we move on." Then he pauses the action to connect to course content. Discussion questions relate to the ethical dilemmas posed in the game. This gives a safe space with which to apply curricular concepts. This approach is similar to screening a documentary film for students, and then pausing to ask questions. Staaby continued:

> If I told them to discuss euthanasia or capital punishment without giving them the correct forum to discuss these things, I suspect they would be afraid to say what they think. If some of them had controversial views or opinions, they wouldn't engage as much as they do now with the proper tools, i.e. the ethical theories to solve these dilemmas. In the game, a girl is bitten and asks you to borrow her gun. That is euthanasia, basically. But at the same time, it isn't, because it's zombies. It's make-believe. Some students get it. They raise their hand and ask, "Isn't this like how some people kill themselves? Isn't this a real-world thing?" Yes, it totally is. But it takes time to get this. I am easing them into ethical moral and philosophical mindset. Easing them into through semiotic domains, as [James Paul] Gee calls it. It is a backdoor in to the semiotic domain that I want them to understand.

Staaby only teaches with commercial games, "not necessarily because I think that educational games are a bad idea in principle, but because many of them are of sub-par quality."

Aside from *The Walking Dead*, Staaby has built lessons around the open world game *The Elder Scrolls V: Skyrim* as a means to discuss Norwegian national romanticism. Students compared and contrasted how Bethesda—the design studio—used vivid landscapes as a narrative tool to what the Norwegian national romantics used in their art and writing. And like Sheehy, students play *Journey*, which literally put them on a hero's journey.

Chapter Summary

Members of The Tribe adapt, appropriate, and contextually transpose games. They may borrow the theme or the core mechanics to drive instruction. These expert teachers twist games intended for education to meet different purposes. Open world games (e.g., *World of Warcraft*) and sandboxes (e.g., *Minecraft*) are particularly malleable to align with curricular needs. These adaptations are sometimes an unintended use of games, whether commercial games or those designed to teach a concept or skill.

References

Campbell, J. (2008). *The hero with a thousand faces* (3rd ed.). Novato, CA: New World Library (Original work published 1949).

Dikkers, S. (2015). *Teachercraft: How teachers learn to use Minecraft in their classrooms.* Pittsburgh, PA: ETC Press.

Gillispie, L., & Lawson, C. (n.d.). *WoWinSchools: A hero's journey.* Retrieved from http://wowinschool.pbworks.com/f/WoWinSchool-A-Heros-Journey.pdf

Haskell, C. (2015). *Play this, learn that* [iBooks]. Retrieved from https://itunes.apple.com/us/book/play-this-learn-that/id1000085917?mt=11

Irvin, G. (2017, January 19). *How to transform your Spanish class with Minecraft: An interview with Glen Irvin.* Retrieved from https://www.prometour.com/how-to-transform-your-spanish-class-with-minecraft-an-interview-with-glen-irvin/

Juul, J. (2003). The game, the player, the world: Looking for a heart of gameness. In M. Copier & J. Raessens (Eds.), *Level up: Digital games research conference proceedings* (pp. 30–45). Utrecht, The Netherlands: Utrecht University. Retrieved from http://www.jesperjuul.net/text/gameplayerworld/

Schrier, K. (2015). EPIC: A framework for using video games in ethics education. *Journal of Moral Education*, 44(4), 393–424. doi:10.1080/03057240.2015.1095168

Sheldon, L. (2012). *The multiplayer classroom: Designing coursework as a game.* Boston, MA: Course Technology/Cengage Learning.

· 1 1 ·

THE CASE FOR EXPERIENTIAL LEARNING

Playful situations for constructivist and experiential learning were baked into The Tribe's teaching. According to John Dewey, meaningful experience should be the goal of schooling (Alexander, Dewey, & Hickman, 1998), and games can be used to create meaningful experiences.

"There are a lot of us that believe that experience is really important—especially those of us on the sociocultural and situated cognition side of things," Benjamin Stokes, an assistant professor at American University, explained to me in late 2016. Stokes was a cofounder of the Games for Change nonprofit. He continued:

> We want our learning to be as close to the experience as possible—partly because of reasons of transfer, reasons of engagement, and passion. It goes back to the authenticity of people—that awful and terrible and great term that gets tossed around so much. To me, I think that experience is incredibly important, but it's also incredibly expensive. It's expensive in terms of time and actual money. A fantastic K12 learning experience might be hiring a private jet for someone and they can fly anywhere around the world they want with 5 of their friends, and 2 teachers. But we're not going to be able to create that, or to have everyone go to the Smithsonian all of the time.

In the children's series, *The Magic School Bus*, the eccentric teacher Ms. Frizzle whisked off children to far-away places in her eponymous school bus.

Her students traveled through time to observe dinosaurs, or they shrunk down to a microscopic level to interact with microbes. But, of course, *The Magic School Bus* was fiction.

Different from passive media (e.g., novels, film), in games, players interact with a system. "In some ways games make these intense and pivotal experiences more accessible," Stokes continued. "It speaks really nicely to this mission a lot of educators believe in: equity. How do we offer those experiences more equitably—not just for the people who can afford to fly to places? In this sense, games help distribute experiences more equitably."

This chapter opens with a recurrent theme I heard from several in The Tribe: games became digital field trips used to provide shared experiences. Digital field trips can sometimes be a virtual tour of a museum or faraway location projected onto a classroom screen or interactive white board. Or it can be a more immersive view of a location, using virtual reality goggles (e.g., Google Expeditions). In games, students have perceived control over outcomes. This interactive dynamic can bring meaning to learning.

Shared Experiences

Piaget (1962) theorized that experiences help minds assimilate new ideas to already known information. When I reference a video game like *Battlefield I* to my students, which is set in World War I, several can contextualize facts. But is meaning making from playing games the same as in noninteractive media, like film or books? "Games have a different meaning compared to watching a documentary or reading a textbook," Sande Chen explained. "If we [as player] have choices, then we get to decide what to do."

A researcher of serious games, Chen also writes narratives for video games. We spoke in late 2016 about how games make meaning for players. "I think there is a lot of debate about how a player feels," Chen said. "We have feelings in games. We have guilt, fear. These are different feelings from watching a movie. We don't really feel guilt most of the time from watching a film, but are allowed to see the depths of the character in an arc." One arc may be the student's personal hero's journey, which is what framed Sheehy's lessons. Chen continued:

> Games have the chance to provide a meaningful experience because you [the player] pay more attention to the experience because you are involved. Because of your interaction, you are not passive. You need to understand what is going on

inside the game and you need to recognize what is affecting other things, and what your actions imply and do within the system of the game. The meaning comes from the interaction with game mechanics. That is to say, there are certain rules within the game's design that affect how you interact, and how you make meaning.

Complex video games situate learning in an equitable manner by applying "distributed authentic professionalism," in which the player "shares knowledge with the virtual world" (Gee, 2007, pp. 207–208). Teachers in The Tribe often used games as a way to situate experiences for their students.

Games as Digital Field Trips

Glen Irvin's *Minecraft*-set high school Spanish classes are now "way different" than before he taught with the game. When he took a traditional instructional approach, Irvin found lessons to be "mechanical;" students "stuck to the script." Students memorized responses within a narrow range, even though language learning can get rather complex.

"My students now want to go beyond the course parameters," Irvin said. "They want different vocabulary and tenses. They want to reach beyond where they are in the language learning process. That is different." Irvin next compared the immersion in the blocky world of *Minecraft* to a field trip. He said:

> The only time I've seen this happen is when I've taken students abroad to a different country. When you take someone to Costa Rica or Mexico or Spain and live there for an extended period of time, you are immersed in the culture. Even though this may be overwhelming at first, you want to consume as much as you possibly can. That's what I feel like we do in class. When we have these activities it's not just about winning the competition, it's about wanting to communicate.

When I spoke to Tobias Staaby in late 2016, he shared the same analogy: games are like field trips. "When I talk to someone who has no idea what a game is, I call it a digital field trip," he said. "You visit someplace, and you do stuff—like you go down to a frog pond and look at tadpoles. Then you take that experience back into the classroom and you talk about it as it relates to the subject matter."

Aleksander Husøy teaches at the same school as Staaby. He echoed the same response. "I use the field trip analogy all the time," Husøy replied. "There are so many places that you can't logistically visit to experience. But through the game medium—while you don't get the full authentic experience—you do get something that is a close replicate to the actual experience, and, to a greater extent, I believe, than film or other forms of literature."

When someone is watching a film or reading a book, he or she is a passive recipient of the story being told. The immersive qualities of games give meaning to learning. "Through the interaction with a game's core mechanics, the player has a significant amount of responsibility for the characters and for the situation that unfolds in the game," Husøy said. This agency—or perceived control over outcomes—can be especially significant when it involves difficult decisions about serious topics.

This War of Mine is a game with serious themes that Husøy uses in his classroom. Set in a fictional war-torn European nation during the 1990s, it puts students into situations that are relevant to the social studies curriculum in Norway—specifically the topics of international relations and conflicts.

"When I use *This War of Mine*, students get emotionally involved and have a very real sense of responsibility to the well-being of the people they are controlling," Husøy said. "In my opinion that gives them a greater connection to the subject matter."

Husøy was "tipped off about the game" from a Swedish colleague who put him in touch with the Polish-based studio: 11 Bit Studios. To his delight, the developers offered the game for free to his class. "It works really well. The game mechanics are really familiar to students. It is similar to *The Sims*."

Curricular concepts are introduced before students play; Husøy frames it all around essential questions. For example, what happens to the rules and norms of a civilized society when the fabric of society breaks down, and there are no police or courts of law? What regulates your action? What is good—and what is evil—when there are no forces to punish or reward society? The game is used to reinforce and exemplify these concepts.

Husøy is using *This War of Mine* as a shared experience—a digital field trip where he can bring students to a place very much removed from the boundaries of the classroom. Students can observe and experience firsthand why the norms they take as a given are not necessarily universal. "With regards to the sociology part of the social studies curriculum, we want students to gain an understanding of what societal norms are, where norms come from, and why do we believe actions to be right or wrong," he said. "Then I ask, 'If someone is placed in a desperate situation, lacking food and shelter, is it morally right, justifiable—or perhaps understandable—that you would take actions that would, under normal circumstances would seem to be a betrayal of societal norms?'"

Lesson Planning for Experiences

Is there anything more cookie-cutter than writing "SWBAT" in a lesson plan book? Teacher shorthand for "student will be able to," it often precedes a (hopefully) higher-order thinking verb from Bloom's Taxonomy. An aligned lesson features an activity that addresses those objectives, and assesses them, as well. "SWBAT compare and contrast perspectives of the British and the American colonists leading up to the American Revolution" is more cognitively challenging than "SWBAT identify New Jersey on a map." But there is a bigger question at hand: In classrooms rich with games, digital media, and personalized instruction, should all students learn the same thing at the same time, all before a bell rings?

Many of the games I observed were inherently unpredictable, giving a unique experience for each student player. I spoke with Dan Curcio about the challenges of writing traditional lesson plans for nontraditional instructional methods. "Here's the problem for a lot of us in Tribe," he began. "There are metacognitive skills that are happening within an experience. You can't put that in a lesson plan. I wish I could say that I sat there and used the format that said the student will do blah, blah, blah." Instead Curcio—like others I interviewed—designs for student experiences. He continued:

> What ends up happening is that I first look at the content and objectives. A lot of it is organic. Let's have an experience and let's do something with this content. A lot of academics do not want to hear that. I can't show you a format to the design, or a plug-in for Bloom's Taxonomy. For the most part, we feel it out. Do I feel like students are handling content they should by 8th grade? Absolutely. Am I necessarily prepping them for the rote memorization that goes with standards-based assessment? I don't feel that is the most important part of education.

Curcio is afforded freedom and agency on how to teach curriculum. He can push experiential learning over drill-and-skill instruction. He starts with the basics, introducing topics with inquiry-based questions. Then he bridges verbal recognition to curricular content. "But then you have to do something with it, whether it is a game or an activity. Sometimes you just have to put fun into your work and see what comes out of it."

Glen Irvin's *Minecraft* lessons aren't cookie-cutter, or one-size-fits-all, either. "When you create a 'normal' lesson plan, you go through your objectives, what do you want your students to be able to do at the end," Irvin began. "Sure, you want to create an engaging lesson in class, but when you're using a game—especially a game like *Minecraft*—you have the ability to do so much more."

To Irvin, planning for meaningful experiences has been the most difficult—yet most rewarding—thing he does. He continued, explaining why designing for experience is so important. Irvin said:

> There is something that goes beyond really good teaching when you have the element of game-based learning. I feel it, and I can see it in almost all of my students who are playing the game. Planning for that—for effecting game-based learning and experiences—is a lot more complex than just a lesson plan.

Computer science teacher Mark Suter shared a similar response. "I know whatever I plan, it is going to evolve," he began. "I ask the class, 'What do you want to learn about?' Or, 'Let's then try out some games to see what we want to make.'"

Suter intentionally doesn't plan an entire semester of lessons. Instead, he refers to social media regularly to see where his lesson trajectory should head. His classroom is stocked with some of the latest cutting-edge technology, and he is trying to stay ahead of the curve. "I go on Twitter to see what Steve [Isaacs] and Lucas [Gillispie] and The Tribe are doing. I went to Minefaire [the *Minecraft*-themed convention Isaacs co-organized] in Philadelphia to see what people are up to. I saw [*Minecraft* content creator] Stephen Reid and 'Vive-craft'—the mod of *Minecraft* using the HTC Vive." Both Suter and Isaacs have had a HTC Vive virtual reality headset in their respective classrooms. "I am totally riding that rail of not planning anything and seeing what the kids are interested in. And I see what other teachers I trust and rely on are doing. The curriculum is constantly morphing."

Suter views his role in lesson planning as being "the course curator." "My planning involves constantly asking, How does this interest the student, and what's going to benefit the student? Start with why—the Simon Sinek thing." (Sinek is a proponent of servant-leadership models, and *Starts with Why* is the title of one of his books.)

By leading his class from behind, Suter is taking a servant-leadership role. Servant-leaders "put their subordinates first, are honest with them, and fair with them" (Northouse, 2013, p. 233). The Sherpa people are an example: they guide people up the Tibetan mountains, leading from behind. "If I start planning by saying, 'I think the student should,' I've already made a mistake. I am not involving the students in the planning."

Games and Mentorship Learning

After observing Isaacs' 20% Time lessons, I adapted it into my social studies classes. For the first semester, students played iCivics' *Win the White House*. After playing, a class discussion and reflection took place, critically analyzing the game's core mechanics, which included fundraising and polling. Students then worked on a project that they proposed, with the goal of teaching others about the election process.

Like Isaacs, I harnessed my community of practice of real world experts, using Skype to arrange mini-mentorships for students. One student wanted to give a TED Talk-style presentation on a big idea, so I connected her with Emma Humphries, iCivics' chief education officer. Humphries had delivered a TEDx Talk at the University of Florida. Writer Mark Cheverton, whom I met at the 2016 Games in Education Symposium, mentored some of my other students, too. Cheverton is the author of a series of *New York Times* bestselling *Minecraft* fiction books. He guided my 7th graders to self-publish on Amazon Kindle using the website Smashwords.

In reality, students were able to accomplish much of what they did because of access to my community of practice. But I was not a typical classroom teacher; by virtue of time spent conducting research, attending conferences, and interviewing game-based learning experts, I had amassed a professional learning network that was just a Skype call away. Clearly this doesn't scale. Surely there are other connected learning educators; however, building networks is time-consuming!

I explained this to game scientist David Williamson Shaffer in early 2017. Shaffer is a researcher of epistemic games, as well as virtual internships. "Essentially what you were doing was creating mini, virtual internships based on students' affinities," he began. "You are inventing for yourself the world I was trying to describe in *How Computer Games Help Children Learn*."

In Shaffer's (2006) prescient book, *How Computer Games Help Children Learn*, he explained how the epistemic learning that takes place from playing video games relates to the epistemic grammar used in professional practice. If someone plays a detective game, the experience might include language specific to that field situated in a narrative context. Shaffer next referenced his research on virtual internships, which are digital workplace simulations. He continued:

> What would help you, as teacher, would be a virtual internship on fan fiction writing, Kickstarter, game design, publishing, and so on. Your student played this game [*Win the White House*] that you essentially treated as a text. You had them play it and

deconstruct it. But then you could have them go into a virtual internship. You could take them to a fan fiction internship. That would provide you with the resources you would need to be able to give these students these kinds of real world experiences, with the mentoring and the feedback and the specific ways of thinking about things that you want them to have. Right now, because you're a really good teacher, you either know something about those domains, or you find someone who knows something about those domains, to mentor them. That is only scalable so far.

Digital tools make it easier to get students in touch with the outside world. Teachers in digital classrooms "are likely to take on a new role in schooling—the coordinator who orchestrates students' interactions within a system of distributed mentoring—a role more like that of a senior practitioner in an apprenticeship or internship than the role of a traditional classroom teacher" (Shaffer, Nash, & Ruis, 2015, p. 18).

Game researcher Benjamin Stokes spoke about Shaffer's notions of mentorships and internships. "Shaffer's claim is the kind of work we do for internships is almost in opposition to the kind of learning we do with textbooks," Stokes began. "The whole point of doing an internship is that you can't get it in a textbook. It's like reading the entire driver's ed book, and then getting tested on it. Passing the test doesn't mean that one can actually know how to drive a car."

For example, a journalism school may graduate thousands of students. But students who graduate may still lack the required workforce skills that internships provide. "They all can't feasibly be expected to attain internships," Stokes continued. "You can't have 1,000 people fill one intern post."

Stokes' analogy of drivers' ed and journalism school reminded me of something Sheehy told me. When interviewed in December 2015, she recounted James Paul Gee's anecdote of how a video game instruction manual only makes sense after one plays the game. A sociolinguist, Gee was among the first to write about the design, grammar, and semiotic language of video games. The story she shared appeared also in Gee's influential (2007) book, *What Video Games Have to Teach Us About Learning and Literacy*. Sheehy said:

> This PhD in linguistics pointed out that he could not make heads-or-tails of the video game manual. It made no sense to him; he was looking up words, and didn't get it. Since he already installed the game, he played it—I think he said for four hours—which is indicative of something. He then returned to the manual and understood it perfectly. He now had the experiential background in his schema to understand what was in the manual—now it all made sense. And then he alluded to school and said, "We give them [students] the manual without letting them play the game."

The "imagined world" Sheehy's students interact with in *World of Warcraft* is experienced, and then connected to the hero's journey narrative in *The Hobbit* (Gee, 2007, p. 105). Sheehy enables her students to associate "words with images, actions, experiences, or dialogue on a real or imagined world" (Gee, 2007, p. 105). Along with the epistemic grammar from the game, students then have an understanding of words *because* they experienced them in a situated context (Gee, 2007; Shaffer, 2006).

Virtual Internships

Virtual internships are a bit like role-playing games. They are computer simulations that allow students—as game players—to engage in the epistemologies of particular disciplines. Students solve authentic problems and look for optimal solutions. This is all done in the language—or epistemic grammar—of those professions.

Like video games, virtual internships can scale to large numbers of students, thus learning is distributed. Virtual internships can also enable teachers to focus on being expert educators—not to be experts of other workforce professions. Virtual internships are defined as:

> Web-based simulations that help students learn to think like scientists, scholars, artists, and workers in the real world do. They simulate not only the content that students are supposed to learn but also the ways of thinking—the epistemologies—that some groups of people use to solve problems. (Virtual Internships, 2017, para 1)

Players of virtual internships become interns at fictional companies or organizations. The platform Shaffer developed helps to mentor students in a way that is consistent with particular fields. "They are doing what happens in any good internship," he explained. "They are doing something people in that field actually do, with guidance and supervision. Students are essentially legitimate peripheral participants in some real-world practice." Legitimate peripheral participation is the "engagement in social practice that entails learning as an integral constituent" (Lave & Wenger, 1991, p. 35).

In a good internship, some work is completed, and then the intern talks to a mentor to get guidance. The interactions on Shaffer's platform mirror that feedback loop, treating student players as if they were at a real company. For example, when players receive email, it is worded to sound like it came from a manager at an actual company. "It is addressed to the role of an intern, rather than the role as student," Shaffer said.

In these simulations, the reflective process is built into the simulation because that's part of a real internship. "We're trying to copy the process of learners going out into the world to try to solve real problems." Thus, virtual internships incorporate a reflection-on-action mechanism (Schön, 1983). Shaffer explained:

> When commercial games—and many learning games—come into the classroom, there is the expectation is that students will play and learn; however, the reflection-on-action happens outside the game. It's the thing the teacher must package around the game. Teachers know that they can't just give students this experience, walk away, and expect that they would understand what was salient about it, and how it connects to the other things that they are doing.

Feedback in virtual internships are in the language—or epistemic grammar—of particular workforce professions. "They [students] are producing deliverables, and those deliverables are part of a larger project," he continued. "The boss in the game doesn't review work and reply, 'This is an A.' The feedback says, 'Here's what you did well, and here's what you need to work on.' Or, 'You need to redo this so you can move on.'"

Teachers can review what students say in text chats. "We have a simplified network diagram that shows what the ideal epistemic frame would look like for someone in a profession during a conversation," Shaffer said. "We know that teachers really care about the quality of students' discussion that they're talking about. We make a model to show what the students are talking about, and to show the critical things and connections they are making back to the teacher."

Like participants in Shaffer's virtual internship simulations, members The Tribe's students reflected on experiences after play—they were engaged in reflection-on-action assessments. "What we know about complex learning is that students have to take action and they have to reflect on that action," Shaffer said. "They have to talk with their teacher or their peers or their mentor about what worked, what didn't, and why. That's what turns actions in a game into an understanding of how a part of the world works."

In Isaacs' classes, game design is used to teach computational thinking and iterative design. His classroom functions more like a game design studio; he even uses Skype to bring in professional game designers.

I shared my observations of Isaacs' praxis with Shaffer. "Essentially what Steve has done was to create a simulated internship," he said. "It's just not virtual—he's a real person. And there is absolutely nothing wrong with that. That is a great pedagogy." Shaffer then remarked about how The Tribe's praxis actually resembles the feedback loop in virtual internships. He said:

Just as you would have the kids read *The Scarlet Letter*, there isn't the expectation that you'd just give the students the book, they'd read it, and be done. You actually have conversations about it. You talk about what was interesting. But those conversations happen outside of *The Scarlet Letter*. It's a text that's brought into this well-established system that schools use for teaching texts. Those could be literary texts, and texts from history. Science is similar, when someone does an experiment. A virtual internship would build some of that more into the simulation because that's the way an internship really works.

Shaffer was careful not to criticize what teachers in The Tribe were doing; after all, both kinds of approaches can run parallel. "Virtual internships are trying to build in things so a teacher doesn't have to. Someone like Steve could put that whole thing online so that kids are engaging with nonplayable characters, rather than just with him."

Shaffer's research led to a discovery that there was actually an advantage of having a virtual mentor, instead of an actual person. He explained:

> In the same way there are certain advantages to be participating in a virtual environment of any kind, students take on the role a little differently when the boss is actually in the simulation. They are not handing it in to the teacher. They are handing it in to someone else. The persistence of the role is deeper than if they know the teacher is assessing them. The teacher has the teacher role, and can only step so far out of that role. If there are nonplayable characters in the simulation, and they are doing those same things, there's an opportunity for it to feel more authentic.

A teacher might tell students that they are actually employed at a company that designs characters for Pixar films. But this narrative shell is likely not believable for many students. Students surely would they are not really designing characters for a Pixar movie.

Shaffer's team discovered that if done remotely, a storyline can become almost plausible. "There really might be somebody at the other end that you were working with. And yeah, maybe they were taking time to get ideas from kids!" The narrative became more believable, and it gave students "a deeper buy-in precisely because it was remote, they were not right there in the classroom." Shaffer continued:

> We used to have someone—a live person—who was in the role of the teacher. That person would mentor the students and work with them face-to-face. And we put it all online in part because it would be easier to scale, and in part because it would be easier to collect the data. We were very concerned that when you went online you would lose some of the tacit understanding of where the students are. You couldn't see their body language. You couldn't stand next to a group to get them to focus. You could do

those things that good teachers do to manage students when they're working. We thought it might degrade the experience. We found that it became more compelling.

Virtual Internship Authorware

A few weeks after I spoke to Shaffer, Peter Quigley—games coordinator for the Epistemic Games Group—led me through a demonstrated of virtual internships—including the free authorware. As of November 2017, there were epistemic games for high school and college levels. At the lab, graduate students conduct research on data that comes out of the games.

The Epistemic Games Group launched free authorware available called VIA. Virtual internships can be created, shared, and modified by any teacher who has an account. When Quigley and I spoke, there were three prepared virtual internship games, which could be used in a classroom "right out-of-the-box," with little adaptation. There was one urban planning simulation aimed towards high school age students, *Land Science*, and two biomedical engineering simulations for college students: *Nephrotex* and *RescuShell*.

In the games on the VIA platform, there are always two main participants: the student players, and a role called "the mentor." The mentor is live, communicating with students, controlling the pace of the action. "It's a real person logged on concurrently," Quigley explained. The mentor is unseen, possible another teacher in the same department, working at another location. "There is teacher in the classroom facilitating the ongoing work students are doing, but he or she takes a backseat." The mentor assesses student work using rubrics written by the teacher. "This holds students accountable. It is an added impetus for students to keep their work together."

Quigley played through *Land Science* for me via Skype. The core mechanic—to balance a city's system—reminded me of *SimCity*'s: players take on the role of an urban planner. The goal is to work together to create proposals for zoning the city of Lowell, Massachusetts. Students follow a particular workflow, which is leveled and scaffolded. They use an email system to retrieve and find tasks. "It is a prescriptive email with tasks to accomplish," Quigley said. Then there is a sandbox where all of the work is housed. This includes resources and a library of documents, and the information is scaffolded. "This sandbox period gets students use to the epistemology."

Land Science has different scaffolded levels—or rooms—of increasing complexity. All student work gets entered into engineering workbooks, which is also modeled on real world practice, and internships have different simulation tools. In *Land Science* it's called "iPlan," which features land parcels overlaid on an interactive Google Map. Students zone land as commercial, industrial, and open space. When rezoned, there is a live bar graph displaying the effects of carbon pollution and housing, which changes in real time.

During play, students use "WorkPro," a fictional workplace platform where they do all of their work: reading emails, consulting documents, communicating with others, and creating designs. "It's meant to emulate streamlined technologies that firms use," Quigley said. "It's their first step in the epistemic game. It's a professional work experience."

Virtual internships also include "Reflection Rooms," where mentors can "facilitate targeted discussion questions that get to closer and closer to a core concept we are trying to get students to understand." This all culminates in a revoice—"a summary of the discussions that changed based on what the students did." The goal is to reinforce or push students in the right direction based on what the mentor wants them to do. "This gets students to reflect on the epistemologies, and to make connections."

The final stage of *Land Science* is an interactive map for students to rezone Lowell. Students make a proposal that must include a written justification for their recommendations. "They do this by reviewing the wishes of stakeholders, reviewing their needs and concerns," Quigley said. "Each stakeholder has different conflicting ideas about what should happen in Lowell. Students work to appease these people with a simulation tool." There is actually no way to satisfy all of the stakeholders, and players learn that multiple stakeholders can be satisfied—but not all.

How The Tribe Engaged Students in Affinity Groups

Going beyond having students publish work online, members of The Tribe engage students in affinity spaces, which are interest-driven communities of practice (Gee, 2005). Peer-supported, interest-powered, and academic-oriented learning are also Principles of Connected Learning (Garcia, 2014).

I spoke to game scholar and lecturer Mark Chen in early 2017 about the value of affinity spaces around games. "The things I want to see in classrooms are similar things what I see in gaming culture—like fan communities around certain games, strategy guides—all of this stuff that is extraneous to the games is all interest-driven work," he said. "Those are the things classrooms could mirror and encourage, on top of using and leveraging the engagement from commercial games."

Many I spoke with in The Tribe make a concerted effort to encourage students to harness affinity groups as mentorship spaces. For example, in the fall of 2016, Mark Grundel brought two of his 5th grade students to speak at

Minefaire. We spoke early in 2017 about how he wanted his students to share his excitement for game-based learning. Minefaire is a *Minecraft*-themed convention that Isaacs co-organized. The event broke a Guinness World Record as the "largest convention organized around a single video game when 12,140 people attended" (Sasko, 2016).

Grundel's students spoke to the crowd about how they built settings for stories. One student "talked about how *Minecraft* empowered him," Grundel said. "He became perceived as a leader in the culture of the classroom. Kids went to him as the expert. *Minecraft* gave them a voice to demonstrate their learning in their own way." Aside from Minefaire, Grundel's students have led teacher professional development sessions on game-based learning. "I had six students stay after school showing staff the games they created."

"In general, getting kids connected to things happening in the real world is good," Shaffer said, after I shared this anecdote. "Kids should connect to something meaningful beyond the classroom—and that's true whether it is sports, clubs, or academics. We want kids to be engaged in things that matter to them in the real world." Shaffer pointed to afterschool clubs, like the Model UN, forensics clubs, and the Science Olympiad.

Isaacs is a vocal proponent of interest-powered learning. This was particularly evident in the 20% Time projects I observed. I also witnessed a system of apprenticeship learning in online affinity spaces in his classroom. These included publishing and critiquing games online, viewing and uploading instructional videos and guides, and remixing online content (e.g., remixing on Code.org). To accomplish this, Isaacs harnessed informal learning spaces, which are typically passion-driven (i.e., affinity groups), into his class' formal learning setting (Gee, 2005). More than just viewing online videos, his students became active practitioners in gamer culture (Duncan & Steinkuehler, 2008; Lave & Wenger, 1991).

What's more, Isaacs considers his students to be part of his personal learning network. In particular, Isaacs relies on student expertise when he began teaching with *Minecraft*. He also plays the same games as many of his students. In the blog post titled, *Minecraft: Zen and the Art of Letting Go*, he wrote:

> This brings me to a point that has had a huge impact on my teaching practice. Minecraft does not come with an instruction manual. Have you ever seen how kids learn how to play *Minecraft*? They go right to YouTube, *Minecraft* websites and wikis. Virtually all of the content they find and use to learn about Minecraft is player-generated. The gamer community has constructed an immense knowledge base and people are excited to share what they know. (Isaacs, 2016, para. 6)

Glen Irvin touts learning in affinity groups to his students, too. "I tell my students that the most powerful thing that they have access to is your voice—not the Internet," he said. "People are out there, and they want to hear how you learn, and what is the most effective." Irvin advises his students to build communities with other people—whatever those communities might be. He continued:

> I tell students my experiences with all of you guys [The Tribe], how different things are for me in the past two years than they were. Could have I done what I was doing just at that point? Absolutely. But there is something to the human experience and the whole growth mindset. There is something satisfying to help other people, and ask for help, and to go back and forth between those two things. My students don't really go on Twitter. But I tell them the power of it for professional collaboration. Even if you don't care about game-based learning, you can reach out to anyone with a degree of expertise. A lot of people are happy to bring you into their group.

To Irvin, it is "super-important for kids to know that the audience is beyond Señor Irvin." He wants his students to present their work to the entire world. Irvin posts his students' game play on YouTube and Twitter. He also freely shares his lesson plans via his blog and on the website Teachers Pay Teachers (as of this writing, his lessons were all available for free: https://www.teacherspayteachers.com/Store/Irvspanish). He does realize the risk of putting work out there, and how it could get criticized. "I tell students that it is because I am super-proud of what they are doing. With the #MinecraftEdu Twitter chat community, I get and share ideas, too."

Chapter Summary

Games are experiences. As such, games can be used to frame content with stories and emotions. When students in a classroom play games, they are embarking on a shared experience which teachers can later reference. In other words, by playing a game, abstract concepts can have meaning to learners.

Those in The Tribe intentionally and purposely create meaningful experiences for their students. Sometimes they go further, arranging mini-mentorships and digital internships, extending game simulations to conditions experienced in the workplace. Members of The Tribe go beyond having students publish work online; they encourage student participation in communities of practice and in interest-powered affinity spaces.

References

Alexander, T. M., Dewey, J., & Hickman, L. A. (1998). *The essential Dewey*. Bloomington, IN: Indiana University Press.

Duncan, S., & Steinkuehler, C. (2008). Scientific habits of mind in virtual worlds. *Journal of Science Education & Technology, 17*(6), 530–543. doi:10.1007/s10956-008-9120-8

Garcia, A. (Ed.). (2014). *Teaching in the connected learning classroom*. Irvine, CA: Digital Media and Learning Research Hub.

Gee, J. (2005). Semiotic social spaces and affinity spaces. In D. Barton & K. Tusting (Eds.), *Beyond communities of practice*. (pp. 214–232). Cambridge, MA: Cambridge University Press.

Gee, J. P. (2007). Game-like learning: An example of situated learning and implications for opportunity to learn. In J. P. Gee, E. H. Haertel, P. A. Moss, D. C. Pullin, & L. J. Young (Eds.), *Assessment, equity, an opportunity to learn* (pp. 200–221). New York, NY: Cambridge University Press.

Isaacs, S. (2016, April 18). *Minecraft: Zen and the art of letting go*. Retrieved from https://blogs.technet.microsoft.com/microsoft_in_education/2016/04/18/minecraft-zen-and-the-art-of-letting-go/

Lave, J., & Wenger, E. (1991). *Situated learning: Legitimate peripheral participation*. Cambridge: Cambridge University Press.

Northouse, P. G. (2013). *Leadership: Theory and practice* (6th ed.). Thousand Oaks, CA: Sage.

Piaget, J. (1962). *Play, dreams and imitation in childhood*. New York, NY: Norton Library.

Sasko, (2016, October 17). *Montco Minecraft fans broke a world record*. Retrieved from http://www.phillymag.com/news/2016/10/17/minecraft-world-record-minefaire/

Schön, D. A. (1983). *The reflective practitioner*. London: Temple Smith.

Shaffer, D. W. (2006). *How computer games help children learn*. New York, NY: Palgrave Macmillan.

Shaffer, D. W., Nash, P., & Ruis, A. R. (2015). Technology and the new professionalization of teaching. *Teachers College Record, 117*(12), 1–30.

Virtual Internships. (2017). Retrieved from http://virtualinterns.org/

· 1 2 ·

OPEN-ENDED ASSESSMENTS FOR OPEN-ENDED GAMES

David Williamson Shaffer (2012) once asked, "How do we know that players aren't just learning how to play the game?" (p. 403). Is what is happening in a game transferable to outside of where play takes place? Playing a game presents a safe-to-fail setting to hypothesize and test affordances without incurring real-world consequences (Barab, Gresalfi, & Ingram-Goble, 2010). Games are situated spaces, in which transfer can take place (Gee, 2007; Shaffer, 2012). But as Sutton-Smith (1997) noted, play is "ambiguous" to define. Therefore, assessing student play in educational games is inherently problematic.

Digital games are particularly adept at aggregating data. They can be used to assess 21st century skills that could be difficult for a teacher to measure such as solving problems, thinking with systems, and collaborating with teams. As a result, game-based learning has the potential to enable teachers to be more effective in practice.

Companies in the educational market are keen on reporting learning analytics to teachers. "There is a push for those requirement for learning games," researcher Sande Chen said, when we spoke in late 2016. "In general, publishers of entertainment games don't have lesson plans because they are coming from an entertainment perspective. Teachers adapting an entertainment product for the classroom need to come up with their own lesson plans."

While phonics workbooks are useful for reinforcing certain literacy skills, they are not the sole means of teaching reading. If children learn to read through whole language approaches, why are educational games still honing in on singular concepts? The culture of getting balanced digital games to classrooms vis-à-vis actionable assessments embedded into the game's design can imply distrust for the abilities of teachers. Use of quantitative game analytics as an assessment tool was also incongruent to what was observed in my research of The Tribe: They embraced reflective practices.

Except for *Minecraft: Education Edition*—which has tools for students to write self-reflections supported by in-game screenshots, much like Darvasi did with his *Gone Home* unit—most games The Tribe used did not have assessment dashboards. BreakoutEDU, an escape the room game kit for classrooms, has taken a similar self-assessment approach as *Minecraft: Education Edition*. BreakoutEDU comes with a deck of cards that have reflection questions. Perhaps the emphasis on self-reflection is because the cofounders—Adam Bellow and James Sanders—are former teachers. Collaborative problem solving is BreakoutEDU's pedagogical goal. "The reflection card deck was created because we wanted to make everything about intrinsic versus extrinsic," Bellow told me, in March 2017. "The other thing was that we wanted teachers to see the learning that was happening after the game."

This chapter discusses how members of The Tribe create assessments to support their particular learning and curricular goals. Of course, this approach is not unique to game-based learning. Teachers use other forms of media intended for commercial consumption, like novels and plays, and then they create and align assessments to meet goals and objectives.

Games, the Curriculum, and Assessments

Teachers today are faced with mounting pressure to have students perform well on standardized tests, a goal that can be incongruent with the playfulness associated in games. Many teachers in the United States adhere to the Common Core State Standards, which place emphasis on more rigorous academic content in earlier grades. While the Common Core State Standards do not dictate pedagogy, they do include what content and skills students need to know at specified grade levels ("Common Core," 2017). What remains is an implied pedagogical approach. Districts then create curriculum based on standards ("Common Core," 2017). At the classroom level, a teacher designs lesson plans to enable students to access curriculum. The current educational landscape can affect a teacher's decision to use nontraditional teaching methodologies, like games.

In the intended curriculum model (ICM), the general curriculum begins at the state level and is disseminated through the teacher's lesson plans (Kurz, 2011). An effective teacher enables students to engage with, to learn, and to display the curriculum (Kurz, 2011). This requires ample time to plan and deliver the intended curriculum equitably (Kurz, 2011).

There remains a gap in the opportunity available for all students to learn the prescribed curriculum (Carter, Ladson-Billings, & Welner, 2013). The "opportunity gap" is "the cumulative differences in access to key educational resources that support learning at home and at school: expert teachers, personalized attention, high-quality curriculum opportunities, good educational material, and plentiful information sources" (Darling-Hammond, 2013, p. 77). Models of teacher effectiveness are based on the central idea that a teacher's role is to enable each student the opportunity to access the curriculum (Kurz, 2011; Polikoff & Porter, 2014).

In The Tribe's classrooms, games were used to give students an opportunity to learn (OTL) the curriculum (Kurz, 2011; Polikoff & Porter, 2014). OTL centers on student access to the curriculum, including general education, special education, and English language learning students (Kurz, 2011). Games have the capability to create an equitable OTL through enabling equal access to the curriculum, which is the heart of effective teaching practice (Gee, 2007; Kurz, 2011).

Teaching is a "complex interaction" between the teacher and his or her students (Archer, Kerr, & Pianta, 2014, p. 1). Currently in the United States, there are value-added measurements (VAMs) that are utilized to assess the overall qualities of an effective teacher. VAMs include student growth from standardized test scores and other benchmarks, such as observed student engagement (Braun, 2005; Glazerman et al., 2010). The Danielson Framework for Teaching is one such measurement, dividing effective teaching into 22 measurable and assessable components, and then further subdividing into 76 more parts (Danielson, 2007).

VAMs run incongruent to gameful teaching practices, in which play takes the lead in instruction. When I spoke to Remi Kalir about teacher observation models and playful learning, he referenced a quote he used in the conclusion to the (2016) book *Teacher Pioneers: Visions from the Edge of the Map*. He wrote, "As the philosopher Maxine Greene eloquently suggests, to neglect imagination and agency as central to pedagogy delimits educators to live and work as 'clerks or functionaries'" (Greene, 1995, p. 1; Kalir, 2016, p. 362).

The Tribe's (Non)Use of Dashboard Analytics

Teacher dashboards that aggregate data on student achievements in games were *not* utilized in any of my observations of Paul Darvasi, Peggy Sheehy, or Steve Isaacs' praxis. While not observed, the topic of assessments and games came up frequently in the coded responses to structured interviews with each. Darvasi mentioned it six times, Isaacs stated it twice, and Sheehy spoke about assessments three times. Referring to assessing play, Darvasi stated, "The 'golden fleece' in game-based learning, [is when] we correspond play with certain learning outcomes." He also professed that there remained "a lack of real knowledge or concrete evidence to show what kind of learning takes place and that you can assess players."

Interviews with other members in The Tribe similarly indicated that knowledge transfer—not play—was assessed. Often, teachers asked students to demonstrate learned knowledge or skills from games to other situations. When Tobias Staaby adapts the commercial video game *The Walking Dead* to teach students about ethical dilemmas, he uses "fairly standard assessments." Rather than rely on game data (e.g., digital badges awarded), or in game progress (e.g., levels attained) to indicate learning, he asks students to apply what they learn from the game to the real world. "It's important for me to not just contain the learning from within the game, but to help students with the abstract knowledge, like utilitarianism and the other ethical theories," Staaby said. "I split them into groups of three or four, and then I give them a dilemma from the real world. I want to see if they can apply what they learned from the game to the real world."

Glen Irvin also reported the use of traditional assessments in his high school Spanish language classes. As students play *Minecraft*, Irvin monitors formative assessments embedded in the experience (e.g., players must chat with one another in Spanish, as well as with the teacher). Because assessment strategies remain intact, students can also elect to not learn with a game-based approach, and still pass the same test. "Overall, the way that I assess formatively and summatively has not changed that much," he said. "Assessments are still the second language conversations that take place in class."

Irvin's assessment strategies are identical as before he taught using *Minecraft*: Students must demonstrate the ability to write and speak in Spanish. "I haven't changed that," he explained. "I ask students to give details about the inside and out of their virtual homes. Are you able to describe the interior of a home, colors, furniture? This depends on the students' level of vocabulary acquisition. The summative assessment is a test at the end—often out loud—as students "prove their learning" by conversing with Irvin.

Self-assessment was one of the preferred methods computer technology teacher Mark Suter favors. His students design their own benchmarks and expectations. He then speaks individually with students to help them to refine their goals. "I ask my students to come up with three measurable goals and three difficult goals," he said. "I've come to learn that—with personalized learning—if they [students] aren't in on it, they're not going to be into it."

Like Isaacs, Suter has 20% Time days for interest-driven projects. "I evolved it to be 80% time," he remarked. "If students prove to me that they go off of the main road and deviate, they're welcome to do that." In one class, a student told Suter that she wanted to eventually work as an accountant. So, he got her the materials to become Microsoft Excel certified. "The caveat is that you have to be independent enough to meet those measurable goals."

Regarding teacher dashboards for digital games, Zack Gilbert has yet to see one that exactly matches his learning targets. "I think most of us in The Tribe will take it [the game] to where the kids want to go," he said. "As students play, they come up with targets I never even thought of, and I can assess those, too."

Teachers in The Tribe are afforded freedom to assess other areas that may come about during play, and they iterate as lessons progress. "It is fly-by-the-seat-of-your-pants, which is my style of teaching," Gilbert said. "I am organized, but I am also organic to when things open up." Reflecting on his praxis, he said,

> With the geography skills I am teaching this year, I've noticed a gap with the 5th grade students. So I altered my curriculum based on my students. I have flexibility to do that, so it is organic. And I am treated like a professional. I came up with the scope and sequence [of the curriculum] with an expert in the building. I am trusted as an educator, so even if I go off the path, it's okay. The Tribe has this common quality: We will go where the game takes us, because there is no canned curriculum. It's not like there are *Civilization* assessments out there!

When asked about his use of teacher dashboards, Aleksander Husøy gave a pithy response: "No, nothing like that." Then he continued, "It wouldn't surprise me if we [The Tribe] all had the same sentiments about educational games." Husøy next leveled a critique of learning games that are packaged with dashboards:

> A significant amount of money goes into these games. This might have value, but only for a very small sliver of the curriculum or knowledge or experience when compared to what you can do with a game not made for education. You, as the teacher, have the authority to use a game in a way that benefits your students—not whatever ideas some game developer at some point in the past thought might be good for classes, or schools, in general.

Members of The Tribe were not only confident about adapting games—they also had several years of teaching experience to support their intuitions. A new teacher might offer a differing opinion on dashboard analytics. Nonetheless, a common problem reported about teacher dashboards was that they promote cookie-cutter, or canned teaching practices.

As a point of comparison, about a quarter of K8 game-using teachers surveyed in the national *Level Up Learning* survey ($n = 513$) also "did not assess student performance with or around digital games in any way" (Takeuchi & Vaala, 2014, p. 19). Instead, game-using teachers reported that they "created their own tests/quizzes (30%) or held whole-class discussions (31%) to measure student learning through gameplay; or interpreted students' game scores as evidence of their knowledge on topics covered in other formats (39%)" (Takeuchi & Vaala, 2014, p. 19).

"The Ultimate Assessment"

The teachers who contributed chapters to Caro Williams-Pierce's (2016) *Teacher Pioneers: Visions form the Edge of the Map* rarely used games specifically designed for learning, or for content delivery. "Just the phrase 'content delivery' makes me cringe," Williams-Pierce said, when we spoke in November 2016. "There is no such thing as a content delivery system—unless the content is peanut butter, and you're shipping it across the country. That's a content delivery system."

The inclusion of teacher dashboards on game achievements has unintended consequences. It can message that teachers need to rely on others to tell them what is important about the game play. "This is one of the things people are still figuring out about learning analytics," Williams-Pierce said. "If you want to design dashboards that are based on sophisticated analytics that are real-time—while students are playing—teachers need to be deeply involved in that design."

There remains a gap between what students as players do, and what that actually means to their learning and understanding. "Every time you put the weird, black box layer between the actual play and what the teacher actually gets to see in the teacher display, you trust random other people who don't know your classroom," Williams-Pierce continued. "They [game designers] don't know your students." The best way to understand and support student learning is when teachers "have the time and leeway to tend to their individual learning in person. Maybe it's just me, but I don't trust people who design teacher dashboards." Williams-Pierce next shared an anecdote about her experience playing the multiplayer first-person shooter game *Destiny*:

> I have a brother who lives in Oregon, and we keep in touch by playing together. He was way experienced than me, and he ran me through some level. And then a number popped up, and it looked like neither of us has killed anybody. I was like, "We just beat this and nothing changed." And then my brother said they [the designers] hadn't fixed a bug. Now that was essentially a dashboard, but it was incorrect. *Destiny* was horrifically buggy when it came out. I think that dashboards that get sent out to teachers don't have such obvious bugs, which can make them slightly more nefarious. You don't know where those numbers are coming from. Maybe they accidentally added a 5 to everyone. How are you supposed to find that out? If *Destiny* can do that with millions of dollars behind it, any educational game can do that too.

In the game-based approaches observed in Darvasi, Sheehy, and Isaacs' classrooms, each stepped back and watched student interactions, which is a Montessorian approach. "This is what teachers do best; they are students of students," Chris Haskell said. "Good teachers pay close attention to what is happening. And then they use their experience to create a narrative for what is happening." He continued:

> A blunt instrument, like a standardized test can't tell you that—even though the student got an answer wrong—he or she actually knew what it was. The student just called it something else. It [the student's answer] might have been a more advanced description that may not have been available in the multiple-choice options. A blunt instrument can't decode that—but a teacher can. Teachers are not good storage devices, but we are really good at meaning making. That is the benefit of a playful environment. We can then step back and take a look.

Williams-Pierce recommended that teachers assess learning by asking students to create something new—"the ultimate assessment." Paul Darvasi did just that when he created assessments around *Gone Home* that were in line with a typical high school literature class. For example, students wrote and published game reviews.

"How do you know that students really learn? They played this game and embedded themselves in an environment," Williams-Pierce said. "Then they create this presentation, and demonstrate what happened."

The Case for Schönian Reflective Practices

GlassLab's *Mars Generation One: Argubot Academy* is a balanced design game, with aligned core mechanics and learning goals. It was designed to teach claims and evidence argumentation schemas. But is playing the game enough to indicate skill mastery? My middle school students tested it when it was first released. Anecdotally, when asked to write argumentative essays—or even to argue out loud in a Socratic-style debate—I observed little learning transfer.

Ultimately, whole class discussions helped foster learning transfer. Glass-Lab marketing materials included a poster of the game's different "argubots" (argument robots), which I used to help students make connections. After giving students primary source texts to read, I then asked which argubots they would use in a battle ("battle" is how argubots argue; the core mechanic of *Mars Generation One: Argubot Academy* is similar to *Pokémon*'s trading card battles). Students thought through argumentation schemes, and most were able to extend the learning from the game to to paper. Of course, this is not to argue that games shouldn't be balanced; rather, game-based assessments should be the starting point for good reflection-on-action practices.

David Williamson Shaffer champions the use of reflective practices when using epistemic games. "We're trying to figure out not just that they [student players] solved a problem, but whether they solved a problem the way a lawyer or a doctor or an architect would, depending on what the problem was," he said.

Donald A. Schön's seminal (1983) book, *The Reflective Practitioner: How Professionals Think in Action*, defined reflection-in-action and refection-on-action. Reflection-in-action is when someone takes an action, reflects, and then continues on (Schön, 1983). A lawyer may reflect-in-action in a courtroom; a teacher may do so during a lesson. Reflection-in-action could be an adjustment in strategy—during a game or at the boardroom. Reflection-on-action takes place after an experience happened (Schön, 1983). A doctor reflects after a procedure.

Teachers in The Tribe tended to construct their own reflection-on-action prompts for students, and they were often posted on learning management systems (e.g., 3D GameLab, Schoology, Haiku, Google Classroom). Students also reflected on actions using the epistemic grammar from games (e.g., role-play as a businessperson in Irvin's *Minecraft* game, and then reflect on the experience in his Schoology page; Shaffer, 2006).

In Sheehy's 3D GameLab quest chain, "The Hero's Footprint," she asked students to create a "Fakebook page," which is a parody of a Facebook profile. Then she asked reflection-on-action questions which were to be written in the language of MMO games and Joseph Campbell's (1949/2008) monomyth. Her stated goal was for students "to show what it might look like if this *World of Warcraft* or *Guild Wars 2* character were using Facebook" ("The Hero's Footprint," 2011, para. 3). Her prompt read, "Share this online for your fellow Heroes to see. In your Hero's Journal, reflect on what your online reputation says about you and how that might affect your future" ("The Hero's Footprint," 2011, para. 3).

In Isaacs' classes, students learned game design through the same iterative design cycle that professional game designers use. They learn the skills and content to code games. Isaacs created charts for students, as well as developer diaries for students to reflect on individual progress. He also mentored students to have the values and identity of the game design profession, as a community of practice (Shaffer, 2006). The reflection-on-action prompt read:

> Every week you should reflect on the experience and your progress. I have been blogging about the overall experience. Check out my blog here. As you continue with the experience it is expected that you reflect on your progress and plan for moving forward. In your blog submission, be specific about what you accomplished and what your next short-term (weekly) goal is. To submit this quest you can simply respond to this quest for the 10 XP or submit a blog post or YouTube video and receive a bonus 10 XP. If you submit a video or blog post please do not include your complete name or personal information. Please include the following:
>
> 1. What product/tool are you working with?
> 2. Share what you have learned so far through the experience.
> 3. What progress have you made so far?
> 4. What is your plan for moving forward? What do you plan to complete within the next week?
> 5. Interesting a-ha moments you have had through the experience of taking ownership of your learning.

Isaacs is quick to share exemplar student work within the community of practice. The following response was from an 8th grade student, which Isaacs shared on Twitter. In the epistemic grammar of the game design profession, she wrote:

> The design document was really helpful. It helped me decide what my game would be like and develop it. The development of my game took a very long time, but it allowed me to express my creativity and was fun to make. In addition, the end product is very enjoyable to play. The betatesting process was useful because the peer feedback helped me improve my game. ("Best Fox Hunter," 2017, para. 1)

"Design document" and "betatesting" are common vernacular in the game design field; it is not common in the lexicon of most middle school students.

For his *Gone Home* unit, Darvasi prepared a chart for his students' formative assessments, asking for screenshot evidence to support claims (e.g., "Does this sort of voiceover affect the realism of the story? How?"). He then prompted students to use language appropriate to publish reviews of the game. He begins by having students read professional game reviews in *The Atlantic* and in *The Guardian*. Then students posted their reviews on gamer community websites (Darvasi, 2014). He wrote:

> This would permit them to genuinely contribute and participate in the knowledge community that the game has generated. Their work would not only be graded by their teacher but, more importantly, their efforts would be subjected to the scrutiny of the legion of invisible eyes that inhabit the real-world of the Internet. (Darvasi, 2014, para. 9)

Reflection-on-action is common in teacher education (Mortari, 2015). To wit is Darvasi's blog, Ludic Learning, which is essentially his reflection-on-action from teaching with games. Isaacs similarly reflects about his experiences on his blog, which features how he designs for student choice and voice.

Narrativizing Game Events

In *Quandary* students are challenged to colonize planet Braxos. Along the way they face ethical dilemmas. *Quandary* is a learning game intended to provide a safe forum to talk about issues like redistribution of income, eminent domain, water problems, and privacy versus security.

When John Fallon adapted *Quandary* into his English curriculum, he included a "hybrid persuasive narrative" assignment. His students chose two of the four episodes of *Quandary*, and then wrote a Star Trek-inspired "Captain's

Log" narrative about situations encountered. "As a Captain's Log, they must consider their audience, provide context, and think about what information would they need to share," Fallon explained.

Knowledge transfer from play can occur when students extend narrative roles from to the classroom (Barab & Gresalfi, 2011; Barab, Heiselt, Hickey, Sadler, & Zuiker, 2007). "A game gives you a safe place to do that because of the fictional layer—but the real-world implications are still very clear," Fallon said. The Captain's Log extended role-play from the game world to the real world. Fallon's reflection prompts included:

- What evidence persuaded you?
- Why did you choose it?
- Why was it particularly useful?
- Why did you make your decisions?
- Was it a populist thing?
- Were you going for what you thought was right?
- Why did you think it was right?

Narrativizing game events became an effective way for Fallon to get a reflection assessment from students. "As a game player, and a teacher, I came up with the Captain's Log assessment. It gave a nice structure, is flexible, and it's fun to experiment with role-playing."

Quandary gives players immediate feedback, thus enabling students to see the consequences of actions in a direct and concrete way. "The most powerful part of the game is this idea that you get to make these choices. "You think you're solving a problem perfectly, and a lot of times the outcome is not what you thought at all—it's a lot messier than you thought."

Unobtrusive Assessments

Zack Gilbert often presents assignments as open-ended problems or questions. He may pose the following prompt: Create an authentic Egyptian village in *Minecraft* during the ancient river time period. Then, as students build, he assesses their progress. "I have to have open-endedness," Gilbert said.

Rather than tell students what their projects are missing, he asks questions. "In a school with very high-level kids, some of them freak when given open-ended questions. They want very clear black-and-white memorization and regurgitation." But Gilbert wants students to figure out answers on their own. He continued:

> They will build a village, and then announce to me that they are done. I then say, "You're all dead." Then I give a hint, like, "food." Then they'll plant crops, but forget to irrigate. So, I'll say, "You figure it out." I also ask them to show me a picture from one of the books in the class.

Students demonstrate knowledge as Gilbert circulates through his classroom. If one group builds a market to sell resources in their virtual world, he may inquire why they chose that particular location. Questions are later aligned to lesson goals.

The curriculum expert at Gilbert's school is supportive of this approach. "She loves the unobtrusive assessment," he said. "As students build in *Minecraft*, I ask what they are doing, and then I jot it down. Like a game, I automatically assess you as you go along."

Gilbert's assessments are modified to the meet the Illinois State Standards, as well as the College, Career, and Civic Life (C3) Framework for Social Studies State Standards, from the National Council of the Social Studies. "I break it down into culture, civics, people, and geography," he said. Gilbert explained:

> Culture is science, math, natural wonders, art, literature, leisure, and religions. Civics is government, theocracies, economics, labor, terrain, resource, and climate. And then you've got the different types of people that are brought into the game—whether it is a great engineer or merchant. I broke all of that down, and then thought about the big events that happen in the game. The kids then take the information and categorize it.

In the past, Gilbert found himself "handholding" students new to playing *Civilization IV*. Nowadays he is less hands-on, trusting in the affordances of the game's designed system. "I do watch so they don't get too frustrated. I put them through the tutorial. But most kids go right into it [playing the campaign]. I want them to solve the problems."

In *Civilization IV*, students track what they've done. "Then I see what the kids come up with and ask, 'Why did you build your civilization here? What resources benefited you in this area? Now break it down into geography or civic categories.'"

Because games are unpredictable, this type of assessment strategy is difficult to plan for in advance. Gilbert must anticipate questions to ask. "With pretty complex games, you need a teacher who knows the game inside and out," he said. "You can't just throw it in there." This echoes Squire's (2011) notion that game-based learning teachers must "know thy game" (p. 138).

"My experience using a game over and over in time is that I create more assessments," Gilbert concluded. "And the assessments change every single time I use the game. Questions have to be open-ended. I want them to think, and work it through."

Games and Dispositional Behaviors

Approximately half of all middle school social studies students nationwide use iCivics, and about 100,000 teachers are registered as site users (Burak & Parker, 2017). Curious about games, assessments, and dispositional behaviors, I spoke with iCivics' director of content, Carrie Ray-Hill, in March 2017. iCivics' offices are in Boston, Massachusetts; however, Ray-Hill works from Filament Games' office in Madison, Wisconsin. Filament designs the games on iCivics' website; Ray-Hill oversees the educational alignment, as well as the accompanying lesson plan materials.

In 2014, iCivics' *Argument Wars* was added to GlassLab's learning analytics platform. Accessing the game on the GlassLab portal—rather than directly from iCivics—enabled teachers to access a dashboard. While there, teachers could track student mastery of the game's balanced core mechanics. But games created for iCivics by Filament are intended to be an experience; the motivation behind design was not the assessments teachers could get from its games.

Two years ago, iCivics added discussion questions to their game materials. "We've experimented with data-driven assessments that were supposed to make life easier," Ray-Hill began. "There are some that think that's the answer—but it actually overemphasizes the use of data. You can't test a kid on their game ability plus their knowledge sets."

Discussion questions come before an iCivics game is played, as well as during, and after. The iCivics team nicknamed this the "iCivics Game Sandwich," which begins with a starter activity and a mini-lesson, then game play, and finally it is all punctuated with post-game activities and assessment questions. Ray-Hill continued, "Questions might be: What was hard about the game? This helps boil down specific learning objectives. It lets the kids look at the game as an entity, from a structure or systems perspective." If students like playing the law firm game *Do I Have a Right?*, they may then create their own cases outside of the game experience. "They can mock it, and play it out. Recreating the game in real-life is an opportunity for open-ended assessments. Students can create their own cases in the classroom about constitutional law, and see where that goes."

But does playing an iCivics game help turn students into participants of American democracy? "I think that's the magic thing we're all reaching for," Ray-Hill replied. In a class period, it is difficult to gauge whether one's tendency to be more active in civic like has changed. "For us, at iCivics, we struggle with that. We can identify knowledge, and where that lives in a game. We can identify skills, and practice skill building."

Playing a game can be more than mastering its system; it can change one's way of thinking, giving them a propensity to take future actions. Dispositions pertain to whether someone may have the tendency to apply what was once learned. Games can possibly alter people's civic dispositions for the better. Benjamin Stokes spoke to me in December 2016 about the potential of using games to positively affect behavior. "Disposition is not that you technically know how to do something, and then you test that skill," he began. "But do you have the tendency to actually enact it?"

When Sheehy's students were observed playing iCivics' *Win the White House*, the purpose wasn't for them to simply become knowledgeable of the election process. Students should leave the experience civically engaged—they should want to participate in American democracy. "It's not like we need to train more people how to vote," Stokes continued. "That skill [pushing a button or pulling a lever] isn't too hard to master."

After playing a civics game, Stokes recommended that teachers ask students why someone would take action in a participatory democracy? Do the students now have a tendency—or disposition—to vote?

In a textbook, an assessment question might ask what chapter students should refer back to. One of the more interesting things about assessments with games is that they tend to look at peoples' actions when there is a wide set of actions. Then choice patterns can be analyzed. "It's what makes games different from textbooks," Stokes said. "There might be some interactive readers that look for choices that people are making, but, for the most part, there isn't much of a landscape for choice in a fixed text."

With games—especially the open-ended complex games in The Tribe's classrooms—students approached choice with a sense of agency. "Those are the things I find most exciting with games. And those are the things that contrast most strongly with traditional assessments."

Of course teachers can ask students outright about changes in dispositional behaviors. They don't have to sit and wait to see if students become more civically engaged. "After a field trip, a museum [manager] might ask the staff, 'Did the student come back on their own time?'" Stokes said. "We don't assess those kinds of questions enough. But those are much more important questions than asking whether somebody memorized a whole bunch of history. If they no longer visit museums, or stop reading the moment they graduate, we haven't really succeeded as educators."

In the long term, dispositions are difficult to assess (Borko, Liston, & Whitcomb, 2007). A multi-year longitudinal study could cost millions of dollars. Yet, the cost shouldn't negate the value of using games to positively affect student outlooks. "Dispositions were unpopular in education and assessment circles 10 years ago, but it's having a little resurgence," Stokes noted.

So how would a teacher know that playing an election-themed game increased a student's tendency to become more civically engaged? Ray-Hill offered up some ideas. She said:

> As a teacher, educator and game person, I look at dispositions as: skills plus knowledge plus relevance and opportunity. You can bring kids to great gaming scenarios to get good skills. But if it's not relevant to them, it doesn't stick. And if it does stick, and they don't have an opportunity to practice, then I believe those dispositions will be lost. If you have a great civics education, but no access to exercising dispositional feelings about the public's role in government, then nothing will happen. So, we work hard to push the skills, the knowledge, and the relevant practice in the games. By playing over and over again, and playing different games, kids might start to think that they do have a voice.

Chapter Summary

The Tribe skews toward open-ended games over content delivery games. By virtue of aligning core mechanics and learning outcomes, mastery of a level in a balanced game could indicate mastery of a learning goal. Then teachers design assessments similar to those used for measuring understanding in open-ended assignments, such as student work turned in for project-based learning assignments.

References

"All Is On." (2017, January 27). *Best fox hunter: Reflection of the game design experience*. Retrieved from http://allison555.blogspot.com/2017/01/best-fox-hunter.html

Archer, J., Kerr, K. A., & Pianta, R. C. (2014). Why measure effective teaching? In T. J. Kane, K. A. Kerr, & R. C. Pianta (Eds.), *Designing teacher evaluation systems: New guidance from the measures of effective teaching project* (pp. 1–6). San Francisco, CA: Jossey-Bass.

Barab, S., & Gresalfi, M. (2011). Learning for a reason: Supporting forms of engagement by designing tasks and orchestrating environments. *Theory into Practice, 50*(4), 300–310. doi:10.1080/00405841.2011.607391

Barab, S. A., Gresalfi, M., & Ingram-Goble, A. (2010). Transformational play: Using games to position person, content, and context. *Educational Researcher, 39*(7), 525–536. doi:10.3102/0013189X10386593

Barab, S. A., Heiselt, C., Hickey, D., Sadler, T., & Zuiker, S. (2007). Relating narrative, inquiry, and inscriptions: A framework for socio-scientific inquiry. *Journal of Science Education and Technology, 16*, 59–82.

Braun, H. (2005). *Using student progress to evaluate teachers: A primer on value-added models.* Retrieved from http://www.ets.org/Media/Research/pdf/PICV AM.pdf

Borko, H., Liston, D., & Whitcomb, J. (2007). Apples and fishes—The debate over dispositions in teacher education. *Journal of Teacher Education, 58*(5), 359–364.

Burak, A., & Parker, L. (2017). *Power play: How video games can save the world.* New York, NY: St. Martin's Press.

Campbell, J. (2008). *The hero with a thousand faces* (3rd ed.). Novato, CA: New World Library (Original work published 1949).

Carter, P. L., Ladson-Billings, G., & Welner, K. G. (2013). *Closing the opportunity gap: What America must do to give every child an even chance.* Oxford: Oxford University Press.

Common Core Homepage. (2017). Retrieved from http://www.corestandards.org

Danielson, C. (2007). *Enhancing professional practice: A framework for teaching* (2nd ed.). Alexandria, VA: ASCD.

Darling-Hammond, L. (2013). *Getting teacher evaluation right: What really matters for effectiveness and improvement.* New York, NY: Teachers College Press.

Darvasi, P. (2014, May 18). *Gone Home lesson 4: Bursting the fantasy classroom bubble with real world reviews.* Retrieved from http://www.ludiclearning.org/2014/05/18/gone-home-lesson-4-bursting-the-fantasy-classroom-bubble-with-real-world-reviews/

Gee, J. P. (2007). *What video games have to teach us about learning and literacy* (rev. ed.). New York, NY: Palgrave Macmillan.

Glazerman, S., Goldhaber, D., Loeb, S., Staiger, D., Raudenbush, S., & Whitehurst, G. (2010, December 15). *Value-added: It's not perfect, but it makes sense.* Retrieved from Education Week website: http://www.edweek.org/ew/articles/2010/12/15/15whitehurst.h30.html

Greene, M. (1995). *Releasing the imagination: Essays on education, the arts, and social change.* San Francisco, CA: Jossey-Bass.

Kalir, J. (2016). Good game: On the limitations of puzzles and possibilities for gameful learning. In C. Williams (Ed.), *Teacher Pioneers: Visions from the edge of the map, Conclusion.* Pittsburgh, PA: ETC Press.

Kurz, A. (2011). Access to what should be taught and will be tested: Students' opportunity to learn the intended curriculum. In S. N. Elliott, R. J. Kettler, P. A. Beddow, & A. Kurz (Eds.), *Handbook of accessible achievement tests for all students: Bridging the gaps between research, practice and policy* (pp. 99–129). New York, NY: Springer.

Mortari, L. (2015). Reflectivity in research practice: An overview of different perspectives. *International Journal of Qualitative Methods, 14*(5), 1–9. doi:10.1177/1609406915618045

Polikoff, M. S., & Porter, A. C. (2014). Instructional alignment as a measure of teaching quality. *Educational Evaluation and Policy Analysis, 36*(4), 399–416.

Schön, D. A. (1983). *The reflective practitioner.* London: Temple Smith.

Shaffer, D. W. (2006). Epistemic frames for epistemic games. *Computers and Education, 46*(3), 223–234.

Shaffer, D. W. (2012). Models of situated action: Computer games and the problem of transfer. In C. Steinkuehler, K. Squire, & S. Barab (Eds.), *Games learning society: Learning in the digital age* (pp. 403–431). Cambridge, MA: Cambridge University Press.

Sheehy, P. (2011, September 7). *The hero's footprint (quest chain).* Retrieved from http://portal.3dgamelab.org/quests/1500?armory=true

Squire, K. (2011). *Video games and learning: Teaching and participatory culture in the digital age.* New York, NY: Teachers College Press.

Sutton-Smith, B. (1997). *The ambiguity of play.* Cambridge, MA: Harvard University Press.

Takeuchi, L. M., & Vaala, S. (2014). *Level up learning: A national survey on teaching with digital games.* New York, NY: The Joan Ganz Cooney Center at Sesame Workshop.

Williams-Pierce, C. (Ed.). (2016). *Teacher Pioneers: Visions from the edge of the map.* Pittsburgh, PA: ETC Press.

· 13 ·
THE ROLE OF THE GAME-BASED TEACHER

No one I interviewed in The Tribe used games just for the sake of using games; instead, they designed experiences for students within their bell schedules. Many of those experiences happened to include students playing immersive games. After students played games, the teachers freely shared their best practices, lessons, and ideas with others. Darvasi provided procedural step-by-step instructions on his blog about the *Gone Home* unit. Sheehy had an open door policy for anyone to visit her classroom. Many others shared out student work on Twitter.

Members of The Tribe "see the learning through the eyes of the students" (Hattie, 2012, p. 111). They were excellent at both teaching and lesson design, adapting resources at hand to meet the goals of each learner (Hattie, 2012). Educational researcher John Hattie described how "excellent" teachers understand the influence they have in guiding young minds. Hattie wrote:

> Teachers need to be aware of what each and every student in their class is thinking and what they know, be able to construct meaning and meaningful experiences in light of this knowledge of the students, and have proficient knowledge and understanding of their subject content so that they can provide meaningful and appropriate feedback such that each student moves progressively through the curriculum levels. (2012, pp. 18–19)

Meenoo Rami, manager of the *Minecraft* teacher community at Microsoft, spoke to me about teaching with games. "Teachers who are nimble, and can think on their feet—and have a few years under their belt—are looking for any and all opportunities to make connections for learning," she said. "It's the teachers that bring the meaningful experiences and depth to lessons. And they have faith in their students. Give students an opportunity to shine, and you will be surprised."

Members of The Tribe were more than facilitators of learning, and they did more than give fun games to students to play. These teachers also met the needs of students by iterating their teaching even as lessons unfolded. These teachers were adept at grasping where smaller lessons fit into the scheme of their overarching goals. And after playing, connections to content were facilitated in whole class discussions.

"Part of being a designer is knowing the constraints and affordances of your environment, and designing within there," Caro Williams-Pierce said. "Expert teachers intimately know the constraints and affordances of their physical context, and they know their students. Therefore, they can design these incredible experiences."

This chapter opens with a discussion of how teachers in The Tribe serve as game-masters, leading students to playful experiences, and how these teachers are experts at learning design.

The Teacher as Game-Master

In the classic tabletop role-playing game *Dungeons & Dragons*, a game-master—or *dungeon master*—navigates player actions. "The teacher as game-master is one of my favorite ways of describing it [game-based learning]," Lucas Gillispie said, in December 2016. "If you get an opportunity, play or watch a *Dungeons & Dragons* scenario." He continued:

> The dungeon master is orchestrating things, creating experiences and situations, and always has the end goal in mind. That person will always try their best to keep their players safe. They are ultimately a storyteller, and kind of playing the other side of the experience. It's a great analogy of what a classroom could be.

Teachers in The Tribe often took on the role of game-master, applying intuition to guide students to learning goals. Like a dungeon master rolling a 20-sided die to decide a hero's fate, Gillispie recommended that other teachers could incorporate chance into lessons—"so it's not so formulaic." He continued,

"Master teachers know which way they want their kids to go. They know what the end goals are. But they must do so without explicitly telling students up front what they are—or even what the path from A to B will look like."

As game-masters, teachers in The Tribe "shared" the role "of a more knowledgeable other with his students and his peers" (Huguet as cited in Sheldon, 2012, p. 127). It was as if they were leading students through challenges, and only they, as teachers, saw the map. Rather than stating to students exactly where to go, teachers-as-game-masters gave students agency to decide.

John Fallon echoed Gillispie's notion of the role of game-based teachers. "A metaphor I've gone back to is that I feel like a dungeon master," he said, in December 2016. "I'm running this game experience with my students. For me, that role is an entertaining and exciting one in a direct game-like sense."

Fallon designs alternate reality games (ARGs) for students, which are played both digitally and in the real world. ARGs have an explicit connection to the teacher as game-master. Based on Homer's *Odyssey*, *Finding the Journal of Odysseus* is an example of an ARG Fallon designed and runs each year. He explained the process:

> I am setting up this narrative experience I have mostly planned out from beginning to end. There are levers—like if this happens, then that will happen. But it is all from behind this metaphorical screen where I know what is going to happen. The students also know something is going to happen—but, they don't know what it is. I help them traverse this narrative experience. It is similar to dungeon master, with a lot of improvisation. I don't know exactly how students are going to interact with it. I don't know if they can solve all of the problems they get. As much as I plan, I have to be on my toes, to react to the experience, all through the lens of making this the most engaging experience the way a good dungeon master tells an engrossing through the mechanics of an RPG [role-playing game].

David Williamson Shaffer also spoke about the teacher-as-game-master model. "I think that—absent of really good artificial intelligence—any good role-playing game needs a good game-master," he said. "Somebody has to manage all of the assets of the game, and coordinate them to the responses that the game system is giving—whether it is what is happening in *Minecraft* or what the teacher says in class."

Teachers in game-based classrooms mediate students as they solve problems, and guide them to reflect on experiences afterwards. As game-masters, teachers have to make sure they say the appropriate things at the appropriate times. "The system [of a classroom] has to have feedback that is appropriately targeted to their level and that is assessing complex work," Shaffer continued.

"When you start getting into complex problems and reflections, and there's not just one solution, then someone has to be able to do the mentoring. Essentially, this is what the game-master is doing."

Flash Lessons and Teaching on the Fly

Many in The Tribe anticipated a "chaotic" rollout when introducing games to their their students (Squire, 2011, p. 113). After all, students need time to learn the interface. "After the first initial dozen quests or so, kids have agency," Peggy Sheehy said, late in 2015. "They have the ability to choose their own direction. So very rarely are they all doing the same thing—almost never."

Sheehy iterated during instruction, and she was observed to be "influential, caring, and actively and passionately engaged in the process of teaching and learning" (Hattie, 2012, p. 19). Her teaching consisted of several mini-lessons—what Sheehy called "flash lessons." Like a video game, her instruction pivoted to enable her to give "explicit information both on demand and just in time" (Gee, 2007, p. 226). If a student had a question, she adeptly seized the teachable moment, in time for students to apply what they just learned.

Sheehy said:

> I'd love to say that I have it down to a perfect science, but I don't. I'm learning and I'm adjusting from day-to-day, from year-to-year. I have to give it a good deal of time because I'm dealing with unique and wonderful little creatures. They're going to respond one way on one day and one way on another day.

Isaacs similarly referred to his iterated lessons as evolving. Regarding the 20% Time projects, Isaacs added more structure to the assignment. "This year it's very clear that it's every Tuesday. That has helped a lot with the structure of it." Part of the structure was setting up mini-deadlines for students, as well as the establishment of a routine. "In middle school, students can have a hard time with long-term projects and can get totally lost." He continued:

> What I do now is take two days to devote some time to what I consider the workflow for quests. I make sure they understand that they have to submit their game, make sure they know where to find the next quest, the link to the game, what to evaluate, where to do their evaluations, and what happens after that. It's a matter of taking students where they need to be, to focus them a bit.

Other members of The Tribe also about how they iterated lessons in class, on the fly. Iteration takes place after student feedback, which involves "formal elements of structured and routine assessment, such as exams and parent-teacher conferences, response to students' comments or questions, and classroom punishments or rewards, but it also includes informal mechanisms, such as body language and casual conversations with students" (Shaffer, Nash, & Ruis, 2015, p. 4). Much of that was a reflection-in-action, while teachers in The Tribe delivered lessons (Schön, 1983).

Mark Grundel spoke to me in early 2017 about how game-based learning requires teachers to be flexible. "A lot of games are not going to have a behind-the-scenes dashboard that's going to pop up and give you [formative assessment] numbers," he said. "Teachers need to be active participants. They need to have conversations with kids, and to make formative assessments and observations as they move around. If a teacher goes off schedule, that's okay, too." Another point Grundel emphasized was the importance of having whole class and small group debrief sessions after game experiences, with time allotted for reflection.

Grundel shared an anecdote about an assignment in which his 5th grade class wrote personal narratives. Some students used Twine, an interactive fiction authoring tool, while others created animated slideshows. One student decided to try the computer version of *Minecraft*. Up until that point, he had only played the Pocket Edition [the mobile version], "which had comparative limitations." In Pocket Edition, players couldn't summon EnderDragons, which are flying, fire-breathing dragons. While on a PC, a more experienced *Minecraft* student showed that student how to summon EnderDragon to his world. Soon enough—just two days before the project was due—his buildings were smoldering in digital flames.

"He had no clue because he only played Pocket Edition," Grundel said. "Half of his project got destroyed. There is no undo, and we didn't do daily backups of his map. The other student didn't intend for that to happen. We talked about the experience—and this goes back to being flexible. The student still learned something, and it was valuable in the end."

Due to necessity, Tobias Staaby teaches on the fly. When using the video game *Rome II: Total War*, the narrative can change based on player decisions. He shared with me how it looks in practice. Staaby said:

> We start at a campaign where you play as Octavian. It's right after when they attacked the people who killed Julius Caesar. It shows them [students] just how fragile a triple alliance based on military power is. We played the game for 40 minutes, and then Pompeii and Sicily attacked Lepidus. Then I asked the class, what should we do? Are we going to go into war on this side, or are we going to back out. They may or may not say that we should back out because wars are expensive.

Because of the nature of the game, Staaby's lessons are unpredictable. He often has no idea where the game is going, and what may happen next. "The A.I. [artificial intelligence] in the game is making new decisions every time we play a campaign."

To prepare himself for a variety of outcomes, Staaby has played through *Rome II: Total War* several times, and he has discovered that the same turning points happen in the game as in the actual historical events. He continued:

> I think the game designers added in the key events. We [the class] wound up with people from Pompeii being at war with Lepidus because the back door was left open when Syracuse was invaded. This turned out to be really difficult because Syracuse had big walls, as many of the cities in the game have. We [the class] then talk about the importance of city walls, and how difficult it was to invade cities when you don't have a battering ram and you don't have ladders. We had to use flaming arrows to burn the gates down—which took forever! Then a girl in class said, "This is just like *Game of Thrones!*" The animation was her frame of reference for this medieval kind of battle, on horses with spears. And then a little more than half of the girls moved their chairs to the screen so they could see better.

In Staaby's classroom, one student plays on a PlayStation 4 game controller, while he guides conversations. He poses questions like, "The people are unhappy, should we lower taxes? Do we need the money for war? Give them circus and bread! It is dynamic—I kind of have my hands off of the wheel for a while. The game makes its own decision, so I have to do much of things on the fly. And that is how I am most comfortable."

The Game Explosion

C. Ross Flatt, manager of programs at the Institute of Play, codeveloped the game *Galactic Mappers* while teaching at Quest to Learn. It has affordances and constraints that charge the teacher with being a game-master. The goal is for students to work together to create a map of an alien planet. To play, teams first draw Land cards, like peninsulas and islands. Students then cut out paper in shapes and glue it draw them on a large blank map. Next students pick Feature cards. Depending on what they select, they may have to draw rivers and mountains on their map. During play, the teacher reviews the maps, and may award more Land and Feature cards (there are Bonus cards too, which award extra points for features like having an archipelago).

"When I rolled out *Galactic Mappers*, it was an exploded experience," Flatt said, late in 2016. Exploding games can mean a variety of approaches, from modding (changing) a game to ramping up the challenges to adding more game levels (O'Keefe, 2012). "The game explosion is what you're doing before during and after game play."

Before his class played, Flatt would have students complete a "Landform Encyclopedia"—they conducted research, wrote synopses, and created illustrations about physical geographic features. Then students completed a "standard, traditional geography activity"—filling in a map of the world with the continents and oceans. The goal was for students to use parts of maps, like a scale and a compass rose. Finally, the night before actually playing the game, he had students read the rules of play. The purpose was to prepare everyone to enter the classroom already familiar with the how to play.

Galactic Mappers is embedded with formative assessments. As the game-master, Flatt asks a series of open-ended questions to his students. The reflection responses often include the importance of the students' experiential learning. "Some would say, 'Now I really get why a map title and compass rose is really important!'" Flatt continued:

> We play the game over a 2 hour period. During play, I ask them questions and I am assessing. They know that I am taking notes. After the game we have a class debrief and discussion, and they have a reflection they have to do at the end. I also have them do a reflection before they play as their ticket to play. They have to talk about landforms and complete some writing. I then measure with the pre- and post-assessment reflection whether *Galactic Mappers* is teaching them anything.

The game explosion includes opportunities for student reflection. Flatt's summative assessment—a test of the geography unit—included open-ended written responses. These reflections asked students to highlight examples about the physical geography they experienced from play.

The Husøy/Staaby Pendulum

In 2015 Aleksander Husøy and Tobias Staaby—who teach together—began to reflect on how they design lessons that include games. The result is a model: "The Husøy/Staaby Pendulum" (see Figure 13.1). Because they continually go back and forth between game play and reflective discussions, they designed it as a pendulum. It starts with the content of the lesson, and includes what they want their students understand. In between, they plan for student discussions and reflections. Husøy explained it to me in December 2016:

> The preconception of most teachers outside The Tribe is the idea that games are somehow "learn-y." Plop the kids in front of these fantastic games and there will be these learning situations. They [students] will grow and develop all kinds of skills.

But, as a teacher, that whole thought doesn't appeal to me at all. If that was what we were using games for, then the teacher isn't necessary. Then why not just have students play fantastic games together in a room without the teacher?

As discussed in Chapter 11, Husøy teaches with the serious game *This War of Mine*. Using it as a concrete example, he walked me through a lesson using the Pendulum model. In *This War of Mine*, players are dropped into war-torn Europe during in the 1990s. The city is in rubbles, and players are left with limited resources. Given this constraint, the game's system illustrates human behavior in particular circumstances. Husøy continued:

> What happens to our societal norms when society breaks down? Why are most people, most of the time, law-abiding? Then we start all the way on the left or right [of the pendulum]. The signifier in the game world [on the far left side of the pendulum] gives students an experience that illustrates the subject matter. Or, I might want start on the right, with a signifier in the real world—to start with a real world experience. I might leave a $20 bill in the classroom, and observe what happens when somebody finds it. That would be an experiment to shed some light on how ethics and morals are when we are not being watched. What are the consequences of our actions? Do we do the right thing, or are we all basically selfish?

Through the dialogical processes, a teacher would facilitate a classroom discussion about the experience. It could be the social experiment of leaving $20 in a room, or from the experience playing *This War of Mine*. "Students move from what the game signifies to the core concepts," he continued. "We draw the parallels from student experiences within the game world to other materials related to the subject in the course. This could be the textbook or cited articles that explain the same concept experienced in the game world."

Husøy and Staaby keep their Pendulum model in mind when they vet games to bring to students. "We look for games that are designed for constructive conversations during and after you play the game," Husøy explained. "Students generally get a better, deeper, more empathetic and closer relation with the subject material when they are able to interact with material—like with a digital game. The most crucial part is when we discuss and debate what it is we experienced in a classroom."

Husøy next shared a scenario from the game *Democracy 3*. In it, players govern and make policy decisions. Husøy uses the game as an experiential approach to teaching about government policies. In simplistic terms, the game provides a visualization of the effects of policy decisions, as well the

The Husøy/Staaby Pendulum

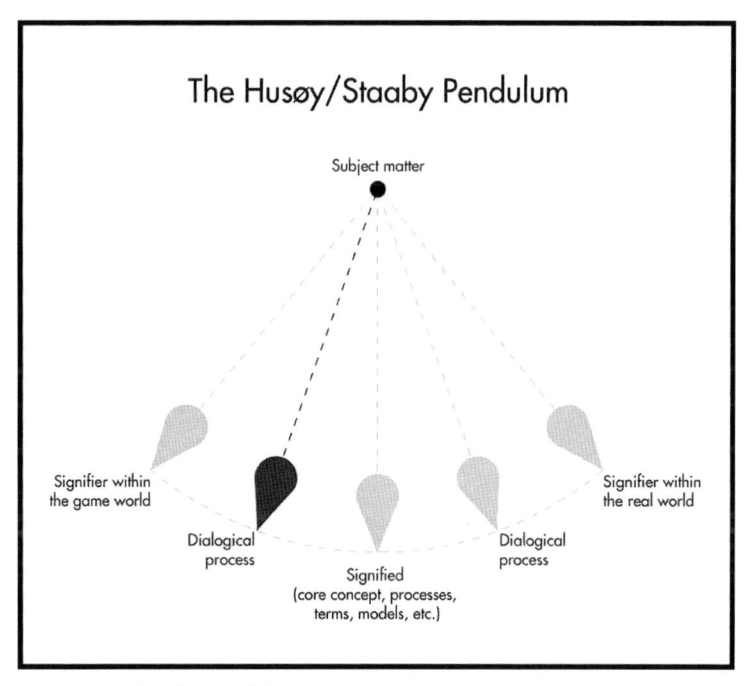

Diagram: A pendulum diagram. At top: "Subject matter". At bottom center: "Signified (core concept, processes, terms, models, etc.)". Left pendulum position: "Signifier within the game world". Right pendulum position: "Signifier within the real world". Between them on both sides: "Dialogical process".

Figure 13.1. The Husøy/Staaby Pendulum.

unintended consequences. The ultimate goal is to improve the country, which would lead to reelection.

Let's say there was alcohol abuse problem in the game's fictional country. The student takes on the role of a policy maker who might decide to reduce the prevalence of alcohol abuse. "One of the ways to do that could be to increase the alcohol tax," Husøy said. "Should you, in the game, make that choice, you will see it visualized: alcohol consumption and alcoholism indeed go down. But, at the same time, the policy may be hugely unpopular among great masses of the electorate."

The dialogic phase of The Husøy/Staaby Pendulum begins as students discover the difficulties of policymaking: there are always winners and losers. Through these discussions around and about the game, students gain a deeper and meaningful understanding of learning goals (Gee, 2007). Husøy may then ask students to predict if a policymaker passed a carbon tax? "You have a huge problem with pollution in your cities. To decrease pollution, you have a carbon tax, but then that results in other effects, consequences both intended and unintended."

Teachers as Learning Designers

When C. Ross Flatt started his teaching career, he observed how other teachers became hesitant to share their lesson plans. "They've made this baby, and it's theirs," he said. "But a designer works in a community that is incredibly open and transparent and wants people to use—for lack of a better word—their product so they can see how it's used."

Flatt defines a learning designer as someone who works collaboratively with other people. "I didn't start thinking of myself as a designer until I started at Quest to Learn [the New York City-based public school founded by the Institute of Play]. It's hard to be a designer when you're just designing on your own. Teaching often times is a lonely and guarded profession."

A learning designer should be open to feedback from collaborators on a regular basis, and they should be receptive to student feedback—particularly on how learning experiences went. They should then use that data to iterate on those experiences. Of course many teachers do this; however, a learning designer always keeps the larger goal in mind. Flatt continued:

> I think it helps when you think about the specific outcomes you want for your students, to think about the steps it takes to get there, and to think about what you, as a teacher, might have to redo along the way. A teacher is often times going to present something for the first time, and students need to learn it so they can move onto something else. A teacher teaches something in a particular way without thinking of the experience. That's because teachers are trying to meet district benchmarks, or tests students have to take, or they don't have time.

Remi Kalir spoke with me about how teachers need agency to become learning designers. "Meaningful experiences—not lesson planning—gets to the heart of the teacher as a designer," he said. Teachers need a feeling of empowerment before they can design student experiences. The act of teaching should not be a series of boxes in a lesson-plan book to tick off. "A sense of [teacher] agency is sometimes missing—even when teachers are adopting game-based learning methods. Lesson planning does not encourage teachers to have a sense of agency. It actually reifies in so many senses the worst of schooling."

So, how does a teacher bring in play within the boundaries of school? Kalir suggested playing within the constraints of classrooms. After all, schools are designed environments. Everything—from the seating arrangement to the bell schedule—is a constraint. "And that is playfulness—you don't have to do that just with games," he advised. "Think playfully to push against the constraints of the classroom—the material architecture." While bells are not as malleable, "there are opportunities that extend beyond the school day because they are online, or into the community, or engage students' culture and history in a unique way that allows them to continue the learning outside of 45 minutes in the classroom."

In his conclusion to Williams-Pierce's (2016) book, *Teacher Pioneers: Visions from the Edge of the Map*, Kalir referred to a "textbookification" of game-based learning, "which is most of what I see, and still see." He wrote, "Games are an unlikely panacea for the shortcomings of either pedagogy or student learning; textbooklike proliferation only further cements the status of certain games as silver bullets" (Kalir, 2016, p. 366). Kalir continued:

> I come back to this metaphor of improvisation. One of the core tensions of high-end game-based learning teachers is that they know the relationships and affordances of tools, typical student responses, and the potential pathways that will play out in a certain scenario. We know from history of jazz that people can only improvise if they are experts. A real tension is how to support this for more novice educators, or for teachers who are veteran and have lots of experience, but are not in the types of schools or instructional environments where they're allowed to experiment and fail free from repercussion.

Kalir's analogy of jazz improvisation echoes Haskell's (Chapter 10) notion of contextual transposition, which similarly referenced how expert teachers rearrange game contexts like music compositions. "This statement of what we call teaching is irrelevant when you see practice being more playful, or—perhaps—more gameful," Kalir concluded. "Teachers should design meaningful experiences in a way that give playful constraints for students."

Chapter Summary

Members of The Tribe are expert learning designers, as well as skilled practitioners. They do not simply write—or execute—traditional lesson plans. Often, learning is personalized, and each student meets different goals than others. Games are not used for competition in all cases; rather, lessons were carefully designed with the students' experience in mind. These playful practices put learners in the zone of proximal development, in which needing to learn content and skills followed.

References

Gee, J. P. (2007). *What video games have to teach us about learning and literacy* (rev. ed.). New York, NY: Palgrave Macmillan.

Hattie, J. (2012). *Visible learning for teachers: Maximizing impact on learning*. London: Routledge.

Kalir, J. (2016). Good game: On the limitations of puzzles and possibilities for gameful learning. In C. Williams (Ed.), *Teacher Pioneers: Visions from the edge of the map, Conclusion*. Pittsburgh, PA: ETC Press.

O'Keeke, D. (2012, December 4). *Collaborate, prototype, playtest, explode! How we design game-like learning at quest*. Retrieved from http://www.instituteofplay.org/2012/12/collaborate-prototype-playtest-explode-how-we-design-game-like-learning-at-quest/

Schön, D. A. (1983). *The reflective practitioner*. London: Temple Smith.

Shaffer, D. W., Nash, P., & Ruis, A. R. (2015). Technology and the new professionalization of teaching. *Teachers College Record, 117*(12), 1–30.

Sheldon, L. (2012). *The multiplayer classroom: Designing coursework as a game*. Boston, MA: Course Technology/Cengage Learning.

Squire, K. (2011). *Video games and learning: Teaching and participatory culture in the digital age*. New York, NY: Teachers College Press.

Williams-Pierce, C. (Ed.). (2016). *Teacher pioneers: Visions from the edge of the map*. Pittsburgh, PA: ETC Press.

CONCLUSION

The purpose of this book was to understand how expert teachers in a game-based learning affinity group used games in the system of their classrooms. These teachers applied Vygotskian and Montessorian approaches, which put students in engaging and playful experiences led by discovery and exploration of content. The goal of using games was often to create meaningful experiences for students, followed by teacher facilitation to connect to the curriculum. Members in The Tribe, as a community of practice, were adroit at designing lessons and assessments. It is entirely likely that the participants would be excellent educators even without games.

The teachers in this book did not teach in isolation. They were passion-driven leaders and practitioners. The Tribe is the unofficial nickname for this affinity group, which is also a community of practice of game-based learning educators. These teachers viewed themselves as changemakers, leading a transformational paradigm shift in modern education. They are vocal leaders in communities of practices. Many have amassed thousands of followers on social media (e.g., Twitter), and are leaders in online game-based learning affinity spaces. Topics discussed in online forums (e.g., design thinking strategies, student choice) were observed being applied to practice. Members of The Tribe shared best practices online, and they also mentored new teachers in professional learning communities.

In the classroom, those in The Tribe led from behind, as servant-leaders. They used games and game design tools rich in playful affordances. Students were colearners with teachers, and often influenced the direction of instruction. Keen attention was paid to student passions and interests.

Lessons Learned

Members of The Tribe were accomplished curriculum designers. They matched their curricular goals and the needs of their students to particular games. They were afforded autonomy to decide what tools to use in their teaching practice. Their students were often participating in personalized environments in which challenges adapted to the learner's ability. This was based on the freedom to explore game worlds, and it served to engage learning. Several of the games used by members of The Tribe were open-ended sandboxes. The trial-and-error of game play, as well as the iterative process extolled from designing games, was effective in encouraging children to learn from failures.

As experts of game-based learning, The Tribe almost never used a game to augment their teaching, or to reinforce a single skill or concept. Games tended to be shared experiences situated as the centerpiece of their classrooms. Related lessons were intended to support learning from a particular game as a designed system. In other words, games were not used support lessons; rather, lessons supported games used as models.

These teachers had a deep understanding of the semiotic grammar of games. They professed their affinity to gamer culture. As a result, they mastered the design grammar and epistemic language of the games their students played. When using games, the teacher-as-game-master model persisted. More than simply selecting or deploying a game for learning, these teachers constantly iterated lessons based on specific student needs. Then they asked students reflection questions regarding in-game decisions, actions, and consequences.

There were commonalities that led me to reflect on lessons learned from these practitioners. I reviewed overall themes to create a list of lessons learned from the expert game-based learning leaders in this book. In no particular order, members of The Tribe:

- *Engaged in game-based learning affinity groups*—The Tribe is a community of practice with social affiliation. They discovered games and best practices together. They also shared student work and their own reflections

on blogs, and on social media platforms. Positive online feedback reduced risk perception in the game of teaching.
- *Played video games and board games*—Teachers played games first, gaining a deep understanding of the mechanics, processes, and semiotic language. Most games observed were commercial, off-the-shelf games—not educational games—that were then tailored to meet curricular objectives. When together, members of The Tribe played games with each other.
- *Had dual leadership styles*—Members of The Tribe were transformational leaders outside the classroom. They mentored and led newcomers to game-based learning, as well as advised game developers, academics, and policymakers. In the classroom, they tended to take on a servant-leadership role, leading students from behind.
- *Used games as the focal point of instruction*—Games were used alongside other more traditional curricular materials (i.e., books, film). Systems were close read like literature, and then analyzed. These experts used some games as the centerpiece for instruction. Games were rarely, if ever, used to teach a single skill.
- *Adapted and appropriated commercial games, as well as games intended for educational purposes*—These experts contextually transposed and repurposed games to fit curricular goals.
- *Taught in a horizontal learning space*—Whether it was *Minecraft* or board games, these teachers played with students. Other times, they took the role of game-master. In both cases, the teacher was as playful as the students.
- *Used games as shared experiences*—Games were like field trips experienced by the class. Teachers used this as an opportunity for experiential learning to help students make meaning of concepts to be learned.
- *Sought games with playful affordances*—Participants selected games that enabled students to have a sense of play. Playful conditions brought students to their zone of proximal development.
- *Valued student interest and passions*—Teaching was not top-down; students' personal interests and affinities were a part of learning in The Tribe's classrooms.
- *Applied self-determination theory*—Considerations were taken to ensure that students had a sense of autonomy, competence, and belongingness. Students had a choice of games to play or authoring tools with which to make games. In cases when the entire class played the same game (e.g.,

Gone Home in Darvasi's class), students had choice to select what the culminating activity or presentation would be.
- *Applied rhetorics of play*—Whether intentional or not, experience and teacher intuition led these educators to include playful learning lenses for students.
- *Created original qualitative assessments*—These teachers were expert in preparing formative and summative assessments on learning outcomes. The Tribe did not assess play; instead, they assessed knowledge transfer. Often, student claims relating to game experiences were backed using empirical evidence from the game. Student reflection-on-action were common, as were journaling and narrativizing game experiences.
- *Included considerations for meaningful role-play in lessons*—Teachers in The Tribe used gameful learning practices, and often engaged students in identity play.
- *Created a culture of iteration over failure*—Fear of failure in games and in game design was not observed. Students were comfortable to test hypotheses. Grades were not based solely on outcome; rather, students were assessed on the process. Applications of Montessorian and Vygotskian learning theories were baked into practice.
- *Designed lessons that put meaningful experiences just ahead of content*—Teachers in this study were experts at designing lessons and adapting resources at hand to meet the goals of each learner. After playing games, teachers facilitated connections to content in whole class discussions. Aside from the game worlds, the lessons were also designed to be meaningful experiences. Student feedback was included in design.

Follow—and Join—The Tribe!

Good game-based learning requires the support of a community of practice. Aside from a list of academic papers and journal articles, many in The Tribe write their own blogs. These resources are where you can find procedural steps to replicating how they teach with games. Also, follow my blog posts, which including my work with Edutopia: https://www.edutopia.org/users/matthew-farber-edd, as well as on my website, http://MatthewFarber.com.

The following list includes links to free resources, lesson plans, Twitter chats to join, and conferences to attend:

- *The Alternate Classroom*, John Fallon's blog about ARGs in the classroom—https://thealternateclassroom.org
- *AWSM*, the blog from the Institute of Play—https://www.instituteofplay.org/blog
- *Doc Haskell*—Chris Haskell's website, blog, and more—https://dochaskell.com
- *EdGamer* blog and podcast from Zack Gilbert—http://edgamer.net
- *Ed Got Game*, BAM Radio show from Matthew Farber and Steve Isaacs—http://www.bamradionetwork.com/game-based-learning
- EXCALIBUR, a new game-based curriculum from Peggy Sheehy—https://peggysheehy.wixsite.com/excalibur
- *Epistemic Games Group*, led by David Williamson Shaffer—http://edgaps.org/gaps
- *Follow the Learning*, from Marianne Malmstrom—http://www.followthelearning.com
- *Gameful Learning Lab*, at the University of Michigan—http://ai.umich.edu/about-ai/gameful-learning-lab/
- *Games4Ed Twitter Chat*, every Thursday at 8:00 p.m. Eastern. Search hashtag: #Games4Ed—https://twitter.com/hashtag/games4ed
- *Games in Education Symposium*—http://gamesineducation.org
- *Games and Learning*, to follow the work of Steve Isaacs—http://gamesandlearning1.blogspot.com
- *Game Design Aspect of the Month*, blog by Sande Chen—http://gamedesignaspect.blogspot.com
- Glen Irvin's *Minecraft*-set Spanish class—https://sites.google.com/view/gamebasedspanish/home
- *Ludic Learning*, the blog—with lesson plans for *Gone Home*, *The Ward Game*, and more, from Paul Darvasi—http://www.ludiclearning.org
- *MinecraftEdu Twitter Chat*, founded by Garrett Zimmer and Mark Grundel, is every Tuesday at 8:00 p.m. Eastern, #MinecraftEdu—https://twitter.com/hashtag/MinecraftEdu
- *Play Educationists* is the blog from Aleksander Husøy and Tobias Staaby—https://spillpedagogene.wordpress.com. It is a terrific resource, written in Norwegian. For the English translation, follow this link in Google Chrome—https://goo.gl/h2DlQm
- *Remi Kalir's* research and blog—http://remikalir.com
- *Teacher Pioneers: Visions from the Edge of the Map*, the (2016) book edited by Caro Williams-Pierce—http://press.etc.cmu.edu/content/teacher-pioneers

- *World of Warcraft in Schools Wiki*, from Lucas Gillispie and Peggy Sheehy. It features blog posts, as well as the *WoWinSchool: A Hero's Journey* curriculum guide—http://wowinschool.pbworks.com
- *Virtual Internships*—http://virtualinterns.org

INDEX

A

A-GAMES study, 53
Academic Business Advisors, 4, 54
Adlard, Charlie, 157
Affinity Group, 7, 9, 12, 24, 29, 39, 56, 121, 221
Affinity Space, v, xiii, 14, 22, 24
Affordance, 12, 33, 47, 52, 111, 113, 118–119, 121, 124, 132, 141, 147, 191, 202–201, 214, 222–223
Agency, vii, 32, 34, 53–54, 111, 122, 139, 132–136, 141–142, 176, 178–179, 194, 204, 212, 218
Ago and Ame (call-and-response), 69, 75
Agra, 159
Alternate reality games (ARGs), 19, 80, 132, 211
Amazon (website), 181
American Revolution, 153–154, 179
American University, 4, 175
Anglican (church), 79, 83
Apples to Apples (card game), 39

Argument Wars (video game), 171, 203
Artificial intelligence (A.I.), 214
Assassin's Creed (video game), 167
Association for Supervision and Curriculum Development (ASCD), 95
The Atlantic (magazine), 200
Attention deficit hyperactive disorder (ADHD), 72
Augmented reality, 122
Autonomy, 32, 34, 36, 132–133, 222–223
Avatars, 10, 43, 64, 115
Aronica, Lou, 13, 24

B

Baggins, Bilbo (fictional character), 148
Balanced design, 46–47, 53, 57, 192, 198, 203, 205
Baldurs' Gate (video game), 139
Barab, Sasha, 42, 56, 57, 58, 117, 124, 130, 142, 191, 201, 206–207
Bartle, Richard, 125, 136, 142

Bartle's Player Type Model, 118
Batman (fictional character), 135, 156–157
Battlestar Galactica (television show), 81
Bellow, Adam, 2, 192
Beowulf (epic poem), 155–156
Bethel University, 3, 36, 137, 161
Bethesda Games, 173
Bill and Melinda Gates Foundation, 44, 55
Bioshock (video game), 85
bitCraft, 98
The Blind Protocol (alternate reality game), 18, 79
Bloom's Taxonomy, 179
Bloomington Boys and Girls Club, 42, 190
Bloxels (video game), 3, 122–123
Blumengarten, Jerry, 21
Bogost, Ian, 28, 121, 125
Boise State University, 3, 16, 21, 165–166
Boss level, 149, 168
BrainPOP, 36, 69, 72, 95
BreakoutEDU, 2, 192
Brevity, 121, 139, 150
Bubbl.us, 141

C

The Cabin in the Woods (short story), 73, 76
Call of Duty (video game), 52
Campbell, Joseph, 67, 77, 162, 174, 199, 206
The Cask of Amontillado (short story), 149
Catcher in the Rye (book), 147
CBC Radio, 1
Chen, Mark, 2, 145–146, 155, 159, 187
Chen, Sande, 120, 162–163, 176, 191, 225
Cheverton, Mark, 181
Choose to Code, 101
Civilization (video game), 30, 64, 72, 141, 148, 152, 160–161, 165, 195, 202
Classcraft, 49, 57, 134
Cleopatra, 39
Cocco, Larry, 55

Code.org, 21, 95, 188
Colonization (video game), 147
College, Career, and Civic Life (C3) Framework for Social Studies State Standards, 202
Collier, Anne, 11, 15
Columbian Exchange, 120
Common Core State Standards, 46, 57, 64, 95, 165, 192, 206
Command blocks, 168–169
Community of Practice, 103, 168, 169
Competence, 132
Competition, 53, 114–115, 136, 177, 219
Computer Science Education Week, 104
Constraints, 9, 35, 52, 119, 121, 128, 132, 210, 214, 218–219
Contextual transposition, 165–167, 173, 223
Core mechanics, 46–47, 128, 152, 155, 157, 161, 165, 172–173, 178, 198, 203, 205
Curcio, Dan, 3, 15–16, 21, 49–50, 136, 167, 179
Corporation for Public Broadcasting, 151
Curriculum, 29, 32, 38, 44, 50, 53, 56, 64, 80, 94–95, 111, 114–115, 122, 124, 134, 140–141, 145–146, 149, 162–156, 167, 178–180, 192–193, 195–196, 200, 202, 206, 209, 222, 226
Cybraryman (see Blumengarten, Jerry)

D

Danielson Framework for Teaching, 193, 206
Dark Age of Camelot (video game), 164
Dark Knight (film), 149, 157
Darvasi, Paul, 1–4, 17, 19–20, 22, 28, 30–31, 34–35, 47, 56, 61–62, 79–94, 111, 115–119, 121, 128, 132–134, 136, 142, 146–150, 159, 162, 172, 192, 194, 197, 200, 209, 224–225
Dawley, Lisa, 140–141
The Death and Life of American Cities (book), 82

INDEX

Dell (computer), 96, 100
Democracy 3 (video game), 216
Design thinking, 50, 148, 221
Destiny (video game), 197
Dewey, John, 41, 57, 175, 190
Digital badges, 38, 49, 140, 194
Digital texts,
   games as, 145
Dikkers, Seann, 3, 27, 36–37, 40, 137–139, 142, 161–162, 166, 174
Disney Infinity (video game), 96–99, 100–102, 104
Dispositional behaviors, 203, 205
Do I Have a Right? (video game), 203
DonorsChoose, 97–99, 102, 105, 110, 116
Drill-and-skill, 53, 179
Dubé, Louise, 127
Dungeons & Dragons (tabletop game), 155, 163, 210
Dungeon master, 211
Durham, Christy, 29, 39, 156–157

E

11 Bit Studios, 178
Ed Games Expo, 55
Edmodo, 49, 101
Educational anarchist, 9, 11–12
Educational technology, 16, 31, 54–56, 122, 145
Edutopia, 135
E. K. Theater, 17
Elder Scrolls V: Skyrim (video game), 167, 173
Electric Funstuff, 153
Electoral College, 153
The Element (book), 13, 24
Empathy, 1, 45, 146, 154, 172
EnderDragons, 213
Entertainment Weekly (magazine), 80
Epistemic frames, 47–48, 58, 207
Epistemic games, 3, 42, 47–48, 58, 181, 184–185, 197, 207, 225
Epistemic Games Group, 3, 48, 184–185, 225

eSports, 171
Ethics, Practice, and Implementation Categorization (EPIC) Framework, 171–172, 174
EverQuest (video game), 164
Experiential learning, 41, 51, 53, 148, 152, 176, 180, 182, 215–216, 224
Extrinsic motivation, 131, 133, 142, 192

F

FableVision, 55
Facebook, 2, 22, 43, 169, 199
Fakebook, 199
Fahrenheit 451 (book), 155
Fallon, John, 3, 19, 31, 81, 149–151, 200–201, 211, 225
Family Quest, 42, 57, 124
Filament Games, 40, 63, 127, 203
Finding the Journal of Odysseus (alternate reality game), 211
1st Playable Productions, 3–4, 14, 16–17
Fishman, Barry, 3, 53, 57, 131–133
Flash lessons, 212
Flatt, C. Ross, 3, 33, 39, 48, 51, 120, 135, 214–215, 218
Floors (video game), 122
Flow channel, 115, 125, 134, 142
Fluxx (card game), 29, 39, 156–159
Forbidden Island (board game), 14
Formative assessments, 84, 137, 158, 194–195, 213, 215, 224
Free play, 84, 116, 119–120
Fullbright Games, 81, 85
Fullerton, Tracy, 46, 57, 135, 142, 152
Future of Education Conference (FETC), 55

G

Galactic Mappers (game), 33, 213, 215
The Game Believes in You (book), 1, 5, 64, 77
Game of Thrones (book, television show), 214

Game-based learning, promises of, 41, 49, 52
GameDesk, 29–30, 168
Game explosion, 214–215
Gameful learning, 12, 13, 127–143, 145, 193, 205, 219–220, 224–225
Game-like learning, 50–51, 57, 82, 107, 137, 139, 141, 190, 211, 220
Game-master, 210–212, 214–215, 222–223
Games4Ed, 3–4, 22–23, 49, 54–56, 108, 225
Games in Education Symposium, 2–4, 11, 14–20, 24, 29–30, 37, 39, 54, 62, 80, 122, 149, 150, 156–157, 163, 181, 225
Games Learning Society (GLS) Conference, 31, 35–36, 65, 128
GameMaker: Studio, 21, 97–99, 101, 103–105, 109–110, 113
Games for Change, 4, 35, 175
Games for Learning Working Group, 35
Gamestar Mechanic (video game), 57, 59, 120
Gamification, 22, 48–49, 56, 58, 95, 116, 131, 143
Gamify Your Classroom: A Field Guide to Game-Based Learning (book), 17, 24
Gandhi, 1, 152, 165
Gaynor, Steve, 81
Gee, James Paul, 14, 22, 24, 29, 40, 47, 50–54, 57, 66, 77, 115–117, 121, 125, 130, 134, 142, 163, 165, 173, 177, 182–183, 187–188, 190–191, 193, 206, 212, 217, 219
Genius hour, 132
Gilbert, Zack, 3, 111, 137, 170, 195, 202–203, 225
Gillispie, Lucas, 3, 14–15, 18, 21, 28, 31–32, 37, 55, 65, 140–141, 163–165, 174, 180, 210–211, 226
GitHub, 101
GlassLab Games, 46, 57, 198, 203
Glazer, Kip, 3, 154–156
Grian (YouTube content creator), 170
Google Docs, 19, 68, 71, 74, 99
Google Sheets, 97, 103

GradeCraft, 131
Greenbriar, Katie (fictional character), 81, 86, 89, 116, 128, 147, 153
Greene, Maxine, 193–194, 206
Growth mindset, 189
Grundel, Mark, 3, 23–24, 45, 136, 187–188, 213, 225
Gone Home (video game), 28, 30–31, 47, 61, 79–85, 91, 93–94, 116–117, 119, 128–129, 134, 142, 146–148, 150–151, 153, 172, 192, 197, 200, 206, 209, 211, 224, 225
Google Expeditions, 176
The Guardian (newspaper), 200
Guilds, 56, 73, 162
Guillotine (card game), 56, 65, 73, 75–76

H

HTC Vive, 180
HTML5, 101
Haiku Learning, 84–85, 87, 199
Halo (video game), 92
Hamlet (play), 147
Hawthorne Effect, 93
Harry Potter, 83, 136, 157
Haskell, Chris, 3, 11, 15–19, 21, 140–141, 165–168, 174, 197, 225
Hattie, John, 209, 212, 220
HedBanz (game), 157
Hergenrader, Trent, 155
Her Story (video game), 149–150
The Hero with a Thousand Faces (book), 67, 77, 174, 206
Hirsch, Emile, 151
Hirsch, Leah, 135
HistoryQuest, 32, 39
The Hobbit (book), 63, 65, 67, 69, 70, 72, 74, 115, 146, 148
Holman, Caitlin, 131
Horizontal learning spaces, 42–43, 58, 223
Hour of Code, 96, 104, 109

How Computer Games Help Children Learn (book), 181, 190
Humanities, 1, 3–4, 63–64, 67, 128, 151–153
Humphries, Emma, 181
Hunger Games (book), 162
Husøy, Aleksander, 3, 30–31, 81, 117, 119, 172, 177–178, 195, 215–217, 225
Husøy/Staaby Pendulum, 215–217

I

iCivics, 73–76, 115, 119, 127, 171, 181, 203–204
Identity play, 111, 130, 141, 224
If You Can (video game), 52–53, 57
Ignorance, 128, 130, 141
Illuminati, 11
In a Grove (short story), 149
Individualized education plans (IEPs), 72
Infamous (video game), 74
Institute of Play, 3, 33, 39, 42, 48, 50–51, 57, 120, 135, 214, 218, 225
Intrinsic motivation, 7, 116, 118, 131–135, 142, 148, 192
iMovie, 124, 145
Intended curriculum model (ICM), 193
iPad, 66, 75, 82, 96, 99, 123–124
iPhone, 66, 102, 104, 107
Irvin, Glenn, 3, 16, 118, 135–136, 166–167, 174, 177, 179–180, 189, 194–195, 199, 225
ISTE (International Society for Technology in Education), 1, 10–13, 24, 54, 122
ISTE Island, 10
Isaacs, Steve, 1–4, 17–18, 21–23, 29–32, 34–36, 56, 61–62, 65, 81, 95–111, 115–122, 124, 132–134, 146, 148, 150, 162–163, 166, 170–171, 180–181, 184, 188, 190, 194–195, 197, 199, 200, 212, 225

J

Jacobs, Jane, 82, 94
JavaScript, 101
Jeopardy! (game show), 51
Jenkins, Henry, 157, 160
Joan Ganz Cooney Center at Sesame Workshop, 25, 95, 207
Jolly Roger pirate flag, 11
Journey (video game), 74, 171, 173

K

KQED MindShift, 17, 21, 79, 81, 94
Kalir, Jeremiah, 3, 128, 130, 142, 193–194, 206, 218–229, 225
Kalman, Robert, 3, 122–124
Kerbal Space Program (video game), 165–166
Kesey, Ken, 70, 94, 132–133, 142
Kickstarter, 181
Kindle, 181
Kinect Adventure (video game), 75
Kirkman, Robert, 157
Kist, William, 35, 40
Kesson, Mallory, 22
Kurosawa, Akira, 149

L

Land Science, 186–187
LawCraft (video game), 76
Lawson, Craig, 140–141, 163–165, 174
Ledger, Heath, 149
Learning, Education, and Games, Vol. I & II (book), 79
Leet Noobs: The Life and Death of an Expert Player Group in World of Warcraft (book), 2, 145, 159
Level Up Learning (survey), 25, 196, 207
Little Big Planet (video game), 74

littleBits, 98
Lone Rangers, 43
Looney Labs, 156, 158
The Lord of the Rings Online (video game), 163
Ludic Learning (blog), 30, 200, 225
Lusory attitude, 128–131

M

Mac (computer), 66, 75, 87, 91
Machinima, 17
Macklin, Colleen, 39
Made with Play (blog series), 135
Magic circle, 119
Magic: The Gathering (card game), 156
The Magic School Bus (book series), 175–176
Makey Makey, 98–99, 103
Malmstrom, Marianne, 3, 10–12, 15, 30, 32, 34, 38, 61, 225
Manegold, Neil, 45
Mario Maker (video game), 99
Marist College, 4, 153
Mars Generation One: Argubot Academy (video game), 46, 198
Marshall, Shelby, 55
Martin, Eric N., 35
Massively multiplayer online (MMO) game, 1, 63–64, 163
Master Chief, 92
Mavis Beacon Teaches Typing (video game), 161
Meier, Sid, 147, 148, 160
Membean, 68–69, 72
Mentor, 2, 9, 23–24, 45, 136, 164, 182–186, 188–189
McLuhan, Marshall, 47, 159
Meaningful experiences, 111, 118, 175, 180, 209–210, 218–219, 224
Merrick, Scott, 11, 24
Metagame (card game), 39
Metz, Ed, 54
Microsoft, 1, 3, 23–24, 42, 44–45, 170, 195, 210

The Migrant Trail (video game), 172
MindShift Guide to Digital Games + Learning (ebook), 79, 94
MineGage, 23
Minecraft (video game), 1, 3, 14, 16, 23–24, 36–37, 40, 42, 44, 46–47, 49–50, 75, 97–98, 100, 103–104, 109, 117, 135–137, 162, 166–168, 170–171, 174, 177, 179–181, 188, 190, 194, 199, 201, 210–211, 213, 223, 225
Minecraft: Education Edition, 44–45
MinecraftEDU Twitter chat, 23–24, 27, 225
Minecraft Mentorship Program, 42
Minefaire, 1, 171, 188, 190
Mission US (video game), 151, 153–154, 172
MIT App Inventor, 103
Monomyth, 140, 162
Monopoly (tabletop game), 157
Montessori, Maria, 121, 125, 139, 143, 150
Montessorian method, 114, 121, 197, 221, 224
Moodle, 141
Moore, Tony, 157
Ms. Frizzle (fictional character), 175
Multiplayer Classroom (book), 58, 66, 77, 174, 220
Myst (video game), 81

N

NJEA Review (magazine), 23
Nadella, Satya, 1
Napoleon, 39, 152
National Endowment for the Humanities (NEH), 151, 153
National Institute of Health (NIH), 55
National Science Foundation (NSF), 55
Nephrotex, 186
Newton's Playground (video game), 52, 58
New Literacies in Action: Teaching and Learning in Multiple Media (book), 35, 40
New York Times (newspaper), 17, 67, 68, 181
Next Generation Science Standards, 46

INDEX

Nicholson, Scott, 81, 131, 143
Nintendo, 99
Nolin, Matt, 3, 11–12, 15–19
Non-playable character (NPC), 108, 167
Nordahl Grieg Secondary School, 81, 117
Nurse Ratchet (fictional character), 133, 136

O

Obama, Barack, 35
Oculus Rift, 96, 103
One Flew Over the Cuckoo's Nest (book), 79, 94, 132, 142
One Night Ultimate Werewolf (board game), 15
Ontario Ministry of Education, 80, 94
Opportunity to learn (OTL), 193
Opportunity gap, 193, 206

P

Pac-Man (video game), 169
Pandaria, 71
PBS Digital Innovator, 1
PC Gamer (website), 81
Pepperdine University, 2, 145, 154
Pervasive games, 1, 4, 19, 79–80, 85
Petri dishes, 9
Piaget, Jean, 53, 58, 114, 125, 176, 190
Pike, Jim, 3, 29, 158, 169–171
Pilakowski, Melissa, 3, 22–23, 49, 56
Pixar, 185
Pixel Press, 3, 122–123
Playfulness, 111, 113, 118, 218
PlayMaker School, 29–30, 156, 168
PlayStation, 66, 73–74, 96, 100–101, 172, 214
Play This, Learn That (ebook), 166, 168, 174
Polygon (website), 31, 80
Poe, Edgar Allan, 17, 149
Pokémon (card game), 198

Pokémon GO (video game), 20
Popplet, 104, 141
Portal 2 (video game), 54, 58
Post-its, 140
PowerPoint, 35, 145
Principles of Connected Learning, 187, 190
Project Spark (video game), 102, 109
Puzzles, 54, 130, 142, 206, 220

Q

Qualitative assessments, 224
Quandary (video game), 200–201
Quarnstrom, Deirdre, 170
Quest Atlantis (video game), 13, 42–43
Quest to Learn (school), 50, 218
Quigley, Peter, 3, 186–187

R

Rashomon (film), 149
Raspberry Pi, 96–97
Rami, Meenoo, 3, 42, 44–45, 210
Ratio Rancher (video game), 46
Ray-Hill, Carrie, 3, 127, 142, 203–205
Red bandanas, 9, 11–13
Redstone, 103
Reflective practices, 184, 192, 207, 215
The Reflective Practitioner: How Professionals Think in Action (book), 58, 198, 220
Reid, Stephen, 180
Relatedness, 132
RescuShell, 186
Responsibility Launcher (video game), 76
Rezzly, 63, 140
Rhetorics of play, 114, 118, 224
River City (virtual world), 43
River Valley Civilizations, 72
Robinson, Ken, 13, 24
RockBand (video game), 96
Rochester Institute of Technology, 155
Rock-paper-scissors (game), 75

Rome II: Total War (video game), 213
Royal St. George's College, 79, 82–83
Role-playing games (RPGs), 71
Rubrics, 80, 139, 186
Ruppel, Marc, 3, 151–153

S

Salem Witch Hunts, 15
Salen, Katie, 42, 46, 50–51, 53, 57–58, 79, 113, 118–119, 125, 127, 131–132, 143
Sanders, James, 192
Serious Play Conference, 54, 65
Scaffolded learning, 113, 137, 149–150, 168, 186
Schön, Donald A., 48, 58, 198, 207, 213, 220
Schönian Reflective Practices, 198
Schoology, 199
Scrabble (tabletop game), 120
The Scarlet Letter (book), 185
Shaffer, David Williamson, 4, 42, 47–48, 56–58, 145, 160, 181–186, 188, 198–199, 207, 211, 213, 220, 225
Schell Games, 65, 119
Schrier, Karen, 4, 79–80, 94, 153–154, 171–172, 174
Severus Snape (fictional character), 136
Sinek, Simon, 180
SMART Board, 66, 84, 87
Smashwords, 181
Snakes and Lattes, 20
Saulnier, Tobi, 4, 11, 17
Second Life (virtual world), 10, 13, 43, 64
Self-determination theory (SDT), 128, 131–133
Servant leadership, 180, 222–223
Shah Jahan, 159
Shakespeare, William, 17, 86, 157
Sharp, John, 39
Sheehy, Peggy, 1–2, 4, 9–13, 15, 17–18, 21, 24, 29–32, 38, 40, 56, 61–77, 79, 81, 111, 115, 117–119, 121, 123, 128, 133, 140–141, 146, 148, 150, 162, 164, 172–173, 176, 182–183, 194, 197, 199, 204, 207, 209, 212, 225–226
Sheldon, Lee, 48, 58, 65, 77, 163, 174, 211, 220
Siri, 147
SketchUp, 104
Signifiers, 52
SimCityEDU: Pollution Challenge! (video game), 46
The Sims (video game), 178
Sisters of Elune, 73–74
Skype, 11, 13, 19, 87–88, 104, 147, 181, 184, 186
Small Business Administration (SBA), 54
Small Business Innovation Research (SBIR) grant, 54–55
SnapGuide, 103, 109
Social media, 21–22, 24, 30–31, 180, 221, 223
Social practice, 28, 183
Socratic Smackdown (debate game), 48
Speakers' Dinner, 18–19, 80
Squire, Kurt, 20, 25, 42, 47, 52–53, 57–59, 113, 121, 126, 136, 143, 148, 160, 202, 207, 212, 220
Staaby, Tobias, 4, 30–31, 117, 172–173, 177, 194, 213–217, 225
Starcraft II (video game), 65
Star Wars (film), 162
Starts with Why (book), 180
Steward (of communities of practice), 21, 25, 40, 122
Stokes, Benjamin, 4, 130, 175–176, 182, 204–205
Stuckey, Bron, 4, 11–15, 27–28, 37, 39, 42–44, 170
Suffern Middle School, 4, 64–65
Suits, Bernard, 128–129, 143, 156
Summative assessments, 195, 215
Super Mario Bros. (video game), 99
Survive and Thrive (tabletop game), 120
Suter, Mark, 4, 21, 113, 141, 180, 195
Sutton-Smith, Brian, 114–116, 118, 126, 130, 143, 191, 207

INDEX

SXSWedu conference, 79
Systems thinking, 50–51, 120

T

20% Time, 109, 181, 188, 195, 212
20% Tuesday, 109
3D GameLab, 63, 69, 72–74, 100–101, 107–110, 115, 134, 140–141, 199, 207
Taboo (game), 39
Taj Mahal, 159
Teacher dashboards, 194–196
Teacher pioneers, 35
Teachercraft: How Teachers Learn to Use Minecraft in their Classrooms (book), 3, 36, 40, 174
Teacher Pioneers: Visions from the Edge of the Map (book), 4, 35–36, 40, 133, 142–143, 146, 159–160, 193, 196, 206–207, 219–220, 225
Teamification, 136
TEDx Talk, 181
This War of Mine (video game), 178
Thoreau, Henry David, 151–152
Theoretical sampling, 2
Toppo, Greg, 1, 5, 22, 63–64, 77, 79
Transcendentalism, 152
Transformational leadership, 1, 9, 33–34, 39, 79, 206, 221, 223
Transmedia storytelling, 157, 160
The Tribe, 2, 4, 9–25, 27–31, 34–35, 37–39, 42, 45–46, 48–50, 52–56, 61, 64–65, 111, 118–119, 121–122, 128, 133–135, 138, 141, 145–146, 157, 159, 162–163, 165, 167–168, 170–171, 173, 175–180, 184, 186–189, 192–196, 198, 204–205, 209–212, 219, 221–224
Troy, New York, 3, 11, 14, 20, 81, 122
Trump, Donald, 35
Twine, 104, 154, 213
Twitter, 3, 15, 21–24, 28, 30–31, 39, 49, 56, 73, 102–104, 109–110, 136, 180, 189, 200, 209, 221, 224–225

U

UNESCO MGIEP, 1
University of Colorado, Denver, 3, 128
University of Florida, 55, 181
University of Wisconsin, Madison, 4, 27, 63, 128, 160, 203
Unreal Engine, 103, 104
USA TODAY (newspaper), 22

V

Value-added measurements (VAMs), 193
Vattel, Lucien, 29
Verne, Jules, 155
Virtual internships, 181, 183–185
Virtual internships authorware (VIA), 186–187
Virtual reality, 96, 176, 180
Vygotsky, Lev, 42, 47, 52, 57, 59, 113, 116, 118, 125–126, 134, 142–143
Vygotskian approach, 116, 125, 168, 221, 224

W

Wakeman, Ted, 30
Walden, a Game (video game), 151–152
The Walking Dead (video game), 30, 172, 194
The Ward Game (alternate reality game), 79, 132–133
Webster, A. J., 4, 29–30, 156–159, 162, 168,
Weisburgh, Mitch, 4, 54–55
Wenger, Etienne, 2, 5, 21–23, 25, 27–28, 40, 42, 58, 183, 188, 190
What Video Games Have to Teach Us About Learning and Literacy (book), xii, 29, 40, 57, 77, 125, 142, 206, 219
Wheeler, Nat (fictional character), 153
Wikipedia, 74
Wii, 73, 75
Wii U, 99

William Annin Middle School (WAMS), 95–96
Williams-Pierce, Caro, 4, 27, 35–36, 40, 133–135, 143, 146, 155, 160, 196–198, 207, 210, 219–220, 225
Win the White House (video game), 74–75, 127
Windows MovieMaker, 145
White House, 35, 163
WMHT, 14
Woodrow Wilson Teaching Foundation, 39
World of Lexica (video game), 64
World of Warcraft (video game), 1–3, 10, 32, 38, 47, 49, 56, 61, 63–67, 69–77, 115–116, 119, 128, 130, 139–140, 146, 148, 150, 159, 162–165, 174, 183, 199, 226
WoWinSchool curriculum, 63, 67, 115, 140–141, 162–164, 174, 226

X

XP (experience points), 63, 108, 115
Xbox, 66, 73, 75, 96–97, 102, 109

Y

Yogibo, 66
YouTube, 13, 24, 45, 100–101, 105, 124, 136, 147, 169–170, 188–189, 199

Z

Zimmer, Garrett, 23, 136, 225
Zimmerman, Eric, 39, 46, 50–53, 58, 113, 119, 127, 131–132, 143
Zone of proximal development, 111, 113, 134
Zoombinis (video game), 99, 109

new literacies
AND DIGITAL EPISTEMOLOGIES

Colin Lankshear & Michele Knobel
General Editors

New literacies emerge and evolve apace as people from all walks of life engage with new technologies, shifting values and institutional change, and increasingly assume 'postmodern' orientations toward their everyday worlds. Despite many efforts to take account of such changes, educational institutions largely remain out of touch with the range of new ways of making and sharing meanings that increasingly mediate and shape the lives of the young people they teach and the futures they face. This series aims to explore some key dimensions of the changes occurring within social practices of literacy and the educational challenges they present, with a view to informing educational practice in helpful ways. It asks what are new literacies, how do they impact on life in schools, homes, communities, workplaces, sites of leisure, and other key settings of human cultural engagement, and what significance do new literacies have for how people learn and how they understand and construct knowledge. It aims to challenge established and 'official' ways of framing literacy, and to ask what it means for literacies to be powerful, effective, and enabling under current and foreseeable conditions. Collectively, the works in this series will help to reorient literacy debates and literacy education agendas.

For further information about the series and submitting manuscripts, please contact:

>Michele Knobel & Colin Lankshear
>Montclair State University
>Dept. of Education and Human Services
>3173 University Hall
>Montclair, NJ 07043
>michele@coatepec.net

To order other books in this series, please contact our Customer Service Department at:
>(800) 770-LANG (within the U.S.)
>(212) 647-7706 (outside the U.S.)
>(212) 647-7707 FAX

Or browse online by series at:
>www.peterlang.com